Union Brotherhood, Union Town

The History of the

Carpenters' Union of Chicago

1863–1987

RICHARD SCHNEIROV

THOMAS J. SUHRBUR

Southern Illinois University Press
Carbondale and Edwardsville

91 90 89 88   4 3 2 1

Library of Congress Cataloging-in-Publication Data

Schneirov, Richard.
  Union brotherhood, union town: the history of the carpenters'
union of Chicago, 1863–1987 / Richard Schneirov and Thomas J.
Suhrbur.
        p.   cm.
     Bibliography: p.
     Includes index.
     ISBN 0-8093-1352-9.   ISBN 0-8093-1353-7 (pbk.)
       1. United Brotherhood of Carpenters and Joiners of America—
History.   2. Trade-unions—Carpenters—Illinois—Chicago—History.
3. Work environment—Illinois—Chicago—History.   4. Chicago (Ill.)—
Social conditions.   I. Suhrbur, Thomas J., 1946–   . II. Title.
HD6515.C2U57 1988
331.88′194′09773—dc19   87-30017
                                                                   CIP

The paper used in this publication meets the minimum requirements of
American National Standard for Information Sciences—
Permanence of Paper for Printed Materials, ANSI Z39.48-1984.

*To the legacy of James "Dad" Brennock
and all his brothers and sisters
who built the carpenters' union
and made Chicago a union town*

Contents

CONTENTS

Illustrations

Preface

This book originated as part of the centennial celebration of the founding of the United Brotherhood of Carpenters and Joiners of America in Chicago in 1881. But what began as a short pamphlet on the history of the Chicago carpenters' union soon developed into a serious, full-length study. For this reason we would like to explain the rationale for the interpretive directions we have taken.

Traditional labor history has been conceived and written as the history of trade unions: their leaders, their policies, and their strikes. In the last two decades a "new labor history" has come into being that treats as central to its focus an entire set of topics that the older labor history treated as secondary. Workplace relations, the culture of working people in their communities, workers' role in local politics, and workers' family life and leisure activities are all subjects of the new labor history. Examining these areas of working-class life has enabled historians to go beyond the institution of the union to discuss the lives of the ordinary workingmen who were never or only temporarily organized, or who were in unions as "the rank and file" but left no written evidence of their thinking.

This book treats a "traditional" topic, a union—in this case the carpenters' union of Chicago—but it attempts to treat it from the perspectives of the new labor history. Readers will find, therefore, that we have been concerned about a variety of issues in addition to the indispensable details of collective bargaining. For one thing, we have tried to discuss the influence on the union of particular ethnic groups, from the Germans, Irish, and Czechs of the late nineteenth century to the Scandinavians and Jews of the early twentieth century. We have also attempted to say something throughout this book about the changing nature of the carpenters' craft, the informal relations between carpenters and their employers in the workplace and the impact of formal union working rules. Particularly we have sought to understand the growth of the union in the late nineteenth century as part of something larger, a *class* movement of workers. Finally, especially in the early part of the book, we have been concerned with politics, both the varied political ideologies of carpenters and the relationship of the union to the local political system, particularly when the union entered politics as part of a labor party.

Some readers will no doubt wish that we had gone further in investigating the social foundations of the carpenters' union history. We have, however, chosen to focus on the institutional narrative for what seem to us to be compelling reasons. First, the carpenters are the only local union in Chicago outside of the printers to have a complete set of records from the mid-nineteenth century through the present. These manuscripts have never before been examined by historians, and we feel that a solid history based on intensive analysis and evaluation of them will serve as a major contribution to labor history. Second, to write a comprehensive social history of rank and file carpenters would be virtually impossible simply because carpenters are too diverse a group. It is hard to think of a single union in the city that throughout its history has drawn its members from such a variety of races and nationalities living in so many different communities as have the carpenters. We have settled for a discussion, where the sources exist, of those social issues that directly impinge on the basic questions of power and control that lie at the heart of any union. In sum, we would like this book to be viewed as a social history of an institution rather than an institutional history.

In the same way that our work attempts to bring together social and institutional history, it is also an attempt to synthesize popular history and academic or professional history. We hope that our book will be accessible to union carpenters: graduate apprentices, union activists, union officials, and retired members. Members of other unions in the city may also be interested in this book, for one of its major themes is that the carpenters are the most representative union in the city and that their history comes close to being a history of Chicago's labor movement in microcosm. To make this book as accessible to unionists as possible we have tried to keep references to disputes among historians to a minimum and to keep our interpretive points within the bounds of the narrative.

In writing this work we have also tried to make a contribution to academic labor history. There are two full-length scholarly histories of the United Brotherhood of Carpenters and Joiners of America now in existence: Robert Christie's *Empire in Wood* (1956) and Walter Galenson's *The United Brotherhood of Carpenters* (1983). Though we have learned from both of them, our thinking has developed primarily within the framework provided by Christie's matchless work, which labor historian Melvyn Dubofsky has called "the finest institutional history" of an American trade union.

We hope that our local study will complement and in some

ways modify Christie's nationally focused monograph. In contrast to Walter Galenson, we share Christie's view that the union's history can be roughly divided into two major eras: an early period when the union was part of a broad-ranging social movement that, to a considerable extent, rejected "the wage-system," followed by a period informed by the philosophy of business unionism. We think that our work elaborates the early period of the carpenters' history in a way that Christie could only hint at in his discussion of the nineteenth century, which relied heavily on the career of General Secretary Peter J. McGuire. In Chicago, there were many counterparts to McGuire; he was far from isolated in his radical views, and they were hardly irrelevant to the path taken by the union itself. Moreover, we believe we shed light on the transition between the two eras in our discussion of the 1900–1901 lockout. Christie's national focus tended to personalize this transition.

Our work modifies the story told in *Empire in Wood* in several important ways. First, Christie took no account of the "new unionism" of the 1912–24 period that, in some ways, represented a resurgence of nineteenth century militancy and radicalism. Second, because so much bargaining in the construction industry is local and not national, Christie's national focus tended to dwell on leaders and developments that were far less relevant to the grassroots level. For example, in *Empire in Wood* the image of the typical twentieth century carpenter leader is viewed through the lens of William Hutcheson. In our own research we have uncovered a picture of the union's leadership more varied than the stereotypical twentieth-century conservative labor bureaucrat portrayed by Christie.

A word about the sources on which this book relies is also in order. For our three chapters on the nineteenth century we have used a wide variety of sources to supplement the records and manuscript accounts supplied by the union. For our chapters on the twentieth century, we have had greater difficulty in finding sources outside union records to supplement the basic bread and butter of collective bargaining. Newspapers, for one thing, did not cover the union movement in as great a detail as they did in the nineteenth century. And there has been less written by labor historians on the Chicago labor movement during the twentieth century than during the nineteenth.

For the post–World War II period, we have relied largely on interviews—oral history. The union's minutes are very thin for this period, and other accounts are almost nonexistent. In most cases we have tried to verify accounts obtained through interviewing either by comparing them with written sources where they exist or by cross-checking them with other oral accounts. We also have attempted to interview a variety of individuals: rank and file carpenters, local officials, District Council officials, and opposition activists.

Finally, though this was a broadly cooperative venture in research and conceptualization, within that context we would like to make known the relative contribution of each author. The research for chapters 1 through 3 was shared: Thomas Suhrbur focused on the developing structure of the union, while Richard Schneirov focused on major events and context. The research for chapters 4 through 6 was done by Richard Schneirov; the interviewing of union members was generally done jointly. With the exception of an early first draft for chapter 3 done by Thomas Suhrbur, the writing of the manuscript from the first through the final drafts was undertaken by Richard Schneirov.

Acknowledgments

This collaborative history of the carpenters' union had its genesis at a time when we were both graduate students in American history at Northern Illinois University. Based on our previous work, we were asked by the Illinois Labor History Society, in cooperation with the Chicago and Northeast Illinois District Council of the United Brotherhood of Carpenters and Joiners of America, to write the history of the Council for the Brotherhood's centennial celebration.

We have a number of institutions and a great variety of individuals to thank for their assistance in the preparation, writing, and publication of this book. First and foremost, we want to express our gratitude to the union for making its documents available to us and for supporting the publication of our work. Not only the District Council but also Locals 1, 10, and 54 allowed us to examine their records. The writing of the book was funded in part by a grant from the Illinois Humanities Council—to which we would like to express our thanks. We would also like to mention that this history was a project of the Illinois Labor History Society.

Many individuals in the union cheerfully gave their time to us for interviews. Without their help in clarifying important issues regarding the carpenters' craft and the operation of the union this book could not have been written. We would like to thank: President George Vest, Jr., Irwin Klass, Stanley Macenas, Leo Beaulieu, Art Holzman, John Libby, Bob Lid; retired unionists Stanley Johnson, the Rev. Joseph L. Donahue, Michael J. Connolly, Joseph McAlinden, and Charles Svec; apprenticeship coordinator Adolph "Duffy" Dardar; and union activists Richard de Vries and Toni Hayes. Other individuals who gave helpful interviews were Joseph Jacobs and Taylor Cotton. General Secretary of the Brotherhood John S. Rogers interceded at a crucial point when the future of this project was in doubt. Later, Secretary-Treasurer Wesley Isaacson lent his assistance to see the project through to completion.

In overseeing this project we owe special thanks to Les Orear, president of the Illinois Labor History Society. Les originated the project, pushed through the funding by the Humanities Council, and set up a special editorial board on which he served that oversaw the writing of the manuscript. For her advice and her many hours of editing work we owe a special debt of gratitude to Fannia Weingartner. Whatever felicity of style this book can claim stems from our response to her critical pen. J. Carroll Moody, who served as our advisor at Northern Illinois University, lent his advice and encouragement throughout the project. Irwin Klass facilitated many of the interviews with union officials, supplied us with back records, and in general negotiated the arrangements with the union.

This book stands on the shoulders of many scholars, all of whom we acknowledge in our Notes. However, we would like to mention one person who made a great contribution to this book. Steven Sapolsky, who at the time was working at the University of Pittsburgh on a dissertation on the Chicago building trades, served as a consultant to the project. Steve most generously shared with us his research material and many of his insights. John B. Jentz, Lillian Moscowitz, and Bruce Nelson also lent assistance at various points in our work. Throughout our labors Archie Motley of the Chicago Historical Society was ever helpful. In the final stages of the preparation of the manuscript Natalie C. Paz-Storey typed and helped organize the appendix matter.

The following persons have also read the manuscript in its entirety and offered helpful commentary: Fannia Weingartner, Steven Sapolsky, Irwin Klass, John B. Jentz, J. Carroll Moody, and William R. Childs. Extensive comments on the final chapter were received from Stanley Macenas and Richard deVries.

We wish to thank the following for illustrations: United Brotherhood of Carpenters and Joiners of America; Institute of Labor and Industrial Relations, University of Illinois; Illinois Labor History Society; Chicago Historical Society; Charles H. Kerr Publishing Company; Chicago and Northeast Illinois District Council, United Brotherhood of Carpenters and Joiners of America. We also want to thank Bart Siegel for his help in photographing illustrations.

One person, though long dead, had a great influence on this work. Paul Hudon, Tom Suhrbur's great-grandfather, was one of the founders of the Chicago carpenters' union. It was the memory of his great-grandfather's life's work, passed down through several generations, that inspired Tom to select the carpenters' union as the topic of a graduate thesis. The research on that thesis served as the springboard for this manuscript.

We want to acknowledge especially our wives—Silvia and Barbara—for their patience and support while we labored over an extended period of time to complete this project.

As a final note: neither the union nor any persons mentioned above bear any responsibility for the interpretation contained in this study. We accept full responsibility for the contents of the book including whatever errors it may contain.

Union Brotherhood, Union Town

CHAPTER 1

The Beginnings of Carpenters' Unionism, 1863–1877

The carpenters of Chicago kind of talked union, and I
suppose I did not keep still any more than any of them.
Finally, they inaugurated a union that kept together
until they had probably 400 or 500 members. Then
came a demand for wages and that was lost—the union
was dissolved. There was no cohesion about it; it got
broke up. Come along, then, until we got to about 1875
or 1876, and there were 4 or 5 or 6 different carpenters'
unions in Chicago, and one was an international, the
other was an independent, and the other was
something else. No kind of cohesion or concert of
action between them at all.

—James Brennock[1]

In 1864, while the nation's attention was riveted on the progress
of the Union army through the South, a thirty-six year old Irish-
born carpenter arrived in Chicago. Six years earlier he had helped
organize the first carpenters' union in Albany, New York. But in
Chicago the carpenter was surprised to find that there was no union
headquarters where he could deposit his union "traveling card." Once
he found work, the newcomer discovered to his consternation that
without a union some carpenters received $.10 more than he did, and
others $.50 less. Though the young journeyman "talked union" as
much as any man, he found that mistrustfulness among the diverse
ethnic groups kept Chicago carpenters in separate organizations. As
late as 1876 he still found that there was "no kind of cohesion or
concert of action between them at all."[2]

In 1878 the carpenter, now a veteran of numerous failed union
organizing efforts, helped establish the city's first carpenters' benev-

1

olent society. In 1881 he helped bring the United Brotherhood of Carpenters and Joiners of America into existence at its inaugural convention in Chicago. Five years later he founded the carpenters' assembly of the Knights of Labor, and the next year was elected president of the United Carpenters Council of Chicago. In the meantime he founded and headed up Chicago's first Building Trades Council. By the 1890s the tramping carpenter who had entered the city as a stranger—a union man in a town of nonunion pieceworkers—was the most revered leader in the strongest union in the city. Known affectionately as "Uncle Jimmie" and "Dad," he eventually wrote the only major history of the origins of the Chicago carpenters' union. When he died at the age of eighty-five in 1913, he was still treasurer of his local, No. 1.[3]

The life of James Brennock, father of the Chicago carpenters' union, is one of the many untold success stories of nineteenth-century Chicago. Unlike the Marshall Fields and the George Armours who sought wealth, fame, and status through self-advancement in the business world, the James Brennocks of the world understood their personal success to be bound up with the idea and practice of solidarity among workingmen. Because Brennock dedicated his life to this goal he was a proud union man to his last day. Properly understood, the story of the origins and triumph of the Chicago carpenters' union is not so much the story of an organization as it is the story of the achievements of thousands of men like James Brennock, men whose lives are rarely recorded on the pages of history books, but who poured their souls into a cause that actualized their best hopes and dreams. This book tells the story of that cause, the union cause, of the Chicago carpenters.

Origins of the Union:
The Transformation of the Craft and Trade

A history of the carpenters union must begin with the great transformation that carpentry as a trade and as a craft underwent in the nation's first century of existence. For it was the response by carpenters to this transformation that brought the union into existence.

The typical American colonial carpenter worked under the age-old artisan system. After a four- to seven-year stint as an apprentice the carpenter graduated to journeyman status. At some point in his life, the wage-earning journeyman expected to set himself up as an independent master carpenter. Unlike the modern carpenter contractor, the old-time master designed the building he constructed and labored side by side with the journeymen he directed. He commonly contracted directly with the building's owner. In addition, colonial master carpenters often formed associations that regulated the prices they charged and the wages they paid.[4]

By the end of the eighteenth century, the artisan system had largely disintegrated in America's eastern cities with the rise of large-scale commercial building. Unable to marshal the necessary capital, an increasing number of master carpenters grew dependent on speculators, promoters, and other middlemen for the financing of construction. Many masters became little more than labor subcontractors. A smaller number of carpenter masters were able to expand their operations to become large builders comparable in many way   modern general contractor. By the time of the American Re   the masters' associations had collapsed and building prices   neymen's wages had become subject to supply and deman   ted by the market. Under the pressures of competition and   odic oversupply of labor, masters began to cut customary wage   ponse to this the first union in the trade emerged in Philadelp   791 to protect the journeyman's interest. By 1840 carpenter   as were active in at least fifteen cities in the young nation.[5]

Because Chicago was born and took shape as a city at a time when the disintegration of artisan labor was fairly complete, there were no masters' associations to block the rise of middlemen and the competitive pressures of the marketplace. Chicago's first great commercial booms of the 1840s and 1850s led to the abrupt rise of large-scale carpenter contracting. There were at least a dozen large-scale builders in Chicago of carpenter origin before the Civil War, several of them prominent citizens such as Amos Grannis, Jonathan Clark, and William Goldie. By the time of the Civil War the bulk of Chicago's established carpenter contractors were organized in partnerships, an indication that the capital requirements of commercial and large-scale residential contracting had become too great for the individual journeymen.[6]

The city of Chicago has long been famous for its leadership in architecture and building techniques. The names of Louis Sullivan and Frank Lloyd Wright are justly well known in this regard. Few realize, however, that the city's first great contribution to building design, the balloon-frame house, was invented by an itinerant Chicago carpenter, Augustine Deodat Taylor in 1833.

Prior to this time, homes were constructed according to the colonial "post and beam" method. The weight of the floors, roof, and walls was carried by a skeleton of heavy posts spaced eight to fourteen feet apart and held together by equally heavy oak or chestnut beams. With the advent of the balloon frame, first seen in St. Mary's Church, originally located at State and Lake streets, a larger number of lighter and easier to handle two-by-four inch "studs," about five hundred in number, replaced the massive beams and posts. The studs were held together by nails replacing the old and costly method of mortised and tenoned joints.

There were several advantages to balloon-frame construction. Architecturally, the dead weight of the building was carried directly to the ground by each of a large number of vertical studs, instead of being transferred to the distant corner posts. Balloon-frame construction also reduced by about 50 percent the amount of wood needed to frame a house. At the same time, the new method reduced the amount of labor, though not the skill, required to construct a simple residential home.

Utilizing this relatively cheap and time-saving method of construction, small nineteenth-century towns such as Chicago and San Francisco mushroomed into major cities almost overnight through their ability to house large populations of migrating workingmen.

Augustine Taylor, inventor of the balloon frame, became one of Chicago's trusted and prominent citizens. One of the city's original trustees, he also served as alderman for two years, and as city collector and assesor.

Twentieth-century home building follows a modified form of the balloon-frame method—called "western" or "platform" framing. In this method the studs rest on separate floors rather than running the height of the structure. By breaking up the building, platform framing is more resistant to fire.[7]

Though the emergence of unions in the carpentry trade was a direct response to the decline of the artisan system and the fluctuation of wages according to market conditions, the modern union evolved somewhat later as a response to the industrialization of journeyman carpentry. America's industrial revolution, beginning in the mid-nineteenth century, affected carpenters' work in two important areas: the nature of the craft and the extent of the labor market.

The carpenters' craft was transformed by the widespread introduction of what was commonly called the "piecework system." The early nineteenth-century journeyman carpenter was still a multiskilled craftsman. When weather permitted, the carpenter worked outdoors, using his adz, saw, chisel, plane, and molding tools to frame the building. Though this "rough work" involved a variety of skills, the real test of a craftsman was trimming. According to James Brennock's description of the old-time journeyman, "window cases, door cases, baseboard, moldings, stairs, nailing newel posts, doors, and every kind of wooden finishing were turned out by hand." A carpenter owned an expensive tool chest worth at least $100 and worked "as much in the shop as he did in the building," especially during the winter months. Though this work was tediously slow, employers seldom attempted "bossing" or rushing to extract more labor because, stated Brennock, "a good carpenter took such pride in the quality of his work that, rather than work beyond what he knew to be the proper limit of his speed, he would pack up his tools and quit."[8]

Beginning in 1839, when Chicago's first sash factory was established, this indoor work was gradually taken over by the planing mills and door, sash, and blind factories. Despite the great growth in the number of such firms during the 1839–49 and 1852–57 periods, there was little mechanization of production, hence factory output remained limited. Following the Civil War a series of improvements in woodworking machinery allowed the semiskilled machine hand employed in these factories to do much of the work of the skilled journeyman carpenter. The number of factory woodworkers in Chicago soared from 352 in 1860 to 2,298 in 1870, while the average number of employees per firm rose from 18.5 to 45 in the same period. Ten years later the average number of employees had risen still further to over 65. In 1873 the two largest door, sash, and blind factories in Chicago, the Goss and Phillips and the Palmer and Fuller companies, employed 600 and 400 men respectively.[9]

The mechanization of much of the work that the old artisan-carpenter had done on the jobsite or in his employer's shop increasingly turned the late nineteenth-century carpenter into a mere installer of factory-made woodwork and enabled the piecework system to invade the trade. Piecework began before the Civil War in large-scale commercial contracting when speculators bypassed the master and his highly skilled journeymen in order to contract out specific tasks such as framing, hanging doors, or laying floors. With the industrialization of indoor work, piecework spread rapidly in the craft. Subcontracting, specialist carpenters could be trained at simple installation tasks in several weeks, and required fewer tools—worth about $10 according to Brennock—to accomplish them. The cost-conscious employer reasoned: why hire fully apprenticed journeymen for the routine work that almost any man could do? Pieceworkers could be employed at a lower rate of pay, for longer hours, and at a more intense pace of work than a fully trained journeymen.[10]

It was common for a subcontracting pieceworker to hire his sons or several immigrant greenhorn laborers of his own nationality to help him in the simpler tasks, thus further undercutting the traditional trade standards of skilled carpenters. Even "legitimate" carpenters sometimes spoke favorably of piecework as a path to self-employment. Explained one Chicago carpenter, "Many of the most successful boss carpenters began for themselves by taking piecework."[11]

Piecework was, in effect, the application to the building trades of the new "sweatshop system" that had taken hold in industries such as clothing manufacture and cigarmaking. Like the custom tailors and skilled cigarmakers, carpenters complained bitterly that competition from the largely immigrant pieceworkers led to the "rushing" of work, the "butchering" of formerly skilled labor, and the lay-off of older men who could not keep up with the frenzied pace of work. In the blunt words of one carpenter union organizer, "Piecework has the effect of flooding the market with men who call themselves carpenters and who know as much about the carpenter trade as a dog does about his father and nothing more."[12]

Thus by the 1870s the ancient and complex trade of carpentry faced the imminent threat of fragmentation into a host of semiskilled occupations. The 1882 report of the Illinois Bureau of Labor Statistics argued this.

> A large percent of the apprentices learn part of the trade, the part which comes easiest to them at which they can earn most immediately, and then follow that branch; the result being that they are necessarily liable to unsteady employment. One report says, "the time is coming when we shall have no carpenters who are able to work creditably at all departments of the trade."[13]

Little wonder that skilled, apprenticed carpenters feared the virtual extinction of their craft.

The numerous attempts by mid-nineteenth century carpenters to minimize the degradation of standards in their craft depended on their ability to organize and regulate the local market. But organization and regulation of the local market proved increasingly difficult with the creation of regional and national railroad networks between 1850 and 1873. As it had altered so many other aspects of society, so too did the railroad interfere with the carpenters' quest for organization. Chicago, which had emerged as the railroad center for the nation, became in the words of national carpenter leader Peter J. McGuire the national "dumping-off place for traveling carpenters who were willing to work for anything." It was these itinerant carpenters, contemptuously called "saw and hatchet men" or "sidewalk men" by local journeymen, who flooded Chicago's labor market during a building boom or strike and supplied the ranks of the pieceworkers. Many also came via the Great Lakes steamers. French Canadians often availed themselves of this cheap form of transportation during the busy season and then returned home during the winter. Thomas Doran, a local union leader, reflected the bitter feelings of Chicago carpenters toward this influx: "Vast hordes of these creatures with skill enough to shove a jackplane would flock to Chicago and form a solid line to the offices of the contractors and . . . bid fifty cents to a dollar less" than skilled resident carpenters. Not surprisingly Chicago carpenters' wages were among the lowest in the country.[14]

By the early 1880s, a time when detailed statistical studies of labor conditions were first undertaken, the average Chicago carpenter had a living standard that approximated that of a laborer, and was barely higher than that of a sweated worker. In 1882 carpenter wages were the lowest for all building trades, a rate that fell below the average for all Illinois occupations. In the next four years that rate fell even farther, while wages for trades such as the bricklayers, plumbers, and printers rose. Carpenters' low pay was compounded by a work year that ranged from an average of forty-two weeks in 1882 to thirty weeks in 1886. Only 9 percent of carpenters with families owned their own homes, compared to 80 percent of all bricklayer family men and 66 percent of all plasterer family men. The carpenter homeowner figure was close to that of the 6 percent for common laborers and 4 percent for hod carriers (bricklayers' helpers).[15]

The ethnic makeup of Chicago's carpenters, like their pay, approximated that of Chicago's newly forming industrial working class. In 1880, 67 percent of all Chicagoans employed in the manufacturing and mechanical trades were foreign born. In the same year, 75 percent of all carpenters were foreign born. By far the largest group consisted of the 28 percent who were German, followed by 9 percent Irish, 7 percent Swedish, and 31 percent others. The relatively low percentage of carpenters who were native born probably reflected the disintegration of the apprenticeship system in America combined with the fact that carpentry, with its low wages, was losing its attractiveness as an occupation for all but the most economically depressed.[16]

Ethnic diversity along with the prevalence of piecework and

the economically depressed state of the trade compounded the problems of union-building. Chicago's foreign-born carpenters generally lived and worked in separate neighborhoods and spoke different languages. German carpenters congregated on the city's Near North side and the Northwest side along Milwaukee Avenue. The Irish were concentrated in Brideport just south of the Chicago River and in a smaller Near West side community west of Halsted Street. Swedish carpenters generally lived in Swedetown on the city's North side, and the Czech community gathered in Pilsen on the Near West side along the Chicago River.[17]

When they went to work, immigrant carpenters, particularly the non–English speaking, generally hired themselves out to contractors of their own ethnic background. Since most of these workmen were pieceworkers with little sense of craft pride, the effect was to reinforce ethnic distinctiveness and further isolate carpenters from one another. Considering this situation, James Brennock was hardly the only carpenter to recognize the difficulty of forming a union. One carpenter remarked ruefully in 1880 that "trade unionism could never amount to much in a city like Chicago, the tradesmen of which had come from all parts of the world, precluding the possibility of bringing them together with any degree of confidence in each other."[18]

Nonetheless, despite the fragmentation of craft skill, despite the rushing on the job, despite the impoverishment, despite the isolation that tradesmen of different nationalities felt, Chicago carpenters made attempt after attempt to form unions and ultimately succeeded. What motivated these union activists to persist in the face of adversity? To listen to the words of the first carpenter unionists, it was not primarily bread and butter or economic goals. Again and again they referrred to values held in common by the vast majority of nineteenth-century Americans: personal autonomy and dignity, economic and social independence, and pride in one's labor. But in contrast to the dominant liberal individualism that sanctioned the unrestricted use of private property in the marketplace as the fulfillment of these values, carpenters questioned acquisitive and competitive capitalism and sought an alternative in "co-operation."

Two words served to symbolize for carpenters what competition had done to their trade: manhood and slavery. Marketplace competition had fastened the piecework system on carpentry, crushing the once-proud journeyman's manhood and reducing him to a slavery not unlike that which had been recently abolished in the Southern states. One carpenter writing in Chicago's trade union paper in 1882 appealed to fellow tradesmen to "crush piece work in the carpenters' trade by all means, and crush every slave who would work by the piece and crush every man who would let piece work." As to the purpose of the union, another carpenter wrote: "We propose to make honest industry the standard of manhood in contradistinction to infidel impudence under the garb of business principles that rides roughshod over all that is holy and sacred, mocks at virtue as if it were a marketable commodity rapidly declining in value."[19]

The crux of the issue was the lure of piecework, which to union-minded carpenters embodied shortsighted selfishness. To the extent that carpenters took this route to economic success, their competition with each other merely worsened the conditions for all. To attain not only better conditions for all but self-respect and dignity in labor as well, a new ethic was required to replace self-interested individualism and competition. Along with other nineteenth-century American and European workingmen, carpenters named this ethic "co-operation," "mutual aid and support," or simply "solidarity." Explained one Chicago carpenter leader in the 1880s: "While we are denied our rights by a monied aristocracy, and not able to attain them by individual effort, the only means left to us is by combination in societies and mutually helping each other." Thus, it was a fusion of older American values and a new working-class ethic that inspired carpenters to build their first unions.[20]

The General Character of the Early Union

In creating an effective union, carpenter activists oriented their organizing efforts toward finding solutions to three major problems: first, how to attract carpenters to the union in the face of the constant temptation to contract for piecework; second, the need to retain the commitment of newly recruited union members at a time when collective bargaining seemed a farfetched goal; and third, the need to forge unity among the different ethnic and language groups among carpenters and the other trades in the construction industry.

The first provisional answer to these difficulties was the simple "protective" union, which characterized carpenter organizing efforts in Chicago between the Civil War and the organization of the Brotherhood in 1881.[21] In contrast to the modern Brotherhood, the early protective union required little in the way of commitment from its members beyond support for the uniform minimum wage. There was no ban on piecework, and unlike later unions it offered no benevolent features such as sick or death benefits, or even a strike fund. Consequently, the union required a minimal or no initiation fee and little dues.

Normally, the protective union was confined to a core of skilled carpenters, men who had the economic independence and craft pride to motivate stable commitment. Only in anticipation of a strike would the protective union sometimes expand into a mass union. During the period of euphoria and high expectations that preceded a strike unskilled carpenters, many of them pieceworkers, often joined the union in large numbers. These men responded to special issues upon which they could focus their hopes for a better life. During the latter half of the nineteenth century that issue most often was shorter hours. Carpenter unions were normally organized as part of mass citywide attempts, and by 1886 nationwide attempts, to attain the eight-hour work day.

Unlike the modern union, the early union had no paid leadership, no bureaucracy, and, consequently, a high turnover among union officials. One reason for this was that there was no need for a stable group of leaders to collect dues and administer benefits. More importantly, there was no collective bargaining and no written contract, consequently no need for skilled negotiators. The typical carpenters' strike began when a small group of the most committed union activists called a series of meetings. This series of meetings would be followed by the formation of a large strike committee. The next stage was often a march led by a brass band and men carrying the union banner. The procession would visit the various building sites around the city, sometimes with other building trades workmen, or alone if there enough carpenters already enrolled in the union. The purpose was to demonstrate to nonunion men the strength of the union and at the same time to solidify the confidence and determination of those in the march.

In the absence of a strong commitment to the union, success depended on keeping up the level of excitement and interest in the strike. Once the strike notice was given, the union drew up a "rat list" of those contractors who refused to accede to union demands. Every day there would be a large gathering at the union hall to hear which "legitimate" employer had agreed to union demands. In the absence of an employers' association, there was little question of negotiating for the entire trade; bargaining was only for those who agreed to terms. If it did not succeed within a few weeks, the strike was in great jeopardy, for after a half-dozen mass meetings laced with inspirational speeches, commitment wore thin, especially with no strike benefits.

To the extent that the union existed beyond periods of strike, it was organized in the branch system. This feature emerged as a such as that between temperance-oriented Americans and beer-drinking Germans, simple language differences made a consolidated union practically impossible. As one Chicago organizer declared, "We have German, French, Bohemian, Scandinavian and English-speaking members. Now how can all these different tongues ventilate before one body? It would take you a week to go through a meeting." To minimize this problem, the early union was divided into branches along ethnic and neighborhood lines, with each branch represented on a central executive board, which together with the president made important decisions and coordinated citywide actions.[22]

By its very nature, therefore, the simple protective union was a makeshift operation and unable to resolve the trade problems posed by piecework. Recognizing the ineffectiveness of their organizations, the leaders of the protective unions often proposed an institution parallel to the union, one that went beyond its immediate goals yet embodied its inner principles of mutualism and solidarity. This was the carpenters' cooperative, which was intended to remove the root cause of piecework, poverty, and unemployment, namely the competitive system of contracting.

In 1875 Chicago's *Workingman's Advocate* briefly stated the rationale behind cooperation:

> The next step in the 'trades unions' movement is CO-OPER-ATION. We do not mean the co-operation of numbers for the purpose of forcing an advance in wages or enforcing the laws or rules we adopt in our "trades unions" for that we are already doing, but a co-operation of labor and money for the purpose of doing business for ourselves. . . . Why can we not through our trades unions form co-operative companies—start businesses for ourselves, and put not only our wages but the entire profits into our pockets? Why work to make other men rich, when by the same labor we can make ourselves rich?

The purpose of cooperatives was to secure to the worker the full product of his labor. Carpenters and other workingmen usually drew a distinction between producers and nonproducers. The latter group, commonly called middlemen, lived parasitically off the fruits of the labor of the worker. From this point of view, unions were only a partial solution to the problem of the "theft" of the producers' labor. Only producers' cooperatives solved the problem completely.[23]

Though support for the fundamental rationale behind cooperatives remained fairly constant, the strength of the cooperative movement varied according to the fortunes of union-sponsored strikes. During the period of mass enthusiasm preparatory to a strike, cooperation was rarely discussed. If a strike failed, as if often did, the union or a section of it commonly constituted itself as a cooperative. In 1864, following a strike, German house carpenters formed the first-known cooperative building society in Chicago; in 1868 the same thing occurred among a larger group of Chicago carpenters following a strike. Again in 1873, 1875, 1879 (ship carpenters), 1885, and 1887, carpenters formed producers' cooperatives.

Carpenters formed two kinds of producers' cooperatives: those intended to reform the trade, and those intended to reform society as a whole. One of the more successful trade cooperatives was organized in 1875 by the Chicago branch of the British Amalgamated Society of Carpenters. Its object was "to do job work and take contracts for building, rent or purchase workshops, supply the members of the society with employment, build or sell for the general benefit and carry on the concern as a dividend paying institution." Share ownership was limited to avoid concentration of control. The Amalgamated's cooperative lasted three years.[24]

In 1885 a large section of the Brotherhood in Chicago formed another carpenter cooperative, intended to purchase land on the outskirts of the city in order to build low-cost homes for Chicago's workingmen, and provide steady work for unemployed building tradesmen. Neither cooperative got off the ground probably due to the lack of capital. Yet, even if the cooperatives had been established, they would have had to compete with large-scale home builders such as Sam Gross who built more than ten thousand homes for workingmen during the 1880s. Gross sold his homes for as little as $1000, asked for a down payment of as little as $10, and offered easy credit terms. Gross himself was an exceptional figure—he seldom foreclosed on mortgages and in 1889 was offered the mayoral nomination on the labor ticket—but cheap home building required large concentrations of capital and its lack undermined the viability of home-building cooperatives.

Finally, both in 1872 and 1887, Chicago carpenters carried the idea of cooperation to its logical conclusion. With other workingmen, they attempted to build a cooperative colony in Arkansas based on common ownership of all productive property.[25]

The early carpenters' protective union and its twin, the producers' cooperative, characterized the carpenters' movement from 1863 through 1877, and to some extent all the way through the 1890s. From the vantage point of twentieth-century unionism there were obvious flaws built into these early methods of organization. But it took Chicago carpenters almost two decades of experience to realize the drawbacks and to create a new kind of union.

The History of the Early Carpenters' Protective Unions, 1863–1877

Before the Civil War the organization of house carpenters in Chicago reflected the relative lack of distinction between outside work and inside work. One of the first associations of carpenters in the city was a benevolent society organized by German cabinetmakers and house carpenters in 1855 known as the Schreiner Verein. The Verein offered benefits to its members and also served as a social society; but it is unlikely that it functioned as a protective union. Among non-Germans, house carpenters were part of the largely Irish "Carpenters, Ship Carpenters, Caulkers, and Ship Joiners Union of Chicago" organized in 1857. This union, which struggled for the ten-hour day in the year of its founding, was reorganized on the eve of the Civil War to exclude house carpenters.[26]

The first citywide attempt of journeymen house carpenters to protect their trade interests came during the Civil War as a response to rising prices. In 1862 carpenters formed a benevolent society, which by next March transformed itself into a protective union. On March 7 a German carpenter published the following appeal to his fellow tradesmen in Chicago's *Illinois Staats Zeitung*.

> You, who have to serve an apprenticeship lasting years and stick a pile of money into your tools before you can work, do you still not want to wake up from your dream? Don't you want to look after your own interests? All businesses have raised their wages, even the day laborers, who don't need anything more than their own hands. And we carpenters, who need so much, are behind them and work for sinful pay. Do we want to go on like this, living so that we must become betrayers of our spirit and our bodies and our families? Because in this way and with these prices we can't hold out, can't think of a better future, if we don't earn more. Should we then be eternal slaves of capital? Can't we also stand on our own, aren't we entitled to our pay for our hard work?

On March 16, 1863, three hundred carpenters employed building a new elevator struck, inaugurating a procession through the city culminating in a short-lived walkout. Though the strike failed, about twenty German carpenters formed a short-lived cooperative society to buy land and build inexpensive homes for its members.[27]

This first protective union sought to deal with the problem of piecework by ridding the trade of "all men who are not in the true and literal sense carpenters and joiners." Until such men submitted themselves to appropriate training, the union proposed that "the names of employers who persist in employing such incompetent workmen shall be handed into the architect's office with the request that such persons be not employed."[28]

The exclusiveness of this approach and the carpenters' reliance on the good sense of architects soon gave way to mass organizing and self-reliance amidst the buoyant mood of Reconstruction and reform following the Civil War. Frank Lawler, president of Chicago's well-organized ship carpenters, led in lobbying for the nation's first state-wide eight-hour law, which passed the Illinois legislature in 1867. On May 1, ten thousand Chicago workingmen and twenty-seven unions turned out for a parade to support enforcement of the law. The *Chicago Tribune* estimated that almost a third of the city's workingmen participated in the festive occasion, which was enlivened by brightly colored union banners, floats, and marching bands. The four-year-old union of Carpenters and Joiners marched behind a wagon bearing a banner displaying a tombstone with the words: "Ten hours: Born 1842, died 1867." The procession also included the Ship Carpenters and Caulkers Union—an independent union throughout the nineteenth century, which ultimately joined the Chicago District Council of Carpenters in 1909 as Local 643. The union marshaled one hundred and fifty men marching behind an elaborate banner depicting a ship being launched, along with the union's motto, "Be Just and Fear Not." The contingent was followed by a horse-drawn wagon carrying a large decked-over yawl with caulkers at work.[29]

The next day the carpenters and other trades inaugurated the city's first general strike for the eight-hour day. For three weeks the union held out, but toward the end of May most carpenters were back working ten hours. The *Tribune* explained the reason: "A great deal of their work is now done by the piece and the [pieceworkers] do not respect the eight hour rule when they are to that extent their own employers." The remnants of the union turned first to an attempt at producers' cooperation. With the onset of the 1868 depression, carpenters participated in a short-lived fling at independent labor politics that ended when the carpenters' candidate for West Town supervisor lost the election.[30]

In 1869, when a handful of carpenter leaders decided to reorganize the union, the *Workingman's Advocate* responded with the old adage:

> "While the lamp holds out to burn, the greatest sinner may return." Though we are afraid the lamp won't long continue to burn for the Chicago carpenters, who as a body ain't worth the price of a bundle of wick. We have sometimes thought that the

importation of a few thousand celestial wood butchers would
prove in the long run an inestimable blessing because there is
a slight possibility that some such visitation might infuse a
little ambition into their ambitionless souls.[31]

The comments of the *Workingman's Advocate* point up an important
truth about the early carpenters. Rather than as proud self-reliant
craftsmen—an image cultivated by union organizers—outside observers viewed carpenters as a weak, scattered collection of individuals
each pursuing his narrow self-interest and, as a group, essentially
unorganizable.

This view of the carpenters seemed to be confirmed during the
year following the Great Chicago Fire when the carpenters' protective
union made its last stand. On the evening of October 8, 1871, a small
fire in the barn behind the O'Leary cottage on the city's Near West
Side raged out of control. When the fire finally stopped twenty-four
hours later, it was from lack of fuel, not from the efforts of the city's
firemen. In one day four square miles were leveled, eighteen thousand
buildings destroyed, and ninety thousand people, mostly workingmen,
left homeless. During the ensuing winter months large numbers of
workingmen either fled the city or resorted to ramshackle huts of
clapboard and scrap. Rents rose to astronomical heights as speculators
cornered scarce housing, land, and building materials.[32]

When, in January, the City Council threatened to pass an ordinance banning wooden-frame buildings in the city, carpenters acted
to protect their own and other workingmen's need for cheap housing.
The North Side carpenters' union joined a march of ten thousand
workingmen, predominantly German, that invaded City Hall. While
Mayor Joseph Medill hid in the cloakroom, the crowd displayed signs
reading, "Homes for the People" and "Leave the Laborer a Home."
One sign from the carpenters' union depicted a gallows, along with
the words, "This is the lot of those who vote for the Fire Ordinance."
A week later the Council adopted a compromise ordinance allowing
wooden residences outside the central portion of the city.[33]

Even when rebuilding began in earnest in the spring of 1872,
carpenters faced major problems as building workers from the East
swamped the city in search of work and high pay. To organize these
men and to advance wages to meet the high cost of housing, Chicago's
carpenters formed a new protective union, the Carpenters and Joiners
Consolidated Union. Within weeks of its founding it had five hundred
members in two branches, and continued to enroll members each day
by the dozens. On May 6 the union demanded a $.50 pay increase to
$3.50 per day. This demand, along with similar ones from other unions,
outraged the city's business community, which accused the building

trades unions of obstructing the rebuilding of the city.[34] Amidst harsh condemnation from the press, an unidentified workingman defended the carpenters and other unions in the *Tribune*:

> Has not this very fire been a pretext used by the moneyed classes to extort, almost rob, the mechanics and laborers of the little they may possess or gain? Are not the men who prate about losses by fire grinding the very lifeblood out of the class they most need to build them up, by compelling them to pay out in rents more than double the former rents and yet have not doubled the wages of those they employ?[35]

In addition to their demand for a pay increase, carpenters asked for a standard, minimum wage. This highly significant demand demonstrated union carpenters' attempts to reverse the trend toward specialization and deskilling brought by piecework. Instead of futilely trying to expel lesser-skilled, lower-paid men from the trade, carpenter leaders now welcomed them into the union on an equal basis. Indeed, the demand for the standard rate appealed especially to those men apt to engage in piecework by offering them higher rates. At the same time, the "minimum" feature of the demand did not prevent fully skilled carpenters from commanding higher than the standard rate. The sharp dissent of this class demand from the conventional notion of individual advancement was reflected in the *Tribune*'s scandalized reaction: "This demand was so manifestly unjust that not a single builder conceded to it."[36]

The May strike was a failure and the carpenters again turned toward cooperation. This time, working with the bricklayers, they tried to establish a "Mechanics Building Association of Chicago." The aim was grand—to see Chicago rebuilt from the ashes by the cooperative labor of its mechanics—but the means were not commensurate with the end, and the attempt proved abortive. During the same period the president of the carpenters' union helped organize the Arkansas Workingman's Co-operative Colonization Society.[37]

In mid-September the strike spirit reawakened when a sudden rush of work promised a favorable outcome. The union revived even faster than it had disintegrated after the spring strike. At one mass meeting over three hundred carpenters joined or rejoined the union, and in less than two weeks it had more than regained its peak May membership. The strike fever climaxed in a procession through the burned-out district. According to the *Workingman's Advocate*, "The men, while passing a building in which carpenters were at work, would point to the banner and invite them to join the union." By the end of the march there were over nineteen hundred carpenters in line. But again the strike failed largely as a result of the influx of unskilled carpenters from Europe and from the East. In a few months the *Advocate* reported that the union was "shattered" and the following July related that "during the winter it wilted away."[38]

The Weaknesses of the Early Protective Union

The protective union's spectacular successes and even more spectacular failures in 1867 and 1872 prompted considerable soul-searching among carpenter activists and leading Chicago trade unionists. What the *Workingman's Advocate* called "laxity of discipline" and "petty jealousy and bickerings"—what amounted to a lack of sustained commitment to the labor cause—led local unionists to look outside their ranks for alternative organizational solutions. In particular, they explored the benefit features of English trade unionism. One supporter of this alternative argued in the *Advocate* that "perhaps the strongest reason why such a feature has proved successful is that self-interest controls to a great extent all human action; and when the benevolent is combined with the protective, as in this instance, selfishness, if no more honorable instinct, prompts to active and continued membership." According to this argument, the problem with the protective union was that, while cheap and easy to join, it was also cheap and easy to quit.[39]

In August 1870 the British Amalgamated Society of Carpenters established a branch in Chicago and its example soon began to exert a decisive influence on Chicago carpenters. The *Workingman's Advocate* marveled at its comprehensive benefit system that entitled members to sick and unemployment benefits, accident compensation, tool insurance, and even retirement payments, all for a weekly dues of $.35 (about one hour's pay). In an extended comparison between American and English trade unions the paper pinpointed h'   `es and extensive benefits as the reason why English unionist   oy their organizations: "A union with a membership of a doz'   and true men is superior to one with a thousand, who are ur   n just so long as the tide carried them along; a good substan'   ,dation is better than an imposing superstructure built on s   ,d this is the great lesson we desire our workingmen to learr

If this lesson was not sufficiently inculcated l   .872 failure, it was indelibly impressed upon Chicago carpen ,ʋ by the catastrophic six-year depression that began with the July 1873 financial panic. The building industry collapsed in 1874, its product falling in value from $25.5 million in 1873 to $5.8 million. Thereafter, it rose to a plateau of between $8 and $10 million before falling again in 1877. According to testimony before an 1879 investigating committee of the House of Representatives, Chicago carpenters suffered a $.39 reduction in wages during the depression years, greater than that of any trade mentioned. In 1876 the *Tribune*, attempting to portray the human dimension of the depression, reported that:

> A carpenter who was employed for only five out of the twelve months last year, says he has not been able to gain "half a living" for his family for five years. His rent is $2 a month and he spent $12 for fuel saying he wanted a great deal more. For clothing and dry goods he could not afford to lay out even $10. He had no recreation or amusement because he was unable to afford it. As to the cause of his condition, the bosses said, "No work, No work."[41]

After a short-lived cooperative experiment at the beginning of the depression, the American protective union withered away, leaving the field to organizations of the foreign-born: the British Amalgamated Society and small German and Scandinavian unions, all of which relied on benefits.[42]

Recognition of the need for benefits, higher dues, and a more stable union structure was only one of the lessons, and not the most crucial one, that carpenters gleaned from their depression experiences. The lack of long-term commitment to the union, which was the basic reason for the failures of 1867 and 1872, originated less in the lack of an attractive benefit system and more in the absence of a broad class outlook capable of uniting skilled craftsmen, who were the core of the union movement, with the large numbers of unskilled men who were easily lured by the promise of piecework. During the depression years of the 1870s such an outlook began to emerge from the older labor reform philosophy that had been dominant in the 1860s.

By the late 1870s a pervasive awareness of class divisions had surfaced in two forms: the radical reform ideas of the English-speaking workers who composed the Knights of Labor and the socialist outlook of the German-speaking workers who composed the Socialistic Labor party. The Knights had much in common with the program that carpenters and other skilled workers had supported before the depression, a program that included the right of producers to the fruits of their labor through cooperatives and radical political reform focusing on government-issued "greenbacks," and anti-land-monopoly legislation. But the Knights made their most distinctive and lasting contribution to the labor movement through their stress on the common interests of all workingman regardless of skill, sex, racial, or national origin. Their motto, "an injury to one is the concern of all," powerfully symbolized this approach. Though the Knights included trade societies in their order, the form of organization they championed was the

"mixed" local assembly that united workingmen of all skills and occupations. The Knights therefore gave a more profound meaning to
the new ethic of labor solidarity that had motivated Chicago carpenters
to enroll unskilled men behind the demand for the uniform standard
wage.

Unlike the Knights, who believed that the organization of all
producers would enable them to win their program without social
conflict, socialist leaders actively supported strikes and, like their
counterparts in the old country, tried to organize a labor party limited
to workingmen. In addition, they differed from the Knights in advo-
cating sweeping government ownership of large-scale industry. Despite these deep political divisions, both the Knights and the socialists
directed a universal appeal beyond skilled craftsmen to the new industrial working class; both also taught that a new era was on the
horizon when "wage-slavery" would give way to new forms of enter-
prise in which workingmen would have a significant voice.[43]

The new outlook of the Knights and the socialists replaced labor
reform as a result of the emergence during the depression of a new
kind of labor movement based on unskilled immigrant workers. The
first evidences appeared during the first winter of the depression when
the socialists mobilized unemployed workingmen to demonstrate for
public-works jobs or public relief. This was followed by a series of
violent confrontations between workers and authorities during strikes.
This series of confrontations culminated in the Great Upheaval of 1877
in which Chicago's predominantly immigrant industrial working class
revolted against wage cuts, long hours, and a host of other grievances.
As thousands of workingmen thronged the streets to enforce the closing
of all places of employment, the police and militia attacked the crowds.
In three July days at least thirty workingmen were killed and over two
hundred were wounded.[44]

Chicago carpenters had good reason to remember July 1877. In
what a judge later called a "criminal riot," Chicago police charged into
a peaceable meeting of German cabinetmakers (now Local 1027) at
Turner Hall, clubbing and shooting wildly. One carpenter was killed
and dozens more were wounded. In 1892 when Illinois Governor John
Peter Altgeld delivered his famous Haymarket pardon message, he
referred to the Turner Hall incident as the origin of a long train of
violent clashes between workers and police that culminated in the
Haymarket bombing.[45]

The entire labor movement was reborn in the fiery crucible of
1877. One month following the bloody affair new leadership surfaced
within the local labor movement as fifty leading trade unionists established the first branch of the Knights of Labor in Chicago; three
months later the socialists ran their first successful candidates for

public office in the city. Because of its transformed character, the post-1877 labor movement was particularly receptive to leadership supplied by the carpenters. Like other skilled workingmen, many carpenters possessed a strong pride in their traditional craft; yet along with most unskilled industrial workers they shared low wages, degraded working conditions, and the need for mass organization. Thus the carpenters were well situated to bridge the older labor reform movement and the modern industrially based labor movement.

In the years from 1877 through the turn of the century, new forms of organization would emerge among the carpenters. The old loosely knit, transitory protective union was now dead, a casualty of the 1872 defeat and the ensuing depression. By 1877 the ingredients for a new type of trade unionism were present. The way was open for a union that combined protective and benevolent features, reflected the influence of Chicago's immigrant groups, particularly the Germans, and was inspired by the new outlook of the socialists and the Knights of Labor. How this new type of union came into being in the turbulent decade of the 1880s and how the carpenters assumed leadership of Chicago's labor movement are the subjects of the next two chapters.

The Forging

of the

Modern Union,

1878–1891

Since Union 21 started it has had a hard time of it.
First we had to contend with civil strife, then
secession, then Knights of Labor meddling . . . and
last of all a secession of the Anarchists. Union 21 has
lived through all this and starts out fresh and full of
vigor determined to be again the banner union
of the Brotherhood. Long live the Brotherhood is
the wish of . . .

—One of the Boys[1]

Few decades in American history have been more socially trau-matic than the 1880s, the midpoint of what historians—fol-lowing Mark Twain—call the Gilded Age. To a nation that unabashedly celebrated the virtues of the unrestricted pursuit of private profit and the sanctity of the individual contract, the ideas of collective bargaining and of trade unions appeared alien and un-natural. Nonetheless, the American labor movement, riding the crest of a powerful mass movement, was able to mount a remarkably suc-cessful challenge to the conventional wisdom of the day. By the close of the decade, with the appearance of powerful national unions and the new American Federation of Labor, the labor movement had achieved a small but permanent niche in American society.

The 1880s also marked the formative period for the United Brotherhood of Carpenters and Joiners in Chicago. This era, that prop-erly begins with the revival of unionism after the 1877 strikes and closes with the signing of the carpenters' first collective bargaining contract in 1891, can be divided into three distinct parts. Between 1878 and 1885 the union struggled through a difficult transitional period. Although the old-style unionism that had marked the 1867 and 1872 upheavals was clearly inadequate, a new brand of unionism had not yet been born. The Brotherhood and other carpenter societies of this time were curious admixtures of the old and the new.

The eight-hour movement and the Haymarket affair, which dominated the events of 1886 and 1887, ended this transitional period by popularizing the ideas of solidarity, mass organization, and militancy. For the first time, the union idea captured the imaginations of thousands of Chicago carpenters of all skill levels and backgrounds. But there was still disunity between the Knights of Labor and the Brotherhood, and among the various building trades. After a short respite in 1888–89, the carpenters resumed their struggle for a contract. This time, led by the Brotherhood and supported by the first unified Building Trades Council, Chicago's carpenters achieved victory.

A Time of Transition, 1878–1885

When citywide carpenter unionism revived in 1878, carpenter leaders began to stress the importance of benefits in achieving stability in their organizations. Following the example of the English, Scandinavian, and German societies that had survived the depression, Chicago carpenters formed their first multiethnic benevolent union.

The new Carpenters and Joiners Benevolent Association, like earlier protective unions, was organized in semiautonomous branches, including a large American branch, and smaller German, Bohemian, and Scandinavian branches. But combining benefit functions with the branch system created a special difficulty. The new commitment to the benefit system disposed rank and file carpenters to be especially jealous of branch autonomy. Given the dreary history of citywide carpenters' unionism, they were fearful that a collapse of the central body might undermine the financial integrity of the benefit system on the branch level. It was probably for this reason that the new benevolent association lacked a common constitution and remained little more than a collection of ethnic benevolent societies, each protective of its right to collect dues and distribute benefits.[2]

In 1879, with the end of the depression, the older protective tendency reasserted itself. A small group of carpenters, dissatisfied with the benevolent society, broke away to form the Carpenters and Joiners Protective and Benevolent Society. Though the "protectives" paid lip service to the idea of benefits, they were more concerned with creating a mass-based union willing to engage in strikes. To this end they constructed a union that was very different from the "benevolents." They set low dues and initiation fees, and to facilitate unity, consolidated all ethnic groups into one body.[3]

As the two rivals competed for members in Chicago in the ensuing two years, the results demonstrated the continued strength of ethnic identification and the absence of a common labor philosophy. Without the drawing power of a strike, the protectives failed to increase their membership beyond 435. The benevolents, on the other hand, attracted three times as many members with their sick benefits and their ethnic autonomy. But even combined these organizations enrolled only a tiny fraction of the trade.[4]

Despite bad feeling the two factions united long enough to host the founding convention of the United Brotherhood of Carpenters and Joiners of America in August 1881. Though a national union of carpenters had existed since 1865, it had ceased to have any influence on Chicago carpenters during the depression. The founding of the United Brotherhood had come on the initiative of St. Louis carpenter leader Peter J. McGuire, who sought to regulate the flow of migrating carpenters from city to city.

The struggle between the protectives and the benevolents continued at the convention, half of whose delegates were from Chicago. The protectives desired a powerful and centralized national organization to support local strikes and to regulate intercity travel. The benevolents wanted a weaker national organization, one which would be limited to serving as a financial clearinghouse for the benefit system of each local. The outcome of the convention was a compromise. The protectives gained the office of a full-time paid national secretary (filled by McGuire), a strike fund, and a national system of working cards. Otherwise, the benevolents ruled the day. The per capita tax was low, disbursement of the strike fund had to be sanctioned by two-thirds of all locals, and the national executive board was weak. In consequence, the United Brotherhood's national organization had little infuence on the Chicago union in the 1880s, other than through the editorials and personal visits of the charismatic McGuire.[5]

For the first year of the Brotherhood's existence in Chicago, the protectives and the benevolents continued their separate lives as Locals 3 and 4. In May 1882 under McGuire's direction, the two locals merged to form Local 21. The new local was truly a union of a new type among Chicago carpenters, a synthesis of protective and benevolent features. Members paid high initiation fees and dues, and with the merger, the new local added a death and disability benefit to the benevolents' old sick benefit. The union adopted a strike fund in 1884, and soon afterward elected its first walking delegate (business agent). The local conciliated its different ethnic and language groups by adopting a branch system, a move necessitated by the Brotherhood's new national policy of one local per city.[6]

An Appeal by the Brotherhood to Non-Union Carpenters

Ye Bohemians from the wilds and forests of your native land, how many times a week do you and your families luxuriate on beefsteak? French Canadians from your snow huts of the Dominions, how much better dwelling places do you now occupy? All you two-and-a-quarter men, how many of your children are going to school? They are more likely to be engaged in picking up coal along the railroad track. If you can live on rye bread and onions washed down with lager, you must understand that decent mechanics cannot, and the boss that employs you and pays you such wages will soon have to do his own work or pay men enough to live on.[7]

In the following two years Local 21 emerged as a power in the local labor movement. Its president, J. P. McGinley, later third general president of the Brotherhood, served as vice-president of the Trade and Labor Assembly and in 1882 ran unsuccessfully as labor's candidate for the state legislature. The carpenters in this period also played the principal role in establishing a new trade union newspaper, the *Progressive Age*, which replaced the more politicized *Workingman's Advocate*. The local subscribed to twenty-one of fifty shares of stock issued by the paper, and contributed six of nine directors to its board.[8]

The union's first great test came in 1884. In the previous two years Local 21 had increased its membership from one thousand to three thousand and the number of its branches from nine to twelve. In the spring of 1884 a local leader wrote that Chicago's carpenters had come to a point in their development when it was necessary to "unfurl their banner and say those who are not with us are against us."[9]

The strike began auspiciously. Under McGuire's personal direction, the local walked out in May for a standard minimum wage of $3 a day. The union set up a strike committee that divided the city into twelve districts. A subcommittee of five visited jobsites in each district to urge nonunion men to join the union. Within ten days the

$3 rate had been secured for two thousand men. Nevertheless, within two months a scarcity of brick and the onset of the 1884–86 depression led to the defeat of the strike. Contributing to the defeat was the inability of the union to attract more than three thousand of the city's six- to eight-thousand carpenters, probably because of its high dues. By August an influx of itinerant carpenters had restored the piecework system in the trade.[10]

As the union retreated, the branch system was unable to prevent the splintering of the local into ethnopolitical factions. In response to ethnic restiveness the Brotherhood's fourth national convention had earlier mandated the establishment of multiple locals per city to replace the branch system. In the case of Chicago, however, the Executive Board required each branch to pay its share of the large strike debt owed by Local 21 to the national union before it could be chartered as a separate local. Rather than do this the Czech carpenter branch, which had helped found the Brotherhood in 1881, left the national union in 1885. They were soon joined in secession by a larger group of Germans. The Chicago Germans, said The Carpenter, "have dodged a settlement and under the lead of a few anarchists, they want to run on their own hook." Several months later The Carpenter reported on the existence of "an armed organization of a dozen carpenters of the anarchist stripe."[11]

Both the German and Bohemian carpenters affiliated with the Central Labor Union (CLU), a federation of unions representing German-speaking trade unionists in the city. Top leadership positions in the CLU were held by members of the International Working People's Association, an anarchist society that in Chicago was an outgrowth of the city's new socialist movement. The anarchists criticized voluntary cooperation and the limited goals of strikes for wages and shorter hours. Unlike the political socialists, who sought to participate in the electoral system, the anarchists advocated revolutionary violence, in the form of dynamite bombs, as a way of abolishing the capitalist state and creating a "free society" of autonomous communes. Almost 80 percent of all Chicago anarchists were German or Czech; and, classified by trade, approximately one-quarter of all anarchists were building trades carpenters.

During this period German and Czech carpenter unionists participated in a variety of anarchist-sponsored activities ranging from celebrations of the Paris Commune of 1871, to participation in armed groups such as the Lehr und Wehr Verein and Bohemian Sharpshooters, to subscribing to local anarchist-socialist papers such as the Arbeiter Zeitung and Budoucnost.[12]

Meanwhile, those Americans remaining in Local 21 secured a

charter from the state to form a building cooperative. As with previous attempts, the cooperative died within the year and devastated the resources of the local. By fall 1885, when McGuire journeyed to Chicago to attempt a much-needed revival of union spirit, the local was almost dead.[13]

With the enfeeblement of Local 21, many American-born carpenters drifted toward the Knights of Labor. The Knights, like the anarchists, opposed the wage system and viewed strikes as diversionary of workers' scarce energies. Unlike the anarchists, however, they had strong roots in the Anglo-American artisan tradition of producers' cooperation. But the Knights updated this tradition. Rather than isolated cooperative experiments, the Knights proposed a vast organization of all workers that would gradually bring into existence a cooperative society. Politically, the Knights saw their order as a vehicle for uniting all producers—workers, farmers, and small businessmen—to counter the growing power of monopolies, trusts, and corporations within the government and to root out the concentration of wealth, social inequality, and political privilege. Though the Knights welcomed trade unions into their order, they advocated the formation of "mixed" local assemblies that would unite workingmen from different trades. It was a Knights' mixed local assembly, Local 1307, which attracted a small group of dissatisfied protectives in 1882 when their local merged with Local 21. With the decline of Local 21 in 1885, other English-speaking carpenters also joined Knights' mixed assemblies, though many retained their membership in the Brotherhood.[14]

The three way split in 1885 represented the final crisis of old-style carpenter unionism and its labor reform philosophy. Despite its renovated structure, the 1881–84 Brotherhood had shown itself incapable of attracting and holding the loyalty of Chicago's carpenters. Meanwhile, the failure of Local 21's cooperative gave credence to the criticism of McGuire and many socialists that it was impractical and diversionary of the union's scarce funds. Carpenters were ready for a new labor philosophy and a new type of union.

The Union Takes Root: the Haymarket Period, 1886–1887

Less than a year before the great eight-hour strikes and the Haymarket affair of 1886, prospects for the carpenters' union seemed dismal. Like the rest of Chicago's labor movement, the union was split into three factions: the Knights of Labor, the Central Labor Union, and the remnants of Local 21 affiliated with the Trade and Labor Assembly. Each rivaled the other for the allegiance of Chicago's carpenters. The

1884 depression had destroyed the city's building boom that had begun in 1880. Piecework was rife, and the dispirited Brotherhood was on the verge of collapse.

Yet, within two short years, beginning with preparation for the eight hour strikes of May 1886, the bulk of Chicago's carpenters turned their back on piecework and subcontracting and embraced unionism.[15] Carpenters successfully enforced their demands for a standard minimum wage and shorter hours with the first systematic use of mass intimidation and other militant tactics; they engaged in their first general walkout and were aided by a sympathy strike; and to weld together Chicago's competing ethno-political factions, the resourceful carpenters developed new forms of unity: the United Carpenters Council and the multilocal system. What made these advances possible was a mighty grass-roots movement for shorter hours and unionism—called by historians the "Great Upheaval"—and a different group of Brotherhood leaders who subscribed to a new and more radical labor outlook.

Two developments energized labor's great upheaval: a new code of class solidarity and an optimistic belief that workingmen could create a better world. During the 1880s two new words became popular among the city's workers. The word "scab" had been used sporadically by skilled craftsmen before this period, but in the 1880s its use proliferated among a broad variety of workingmen affected by industrialization. The use of the word scab implied that there was a moral community of workers and that the men or women who crossed picket lines of strikers or who took jobs at lower pay were traitors to this community. It was during strikes of this period that the word acquired a kind of superstitious power; few workingmen—whatever their ethnic background—wanted to be called a scab. During the streetcar workers' strike of 1885 Police Captain John Bonfield instructed his men to arrest any bystander who shouted the word at the strikebreakers they were protecting.[16]

A word of similar meaning that became popular during this period was "boycott." Captain Boycott was a hated British land agent in Ireland who became the focus of the Irish Land League's struggle in behalf of tenants. Instead of employing violence, the League advocated that Irish patriots refuse to associate with him, in effect ostracizing him from the community. The tactic worked and spread like wildfire across the Atlantic where it was adopted in the early 1880s by Irish-American labor leaders and popularized by the Knights of Labor. Like the word "scab," boycott presupposed the existence of a moral community among workingmen.

In 1881 a Brotherhood leader argued that boycotting could be used to destroy the piecework system:

As the carpenter trade suffers more from piecework than any other cause, it is what should be first abolished, but without the aid of Captain Boycott it will take some time to do it. . . . Let no Union foreman give a job to a man who is known to take piecework; let no union man work with a man who takes piecework, and neither union nor non-union man should raise a hand for a boss who is known to let piecework. Is this boycotting? If so let it come, and soon. When a man is mean enough to try to crush our trade at every opportunity, I say *crush him* in every legal way in our power. One grand union must be formed—and that is a union of all the trades. Then, when a boss will not listen to reason, notification thereof should be given all the unions. Then let no man purchase from a grocer who sells him provisions, nor from the butcher who sells him his meat. Will I go further?[17]

The sense of power and possibility unleashed by the notion that all trades could unite in one organization and use their collective power legally to right the wrongs of Gilded Age capitalism found an outlet in the eight-hour movement. Since the 1860s eight hours had been the central goal of the labor movement and of carpenters. In several ways the demand had revolutionary implications. The ten-hour day was seen by union leaders as the reason why workers were physically and emotionally exhausted and discouraged from seeking redress of their grievances. A 20 percent reduction of hours would allow workers to redirect their energies to improvement of themselves and of their class. By the 1870s and 1880s labor theorist Ira Steward argued that eight hours' work for ten hours' pay would allow workingmen to appropriate the largest share of profit to themselves, which they could use to establish cooperatives. It was in both senses that P. J. McGuire called the eight-hour movement "the Lexington of the coming revolution and it would go on until the capitalists were driven from power."[18]

In 1884, led by McGuire, the tiny Federation of Organized Trades and Labor Unions—forerunner of the American Federation of Labor—called for a national strike for the eight hour day on May 1, 1886. To implement this goal Chicago's labor leaders formed the Eight Hour League in the fall of 1885. But the idea did not catch fire until the city's workingmen had concrete evidence of the power of solidarity in a single organization, the Knights of Labor. In the spring of 1886 the Knights engaged in the nation's first great sympathy strike in which all trades on the Southwest Railroad lines united against the most notorious of the late nineteenth-century Robber Barons, Jay Gould. Immediately following this victory the Chicago Knights won two local boycott victories. At last it seemed possible to put the dreams associated with eight hours into action.

In the spring of 1886 the Knights became the vehicle for workingmen's aspirations in Chicago and throughout the nation. Locally, the Knights grew from two thousand in 1885 to over twenty thousand in 1886, with most of this growth coming in the spring of 1886. English-speaking carpenters flocked to the Knights in the same way that they had flocked to earlier protective unions in 1867 and 1872. Brotherhood leaders James Brennock and R. C. Owens withdrew from their mixed local assembly, and along with James J. Linehan, formed Knights' carpenters' Assembly 6570. According to Brennock: "The result of the establishment of the Knights of Labor assembly was that they flocked in there by the hundreds every meeting; some nights in fact 200 members got in there. The Knights of Labor carpenters went up spontaneously."[19]

In March 1886 the Chicago *Knights of Labor* newspaper reported that the carpenters were rapidly joining assemblies. "There are assemblies nearly wholly composed of carpenters and two more assemblies principally carpenters, are in the process of organization, and quite a number of members of Union 21 belong to the Order, and from the best information we can get there appear to be more carpenters in the KOL in the United States and Canada than in the Brotherhood."[20]

Local 21 had languished until the Knights began to grow. "Then," recalled Brennock, "the result of that growth was that the Brotherhood of United Carpenters and Joiners of America began to prick up their ears too, and say now we must begin to do something. . . . After the Knights were established they grew on apace together."[21] Meanwhile, many German and Czech carpenters joined unions affiliated with the anarchist-led Central Labor Union.

The resurgence of the Brotherhood was due in large part to a change in leadership in Local 21. The 1884–85 debacle had discredited older leaders such as J. P. McGinley, Thomas Doran, and Thomas Blair, and along with them major tenets of their labor reform philosophy, which shunned militancy and espoused temperance (prohibition of intoxicating drink on Sundays) and producers' cooperatives. In their place arose a new group that focused the hopes of the organization on the eight-hour demand as a means of unifying carpenters of different political beliefs; and, unlike the old leaders, they were willing to sanction mass militancy based on labor solidarity to win carpenter demands. The break with the past was dramatic. Between 1881 and 1882 the *Progressive Age* listed eighty-five Brotherhood officials; during the late 1880s not one of these men held positions in the city central body of carpenters.[22]

The new Brotherhood leadership consisted of a triumvirate composed of James Brennock, William Kliver, and Robert Swallow. These men, like national leader McGuire, were attuned to the radicalism of the mid–1880s and were willing to work closely with the Knights of Labor and anarchists in the CLU. Though they disapproved of violent revolution, they strongly defended the civil rights of the condemned anarchists after Haymarket. They also played a vigorous role in supporting labor's independent political thrust, the United Labor party, led by machinist Thomas J. Morgan, Chicago's leading socialist. The carpenters contributed thirty-six delegates to the party's founding convention, more by far than any other Chicago union. Finally, the triumvirate promoted the political climate that allowed the Germans and Czechs to return to the Brotherhood in 1886.[23]

Each of these leaders was also active in the Knights of Labor. Doubtlessly they were attracted by the Knights' motto, "an injury to one is the concern of all," and its expression in the sympathy strike. Brennock helped organize Assembly 6570; Swallow represented mixed Assembly 6561 at the founding convention of the United Labor party; Kliver was a member of mixed Assembly 1307. As part of their strong commitment to class solidarity beyond their trade, these leaders also provided leadership to the city's labor movement. In early 1887 the Trade and Labor Assembly elected Kliver as its president, and he was succeeded by Swallow. During the same year Brennock was elected first president of the new Building Trades Council.[24]

On the eve of the eight-hour strikes, Brotherhood leaders worked diligently to unify Chicago's diverse carpenter factions. By late March nine groups within five different carpenter unions including Local 21, the Amalgamated, and three CLU unions had combined to form the United Carpenters Committee. Though the Knights were not represented because their national office opposed the eight-hour strike, their local assemblies generally cooperated in the movement. By April 24, the committee could claim that 80 percent of all carpenters belonged to various carpenter unions. Confronted with this strength the contractors, who had also organized in the meantime, agreed fully one week before the May 1 deadline to reduce hours to eight and appoint a joint arbitration committee to determine wages. Within a month of frenzied organizing, Chicago's carpenters had won the great goal that had eluded them in two decades of struggle.[25]

On May 3, 1886 R. C. Owens, carpenter leader of the Brotherhood and the Knights, proudly addressed a mass meeting of carpenters to hail the contractors' adoption of eight hours. Less than twenty-four hours later an event occurred that fairly snatched this momentous triumph out of the hands of the union. On the afternoon of May 3 police had killed one worker and wounded several others who were attempting to stop strikebreakers at McCormick's Reaper Plant. In response, the anarchists convened a protest meeting the following evening at Haymarket Square. The crowd of about three thousand—relatively small for those excited times—had dwindled to less than a third its original size and was in the midst of dispersing when a squad of police arrived. They were under the command of the notorious Captain Bonfield, known for his motto, "the club today saves the bullet tomorrow." Minutes before his police advanced, Mayor Harrison had told Bonfield that the meeting was harmless and that police intervention was not necessary. Nonetheless, 176 policemen soon advanced to confront the crowd of workingmen. In the charged moment when Bonfield commanded the crowd to disperse, someone—no one knows who—threw a bomb into the ranks of the police. Seven officers were killed and 70 wounded. The remaining policemen responded to the explosion by firing into the panic-stricken crowd, killing seven workers and wounding dozens more.[26]

Though the prosecution never established the identity of the bomb thrower, and all the city's unions condemned the act, Chicago's press, business, and political leadership used the Haymarket incident to destroy the anarchist political organization and discredit the labor movement. In the hysteria that followed the bombing, freedom of speech and press were temporarily suspended. Within two days two hundred labor and socialist leaders were arrested in a police dragnet operation. According to one unionist:

> After May [4] picketing became absolutely impossible. The police arrested all pickets, even two or three. The attitude on the part of the police was practically the same as though the city was under martial law. Labor unions were raided, broken up, their property confiscated, the police used their clubs freely. Arrests were made without cause, and the life of the workingman was not quite safe when out on strike.[27]

The experience of Chicago's highly skilled cabinetmakers and furniture-workers was typical. German socialists had organized the International Furniture Workers Union in 1872. On the eve of the eight-hour strikes the union had increased its membership from eight hundred to approximately four to five thousand, many of the workers semiskilled machine-tenders. On the night of May 4 after the Haymarket bomb exploded, the Chicago local experienced a police attack similar to that of July 1877. Captain Bonfield and his men stormed into Sepf's Hall, tore to shreds the union's flag, and partially destroyed its library. Aware of the Turner Hall court decision favoring the union, the city forestalled a lawsuit by voluntarily paying the union $250 in damages. But the union was a shambles; a year after the May strikes, the Furniture Workers Union had only three hundred members.[28]

Beginning in June eight anarchist leaders were put on trial for violating the state's criminal conspiracy law. According to this law the prosecution did not have to demonstrate that the anarchists threw the bomb or even conspired with those who threw the bomb, only that they advocated revolutionary violence and contributed to the climate in which the bomb was thrown. Because of the antilabor and antiradical hysteria, eight anarchists were convicted and seven were sentenced to death. On November 11, 1887, four of those sentenced were hanged—two had their sentences commuted by the governor and one, Louis Lingg, an organizer for a carpenters' union affiliated with the CLU, committed suicide—in one of the blackest episodes in the history of Chicago and of the American labor movement.

One week after the bomb at Haymarket exploded, the contractors' association, using the incident as a pretext, declared its intention of restoring the ten-hour day. By early June over one thousand carpenters were locked out. The union responded with a strike and enforced its demands with militant action. But it took a daring and charismatic immigrant to organize this action.

William Henry Jackson was a young, well-educated British Canadian, who had aligned himself with the 1885 rebellion of the Métis, mixed blood French Indians, in northwestern Canada. After initial success, the armed rebellion was defeated by Canadian troops, and Louis Riel, its leader, was executed. As Riel's secretary, Jackson was consigned to a lunatic asylum. In November 1885 Jackson escaped and made his way on foot to the United States. Arriving in Chicago shortly before the Haymarket incident Jackson changed his name to Honore Joseph Jaxon, laid claim to French-Indian descent, and gained fame by lecturing on the Métis Rebellion. Meanwhile, he joined a French-Canadian carpenters local of the Knights of Labor and rose to the post of secretary of the United Carpenters Committee.[29]

When the May strike seemed about to fail, Jaxon turned his Métis military experience to good use. He became the strike's "general," mapping out the locations of ten hour jobsites and arranging for union men trained in the use of the slingshot to "clean out the scabs." In all cases he concentrated his forces so that his men outnumbered their foes. Because these guerrilla skirmishes occurred simultaneously at different locations, there was little the police could do to interfere. "It worked to perfection," recalled Jaxon many years later.

It struck terror to the hearts of the scabs and bosses at the same time. They didn't know when the lightning might strike again. And there was little actual violence. Most of the scabs ran when we entered the buildings and not a man was arrested. The scabs joined the union in hundreds in the next few days. That was the first organized violence in the building trades in Chicago.[30]

With such tactics the eight-hour movement defeated the smaller contractors; but the larger millmen-contractors, employing a majority of Chicago's carpenters, continued to defy the union. The building season closed with their men still working ten hours.[31]

The mixed outcome of the 1886 strike proved to be only a momentary setback. The union did not melt away or break up into its ethnic components as it had done following previous defeats. Instead, the upsurge of the spring of 1886 continued past the Haymarket reaction into 1887, culminating in new and higher levels of carpenter solidarity around the union.

Two important developments enabled the carpenters to renew the eight-hour struggle. The first was the return of the anarchist-led Germans and Bohemians to the Brotherhood's fold. In all likelihood, their decision to give up their short-lived independence was a defensive response to the sharp turn in public opinion after Haymarket. According to their own account it was a consequence of their commitment to class unity. Facilitating their return was the Brotherhood's national policy of allowing multiple locals in each city. In the fall of 1886 the anarchists rejoined the union, the Czechs as Local 54, and the Germans as locals 240–44.

Their return marked the origin of the vital ethnic local tradition among Chicago's carpenters. By permitting separate ethnic organizations at the neighborhood level, each local could pursue its own cultural interests and politics. For example, Czech Local 54 consisted largely of anti-Catholic "free thinkers," followers of a suppressed Bohemian nationalist tradition that flowered in America. Local 54 contributed to the defense fund of the anarchist carpenter Louis Lingg and later sent delegates to the annual memorial service for the executed Haymarket martyrs and worked for the release of the imprisoned survivors. In one episode the union moved its headquarters rather than take the portrait of one of the Haymarket martyrs off the wall of a school from which it rented its hall. Ethnic local autonomy also fostered a strong camaraderie among members through picnics, parades, and dances and encouraged rank and file participation in the union.[32]

With the return to the Brotherhood of the ethnic independents, the main impediment to unity among carpenters came from the rivalry between the Brotherhood and the Knights of Labor. The Knights continued to grow phenomenally during the last three months of 1886 after the decline of the Brotherhood-run strike. By the end of December the *Knights of Labor* newspaper boasted that its organization controlled between five and six thousand of the city's carpenters, divided into four local assemblies, including French- and German-speaking ones.[33]

As the carpenters prepared to renew their demands on the contractors in 1887, the need for a new organization that included Knights as well as Brotherhood members became clear. James Brennock, member of both unions, was well placed to lead such a movement. In January 1887 he pioneered the formation of the United Carpenters Council including members of the Knights, the Brotherhood, and the British Amalgamated Society of Carpenters. The UCC was an important advance over the old carpenters' committee. It was the largest carpenters' organization ever formed in Chicago up to that time, representing some six thousand of Chicago's approximately eight thousand carpenters. More significantly, the new UCC was more unified and centralized than the loosely knit committee. Each member union exchanged working cards with all others; and leaders attempted, with some success, to persuade the constituent unions to adopt uniform initiation fees and dues to avoid membership rivalries. The UCC hired three walking delegates—the first one being James Brennock—paid through a per capita tax on the unions. Finally, decisions by UCC delegates were not referred to each union for ratification as before. By concentrating the essential powers of each union in a powerful executive council, the UCC was the immediate forerunner of the modern Brotherhood's District Council.[34]

The spring and summer of 1887 represented the high tide of labor unity and militancy among carpenters in the 1880s. The carpenters' demands were more ambitious than ever before. Not only did the UCC ask for eight hours, a standard minimum wage, and a wage increase as in 1886, but it now demanded union recognition in the form of a closed shop. When negotiations broke down in March over the latter two demands, the UCC called a strike for April 1. On that date 90 percent of the city's carpenters walked out. Recalled one observer, "The bosses were stunned, they had not expected any but the organized men—and probably not all of them to obey the strike order." Ten days later the small contractors split from the the bosses' association, which was dominated by the large millmen-contractors, and agreed to the UCC's demands.[35]

Yet, when the UCC accepted this capitulation in order to pressure the large contractors, a large sector of the union's rank and file revolted. Refusing to go along with a divide-and-conquer policy, the radical Germans, Czechs, and others argued that without a general strike of all carpenters there would be no way for the union leadership to tell who was working more than eight hours or for less than scale. Though the disagreement was tactical in nature, it had ideological overtones, for the German carpenters' strong commitment to this tactic stemmed from their political position favoring uncompromising class warfare. The less militant *Knights* newspaper was outraged at this turn of events, calling the rebels "men wild with excitement, foolhardy and hotheaded . . . placing themselves on a level with an utterly unorganizable mob strike." The UCC was in a quandary, fearing that the revolt would reunify the contractors. In taking their original position, carpenter leaders may have estimated that the strikers were not strong enough without building trades unity to win a contract from the large contractors, and realistically strove to employ members with the small contractors. Several days later the UCC resumed this policy and concluded an agreement with the smaller contractors.[36]

The successful agreement soon provoked a reaction from the large contractors. In early May the mason contractors, backed by Chicago's large builders, material manufacturers, and the National Association of Builders, declared a lockout of the bricklayers and vowed to "crush out the walking delegate" and institute the open shop. They were soon joined by the major carpenter contractors. The joint lockout represented the first general reaction of construction employers to the 1886–87 labor upsurge and its successful use of new tactics such as the boycott and organized intimidation.

According to the *Tribune's* labor correspondent:

> The strike of a year ago marked an epoch in the history of industrial affairs in the city. The Haymarket bomb changed the situation and put new ideas in the heads of the men who furnished the brain and the capital. They realized for the first time that unless active measures were taken business would be ruined and the triumph of the walking delegate would be complete.

The contractors' lockout was backed by a material manufacturers' boycott of all construction work. This was clearly an attempt to force the smaller contractors to hew the line drawn by the large ones. In a broader sense, the lockout and material boycott was the reply of the big builders to the use of divide-and-conquer tactics by the UCC and the bricklayers' union.[37]

To many building trades workers, particularly the carpenters, it was obvious that only a Building Trades Council composed of all trades and willing to engage in sympathy action could successfully repel the employers' onslaught. Hitherto, the bricklayers—the only union among the building trades with collective bargaining—had remained aloof from the trades unity movement. On June 22 a successful rank and file German revolt against the union leadership led the bricklayers to join the new council that the carpenters had helped start earlier in the year.[38]

Thereafter, the situation improved considerably. In early July the bricklayers settled their dispute with the masons by arbitration, leaving only the carpenters locked out. This time the carpenters could rely on sympathy action from the bricklayers, who offered what they called "moral support." According to the *Tribune* account, "moral support with the average bricklayer means the dropping of a brick upon the head of an unwary nonunion workman." Help from the bricklayers, plus a longstanding and turbulent boycott of the downtown Haymarket Theater, helped the carpenters to turn the tide. By the end of the summer the leading contractors had conceded the eight hour demand, though the UCC was not able to secure a compensatory hourly wage increase or union recognition.[39]

The 1887 triumph was an important turning point for the union. The centralized UCC had proven its effectiveness and continued to run trade affairs in Chicago until 1894. Though they did not achieve union recognition, the carpenters had played a major role in bringing unity to Chicago's building trades and in defeating the first open-shop attack on unions by united employers. Not until 1921 would employers initiate another open-shop campaign. Most importantly, the 1887 struggle pointed the way to new tactics: the intertrade sympathy strike and boycott and the general walkout designed to secure an agreement with a unified bosses' association, as well as the consolidation of older institutions such as the "walking delegate."

On September 5, 1887, the Trade and Labor Assembly held its annual Labor Day parade. Two years earlier only fifty carpenters had appeared; now over two thousand Brotherhood men marched down the city's streets in a mile-long contingent while they quaffed beer and sang "Marching Through Georgia."[40]

The Brotherhood versus the Knights and the Winning of the First Contract

The high tide of 1886–87 unified long-isolated and antagonistic ethnic factions among Chicago carpenters behind a more inclusive and militant class outlook. In contrast, nonethnic organizational divisions remained more durable. Beginning in late 1887, the Brotherhood and the Knights entered into a bitter rivalry that concluded several years later in the practical defeat of the Knights. Only after the substantial resolution of this conflict in 1890 was the union able to summon up the strength to win its first contract.

The dispute between the Brotherhood and the Knights stemmed only partially from the Knights' aversion to strikes and practical trade union politics. More basic were issues of organization and the resulting conflict between local and national Knights' leaders. Brotherhood members initially viewed the Knights as principally an educational and labor reform organization, rather than a "dual union." Indeed, Brotherhood leaders found the Knights' political reform orientation quite compatible with their own, as indicated by their membership in Knights' mixed assemblies. In 1886 the establishment of the first Knights' carpenters' assembly represented a break in this congenial division of labor. According to James Brennock, it was "the first seed of its destruction." The reason was that in matters of strikes and union organization the Knights were bound by the dictates of a centralized command system passing from the General Executive Board to the district assemblies to the local assemblies. The leaders of the higher bodies represented a broad class constituency, and could not put the interests of the carpenters' trade paramount.[41]

This potential problem became a stumbling block during the 1887 lockout, when the carpenter Knights and the Brotherhood locals appealed to their respective national organizations for strike benefits. When the Knights' General Executive Board refused to pay benefits as part of its policy of reining in strikes by new members, Knights' members deserted in droves to the Brotherhood, which received funds through McGuire. The Knights' action in 1887 solidified their reputation for losing and even sabotaging local strikes first earned in the packinghouse workers' strike in the fall of 1886. James Brennock exaggerated only slightly when he recalled that the Knights of Labor "has never been known in history [to have] gained one strike; they were all failures."[42]

In the last months of 1887 Knights' Local Assembly 6570 declined from 500 men in January 1887 to 180 by the end of the year. In the same period Assembly 9272 was reduced from 73 to 44. The German carpenter Assembly 9266 went out of existence. In mid-December a Knights of Labor member summarized the radical shift in organizational strength: "A year ago the Knights and the carpenters' Brotherhood were on equal footing as far as members were concerned. The carpenters' Brotherhood have now swallowed the Knights and have more than doubled their membership. Nothing succeeds like success and nothing fails like failure."[43]

Following this decline, the issue between the Knights and the Brotherhood became one of dual unionism. In the fall of 1887 several

Knights' carpenters' assemblies withdrew from the UCC and helped form a separate Knights' national Trade District Assembly, operating independently of the General Executive Board. When the UCC renewed its demands on the contractors in February 1888, the local Knights' council undercut the union by accepting a lower wage settlement from the contractors. This action, plus the dissolution of the Building Trades Council in May 1889, forced the UCC to suspend its strike plans and turn its attention to a municipal campaign to secure government support for the eight-hour day. On June 8, 1889, the City Council adopted an eight-hour ordinance drawn up by the soon-to-be-famous trial lawyer Clarence Darrow at the behest of the carpenters. On December 9 the School Board and Board of county Commissioners also accepted the eight-hour principle.[44]

The year 1889 was the landmark for another crucial development for the Brotherhood. Previously all carpenter unions, with the short-lived exception of the tiny "protective" faction (1879–82), had been internally differentiated by ethnicity and language, either through branches or ethnic locals. In the spring of 1889 former German anarchist Locals 240 through 244, 284, and 291, as well as top CLU official Adolph Stamm, combined with the English-speaking Progressive Carpenters Union, along with a number of important leaders from Knights' Assembly 6570 to merge with Local 1. With almost half of all Brotherhood members, the local was easily the largest in the Brotherhood's District Council and the UCC. From its inception Local 1, headed by former Knight James J. Linehan, was the most politically radical and militant of all carpenter unions. Along with Local 28, which to a large extent shared this perspective, Local 1 dominated the leadership and determined the policy of the UCC throughout the early 1890s.[45]

Chicago carpenters began preparing for their 1890 campaign in the role of standard bearers for the American labor movement's second great attempt to win the eight-hour day. The decisive question in the great 1890 strike, however, was not hours; that had been conceded by most large employers in 1887. Rather, it was wages and, most of all, union recognition in the form of the UCC's demand for a joint arbitration committee. Under the influence of Local 1, the carpenters learned well the lesson of 1887 taught by the Germans. A stable agreement with the contractors' association was a prerequisite to enforcing all other demands. One UCC leader put the matter succinctly, stating that, "If we wanted to, we could get 100 contractors [signed up] in one day to employ our men, but we have to stand out for recognition of our organization."[46]

On the eve of the strike, the union had reason for confidence.

The previous week the Knights, who had given indications of under-cutting the UCC's wage demands again, rejoined the council with their three assemblies and five hundred men. With the inclusion of the Knights, the UCC now represented between 70 percent and 90 percent of the trade. Moreover, the bricklayers promised not to work with nonunion men. On April 7 about six thousand men struck, virtually the entire trade.

The Master Carpenters' Association secretary candidly admitted the employers' astonishment at the strength of the union. The Association's president, William Goldie, however, was not willing to concede: "I do not think the union is as strong as it claims. Many of its members joined within the last week."[47]

But the carpenters were indeed far stronger than in 1887. Not only were the vast majority signed up, but, with the help of the Brotherhood in other cities, they had devised a way of insulating Chicago from the usual influx of nonunion men who inundated any city when a strike was afoot. The *Tribune* described the system this way:

> The strikers have a system that works like a charm. There is not a point of any consequence in the United States from which any man can start with a kit of tools without notice being sent at once to Chicago. In a radius of sixty-five miles around Chicago members of carpenters' unions are stationed at every town along every railroad, and no carpenter can pass them without having the fact wired to the strike committee. In this way the local men can meet every new arrival and in most cases capture him for the union.

UCC President James O'Connell, from Local 1, explained the source of the national support Chicago carpenters were receiving in his ringing declaration that: "We are not fighting the battle of Chicago carpenters alone. We are fighting for united labor all over this land."[48]

Within the city the carpenters were equally well organized. Squads of union men visited "scab" building sites around town, intimidating strikebreakers by force of numbers and by "causing" their tools to disappear permanently in the walls of buildings under construction. By the end of the strike the contractors' assocation claimed that thirty-five buildings had been "raided" and ninety-seven men physically attacked by the union.[49]

The carpenters were aided by a hands-off police policy. This was the fruit of a budding alliance with the local Democratic party that had its origins with Mayor Carter Harrison, but had become more formal with the union's support of Democratic mayoral candidate De Witt Cregier's nomination in 1889 and the city's subsequent endorsement of the eight-hour day. During the strike fifty-six union men were arrested, but none were convicted by local judges. As the strike progressed the contractors turned to Bonfield's Detective Agency (Bonfield had resigned from the police force in scandal) for men to serve as witnesses, and to act, according to the union, as agents provocateurs. The value of the aid given the union by the Democratic administration was indicated two months later when the carpenters refrained from joining a movement for an independent labor party, because, as the *Tribune* remarked, "This would exasperate the Democratic city administration and bring on the active opposition of the City Hall officials and the police."[50]

Just as in 1887, the smaller contractors began to weaken within a week of the strike. On April 11, fifty of them formed a new association and offered to meet the UCC's demands. There were in Chicago between one thousand and sixteen hundred employers of carpenters, all but 120 of them employing between five and fifteen men. However, the 120 large contractors employed two-thirds of all Chicago carpenters. The problem of the union was to determine whether the new association was large enough to employ most of its members. The union solved this problem by refusing to negotiate until the small-contractors' association could guarantee employment for four thousand carpenters. This tactic was undermined on April 26 when the national Brotherhood refused to appropriate strike funds unless the UCC abandoned its high employment requirement for the new association. On April 30 the union relented and signed an arbitration agreement with the new association.[51]

The UCC was still committed to a contract. In contrast to their stance in 1887, the new leadership viewed the agreement as a stopgap measure that would enable the union to put its financially strapped men back to work while continuing to pressure the builders to switch contracts from the large contractors to the small ones. As part of this tactic, the association and the union had a secret agreement whereby contractors would subtract $.025 cents from each carpenters' hourly wage and give it to the UCC to help organize nonunion men working for the large contractors. In sum, the UCC had gone as far as it could with the radicals' "general walkout for a contract" tactic and had fallen back on a divide-and-conquer tactic with several important safeguards.

Unfortunately, the small contractors were too weak to win contracts away from the large, well-connected contractors, and therefore were unable to employ all the union's members. By mid-June they could not afford to pay the wages they had agreed to in the spring, and consequently, they abrogated their agreement with the UCC.[52]

The UCC wisely waited until September to strike again. The rank and file needed time to build up its savings. In September some six thousand carpenters walked out again, but this time the UCC returned to a divide-and-conquer tactic immediately. The Germans in Local 1 were incensed by this decision of the American leadership of their local. At their weekly meeting on September 3 a row began. "For fully twenty minutes there was a free fight all around," reported the Tribune. "Men tumbled over chairs, clinched and rolled on the floor." When the smoke cleared, the Germans had taken over the leadership. But they could not prevail within the UCC. As the season drew to a close, the carpenters were still without a contract. Yet, the UCC policy of selective agreements had insured that the union was able to provide work for most of its members; when the year 1891 began the union's numerical strength exceeded that of the previous year.[53]

In this situation the union needed only a small push to get over the hump. It came from two sources. In October 1890 the carpenters initiated the formation of the first enduring Building Trades Council. Including the bricklayers, it was governed by the walking delegates from each trade. The formation of an effective BTC represented a major turning point in the ability of Chicago's building trades unions to carry out successful strikes. Between 1886 and 1890 only 43 percent of all building trades strikes were successful; from 1890 through 1894 the percentage rose steadily each year reaching 85 percent in 1894.[54]

While labor was consolidating its unity, a split appeared among Chicago's businessmen. The long tie-ups of 1890, coming on the heels of similar tie-ups in 1886 and 1887, had convinced many Chicago capitalists that the union would not go away. They realized that the World's Fair, then under construction, could not be built without labor's cooperation. On March 7, 1891, the World's Fair Directory voted to mandate compulsory arbitration and eight hours in all World's Fair contracts. With the threat of another carpenters' strike backed by sympathy action and the loss of support of the city's business community hanging over them, the leading contractors capitulated on March 21 and signed a two-year agreement with the UCC for arbitration, eight hours, and a $.35 an hour wage. For the first time collective bargaining was a reality in Chicago's carpentry trade.[55]

In the twenty-eight year period between 1863 and 1891 the loosely knit, short-lived, simple protective union had given way to the unified and disciplined United Brotherhood of Carpenters and Joiners of America. Where the old protective union required little or no monetary contribution from its members, the Brotherhood required the commitment of high initiation fees and dues, and paid a variety of benefits. Where the simple protective union relied on mass demonstrations and the enthusiasm of the moment to rally nonunion men to its banner, the Brotherhood employed the paid walking delegate, systematic and focused intimidation, and the attraction of benefits. Where the older unions, including the early Brotherhood, were divided into language and ethno-political factions, the Brotherhood's Locals 1 and 28 proved that long-antagonistic cultural groups could work together in a single organization. With this foundation the modern union was able to break the back of the piecework system that had earlier threatened to undermine the skill of the general carpenter. By 1899 P. J. McGuire could boast of the fact that piecework had disappeared in all but seven American cities. Though piecework remained as a constant threat, the strength of the union limited it to a minor role in the trade.[56]

The great watershed in this transformation had occurred in the mid–1880s, a fact highlighted by the changing character of union leadership. In a sample of forty-four carpenter union leaders from the 1881–82 period only fourteen were still working at their trade in Chicago by 1888; and ten were listed as contractors. By contrast, in a sample of forty-four UCC officers and delegates from the late 1880s, thirty-two were still employed as journeymen carpenters in 1894 and only three had become contractors. Five other leaders held political patronage positions, while one had been elected to public office. All this suggests that a significant segment of the pre-Haymarket carpenter leadership still identified self-improvement as much with self-employment as with the union, while the newer leadership identified its fortunes with collective advancement through the union. It also suggests that the success of the union by the end of the decade had created the conditions for the maintenance of a stable core of leaders who were firmly committed to their local trade, their union, and their class.[57]

Following the decline of the Knights and the demise of the anarchists, the Brotherhood of Carpenters of the 1890s has often been viewed by historians as a constituent element of a more exclusive and conservative American Federation of Labor emerging under the leadership of Samuel Gompers. This study of the union's origins reveals, however, that Brotherhood carpenters took at least as much from the old Knights of Labor and the socialists and anarchists as they discarded. The German and Czech socialists and anarchists taught the need for a general walkout for union recognition, and it was their militancy that gave backbone to the great strikes of the 1886–90 period. The English-speaking workingmen of the Knights of Labor were just as important for they gave form and substance to the new ethic of labor solidarity. More than any group, it was the Knights who popularized intertrade solidarity that took shape in the Building Trades Council and in the sympathy strike.[58]

Surveying the past in 1905, Ed Nockles, secretary of the Chicago Federation of Labor, observed that the sympathy strike was based on

> the truths expounded by the Knights of Labor, in effect that the "Injury of one is the concern of all," [which] seems more true today than when first announced, and upon this principle rests all the progress of our upward and forward march, and if the self-sacrificing men and women of our country did not accept and place all their hopes and aspirations upon this principle, slavery would still be extant in the country, not alone among the blacks, but among the whites.[59]

CHAPTER 3

Moderates

and Radicals

The Struggle for Control,

1891–1901

I know of contractors, men that have gone to contracting in this city at my business since I came to this city, and they had no more dollars and perhaps not as many as I had, and now they are worth their hundreds of thousands. Who has done that for them? Nothing more nor less than the labor of my hands and everybody else's that labored for them. Since that time they have never taken off their coats to produce one dollar; never done an hour's work; as I told you before, they employ drivers to get the utmost out of the muscles of those they hire. They have never done a day's work since they went to bossing, and they hold the workingman today in contempt, these same men, and then they say that workingmen and the labor unions are tyrannous.

. . . It is just like this with me: I have got now to be a pretty old crab. I believe the time is very near at hand when the world can get along without that animal the world calls a contractor. I believe it would be better for the community if there was not a contractor on the face of the earth. They would have better value and they would do more justice to one another.

—James Brennock[1]

In 1891 the carpenters' union had achieved union recognition, a two year contract, control of piecework, the eight-hour day, and a compensatory wage increase. Only the closed shop and the enrollment of the vast majority of carpenters still eluded the union. Yet these existing and hoped for achievements in the realm of collective bargaining hardly encompassed the purpose and meaning of unionism as it was then understood. To the activists who had brought the union into being, unionism was a transcendent cause that still conveyed the utopian and world-renewing expectations that had been nurtured by the Knights of Labor and the socialists in the previous decade. These leaders infused the 1880s "religion of solidarity"—a phrase popularized by Edward Bellamy in his influential utopian socialist novel, *Looking Backward*, published in 1887—into the unionism they built in the 1890s. Understood in this way, the early union was a kind of labor church institutionalizing the spirit of solidarity.

The solidarity religion, symbolized in the Knights' motto, "an injury to one is the concern of all," became an integral part of the daily union lives of Chicago carpenters in a variety of ways. By the late 1890's the boycott became something practical for workingmen with the emergence of the union label movement. No good union man was to work on or purchase materials or goods that did not display the union-made label. Furthermore, the principle of mutual aid and sympathy took on a living reality with the establishment of a viable Building Trades Council. There would be no more crossing of other trades' picket lines during strikes. Thereafter, the sympathy strike did not rely on spontaneous sentiment but on loyalty to an organization that enforced sympathy. Finally, union power in the workplace aimed at defending the carpenters' freedom from overwork and petty tyranny became codified in this period in a set of work rules legislated by the union. Adherence to each of these practices in the 1890s became a sacred test of one's character as a good union man. To violate any of them was to advertise oneself as a scab, that is, a traitor to one's fellow workmen and to one's class.

At the heart of the union's solidarity religion lay a widely held myth that seems to have animated the thinking of leading activists. It is important to recognize that the degree of correspondence of a myth to social reality may be less important than the ability of a myth to infuse daily action with a deeper meaning and significance, and therby endow it with more potency. As reconstructed from the words of James Brennock and others, many carpenters believed that the trade had been peopled by proud, independent, and free artisans. But, with the emergence of the snakelike competitive business system, the artisan had fallen from this high state. Robbed of the fruits of his labor by the money power, degraded in his craftsmanship by the division of labor, and debased in his manhood by bossism, the once-proud artisan turned to the union for salvation. The union, in this heroic saga, was the mainspring of a class movement engaged in an upward and forward march toward the cooperative commonwealth of labor and the abolition of the wage system. This story of fall from grace into degradation and faith in an ultimate redemption in a future of harmony and freedom clothed the daily struggles of carpenter unionists with a higher purpose. All events, it seemed, were bricks in an unfolding path leading toward the City of Labor.

In 1899 Charles Spahr, a British observer of the inner workings of the Chicago labor movement, including that of the carpenters, captured something of the optimistic tenor and tendency of the movement when he commented:

> Here, then is the possible outcome for the future. The unions are accumulating reserve funds, and, in spite of immigration, are increasing rapidly in discipline and intelligence. The time is coming when the unions may be able to manage business co-operatively. . . . The time is yet coming when historians will look back upon the present day struggles of trade unionists as the town meetings of the despised Puritan levellers of the seventeenth century. The men may seem commonplace and the measures petty, but it is through just such instrumentalities that the great designs for human advancement are always worked out.[2]

The kind of future glimpsed by Spahr through the eyes of Chicago unionists was different in important ways from the advocacy before 1886 of experiments in producer cooperatives. The Carpenter pointedly dismissed such experiments as "folly," arguing that "in the few instances where carpenters have formed such co-operative associations to take contracts, they have ended in landing the business in one man's hands, or it became a joint stock partnership, or ended— a dismal failure." Instead of this shortsighted strategy The Carpenter stated:

> We propose to prepare for a more general system of co-operation through association and unity of action, so as to supplant the entire system of bossism and of wages, and in its stead establish a co-operative Democracy of Industry, through which the worker will receive the full result of his toil, and not the mere beggarly market price, in the shape of wages.[3]

During the 1890s virtually every Chicago carpenter leader on record on this subject gave assent to the long-term goal of abolishing the wage system and establishing a cooperative society. There were, however, two increasingly divergent interpretations of how this goal would be achieved. One group led by the still-influential James Brennock, believed that "the time is very near at hand when the world can get along without that animal the world calls a contractor." According to UCC President O. E. Woodbury, one of the prime goals of the union was to do "what lies within their power to educate the masses up to where they will get out from the thralldom of the wage slave system under which we labor to-day." The radicals sought an independent labor party dedicated to reversing the concentration of wealth in the hands of the "money power" and establishing cooperative control of industry. In the early 1890s the radicals were the dominant wing within the United Carpenters Council based upon the alliance of radical Brotherhood Locals 1 and 28 with the Knights of Labor locals.[4]

The moderate to conservative wing of the union leadership did not openly repudiate the goal of a cooperative society. If the words of the more articulate national labor leaders of this period who originated the theory of "pure and simple unionism" are any indication, they rather placed this goal in the far-off future. These leaders believed that the union should not propagate utopian goals but should concentrate union efforts on the immediate needs of increasing wages, bettering conditions, and strengthening the labor movement. By doing these things, labor would create higher hopes and generate impetus toward labor's long term goals. A.F. of L. President Samuel Gompers articulated this philosophy best: "Unions pure and simple are the natural organization of wage workers to secure their present and practical improvement and to achieve their final emancipation. . . . The way out of the wage system is through higher wages." In Chicago the moderates opposed independent labor politics and instead allied with the ruling Democratic party, which allowed them to carry on strikes for immediate improvements without police intervention.[5]

During the 1890s these two positions clashed in a battle for supremacy within the carpenters' union. Three critical episodes marked the conflict for "the soul" of the union. During the World's Fair construction boom, the carpenters for the first time came face to face with a power outside the local arena. As sponsor of the fair, the federal government backed a powerful coalition of antiunion forces that undercut the union's growing influence within the city. Immediately following this confrontation, the great 1893–97 depression propelled the union under radical leadership into the midst of the Pullman sympathy strike and a second great attempt to emancipate labor from the Democratic party in local politics. These two great attempts to broaden the horizons of solidarity of carpenters ended in failure. Finally, between 1898 and 1900 the carpenters were able to turn the tables on the contractors, forcing them to accept individual agreements drawn up by the union. This short period of unprecedented dominance seemed to foreshadow a future of industrial democracy rather than corporate tyranny. It was immediately followed, however, by a thirteen-month lockout that resulted in a historic defeat for the Brotherhood forcing the union to reconsider its long-term goals.

The Carpenters and the World's Fair

In the three-year period beginning in March 1891 and concluding with the start of the 1893 panic and depression, the Chicago carpenters' union attained an unprecedented level of influence and prestige within the city's labor movement. In 1891 the union could claim between six- and seven-thousand members, a figure that mounted steadily during the World's Fair boom, reaching between nine and twelve thousand in 1893. This made the carpenters the largest union in Chicago. In 1891 the carpenters held top leadership posts in all of Chicago's central labor organizations. James O'Connell of Local 1 was president of the Building Trades Council; Robert Swallow of Local 28 (now Local 10) was president of the Trades and Labor Assembly; and Adolph Stamm of Local 1 was secretary-treasurer of the Central Labor Union. On the national level, William Kliver of Local 28 was president of the Brotherhood.[6]

The prominence of carpenters as marshals and participants in the city's Labor Day parades, as speakers in union organizing drives for other trades, and as political activists in local electoral campaigns further testified to their commanding position within the Chicago labor movement. Indeed, it is no exaggeration to say that Chicago's reputation as a "union town," which originated in these years, was gained under the leadership of the carpenters.[7]

The carpenters' prominence within the labor movement was derived from their peculiarly strong collective bargaining position. Yet their relationship with employing contractors combined elements of cooperation as well as conflict. Contractors had self-interested reasons for accepting collective bargaining. In an industry with low capital requirements for entry and relatively high labor costs, large contractors had little advantage over smaller competitors who could outbid them by using cheaper labor. The need for stability became particularly acute for larger contractors with the rise of the central business district after 1889. To standardize wages and thus stabilize competition, the major contractors, particularly the new general contractors who built the skyscrapers, department stores, hotels, and elevated lines, had to maintain an agreement with the union. In 1891 one carpenter leader explained: "If a minimum [wage] rate were fixed, the contractor would know what to calculate upon in making his bids. Each would know the other would not underbid him in securing cheaper labor."[8]

Yet the experience of the 1880s had demonstrated that contractors were unwilling to jettison their traditional antipathy to collective bargaining, even in the face of competitive pressures, until the union could control piecework and prevent the overwhelming majority of carpenters from accepting work at below union scale. Only when the union's strength had been clearly established in the 1890 strike were the large contractors willing to sign a collective bargaining agreement. Significantly, this agreement included an article stating that "any journeyman carpenter being a member of any organization represented in the United Carpenters Council may work for any person who does not pay less than the minimum of wages."[9]

Though this cooperative relationship, underpinned by the union's ability to set a floor under wages, was the bedrock upon which rested the soil of collective bargaining, the adoption of any particular level of wages and conditions was dependent upon the shifting balance of forces between the union and the contractors' association. In the 1890s the carpenters' strong bargaining position stemmed in large measure from the many independent contractors outside the association who were willing to employ union men at union rates in the event of an unresolvable dispute between the union and the contractors. The number of these "independents" and the consequent ability of union men to find employment during conflicts increased significantly during the first three years of the 1890s when the World's Fair stimulated a vast construction boom of apartment buildings and small residential homes on the city's South Side. The existence of this boom and the bargaining leverage it gave to the carpenters allowed the union to refuse the contractors' association's request in 1891 for an article in the contract preventing union men from working for nonassociation contractors. Thus the union avoided an "exclusive agreement," which would have unified the contractors' association. In this way the union maintained its ability to play off the contractors against each other and consolidated its advantage in collective bargaining.[10]

But, at the same time that the building boom generated by the fair strengthened the union's hand, the management of the fair limited the reach of the union's grasp. Unlike most construction projects, which typically involved the owner, banker, contractor, and union, the World's Fair was a national project chartered by the United States Congress and overseen by a national commission. That commission controlled the World's Fair Directory, which was composed of leading

Chicago businessmen under the leadership of Lyman Gage, president of the First National Bank. For the first time the union stood face to face with a powerful combination of government and business.[11]

With labor allowed only a token representation on the World's Fair Directory, the city's unions, acting on behalf of the workmen employed in building the fair, established a Joint Labor Committee. The prime issue was the request by the unions that the federal government not use its power to undercut existing collective bargaining standards. If such an agreement could have been secured, it would have been a powerful weapon in maintaining and spreading unionism. The Committee made five demands on the Directory: an eight-hour day; arbitration of all disputes; preferential hiring of union men; a $1.50 minimum wage for unskilled, nonunion labor; and the prevailing union wage for trades with collective bargaining agreements in force.[12]

The Directory responded in May 1891 by agreeing to arbitration and offering informal support for the eight hour day but denying the wage demands. Had the Directory adopted the minimum wage, fair contractors would have had little incentive to flood the labor market with less-skilled, nonunion men from out of town. Moreover, the prevailing wage principle would have forced those employers not party to union agreement to abide by its terms at risk of losing their contracts with the fair. The rejection of the minimum and prevailing wage principles threatened the carpenters' new agreement with the contractors' association. The *Chicago Tribune* summed up the situation this way: "The World's Fair Directorate seems to want to break down the union price paid in Chicago and unless all employers are compelled to pay the price agreed upon by the bosses and the journeymen's association, [the contractors] will break away and secure carpenters as cheaply as possible."[13]

In the late spring of 1891 both the union and the Directory squared off to fight. Before construction began, the Directory had erected a high fence around the fairgrounds with guards at every gate to keep out labor agitators. Meanwhile, the chief of construction had set up barracks and commissaries to house and feed thousands of out-of-town, nonunion, low-wage laborers. Still, by various means, the carpenters began to organize the fair laborers and in April these men walked out demanding a daily wage of $1.75 for an eight-hour day. Although they had the support of the carpenters and other building trades, the laborers were unable to sustain their strike. The Directory enjoyed broad support within the city and commanded the aid of the Chicago police.[14]

The defeat of the laborers' strike and the recognition of the favorable position enjoyed by the Directory led the carpenters to sidestep a direct confrontation. Thereafter, working through the Joint Labor Committee, the union began vigorously lobbying the state legislature, Congress, and the president for a minimum wage at the fair. Within the city the UCC directed a steady stream of complaints at the Directory and chief architect Daniel Burnham for failing to enforce the eight-hour rule.[15]

Without a general walkout, there was little the union could do to enforce its work rules on the men working under its jurisdiction at the fair. Business agents' reports to the UCC indicated that as many as one-third of all carpenters working at the fair were nonunion men, virtually all working below scale. This affected the behavior of union carpenters. One frustrated business agent was quoted as saying that "it was impossible to control these people working out there . . . that he got statements from some foremen out there that union carpenters were working all hours from eight to sixteen." Compounding the situation were unsafe working conditions created by the frantic rush to complete work on time for the opening. In the first six months of fair construction alone, seventeen building tradesmen were killed or permanently disabled.[16]

Stymied by the powerful Directory, the union turned to A.F. of L. President Samuel Gompers for assistance. In February 1892 Gompers interceded with the fair's superintendent to discuss union grievances. Gompers, however, came away from the meeting with the Directory defending its decision to leave the minimum wage and union hiring as open questions. Moreover, Gompers neglected to press the safety issue and completely absolved the Directory from blame in failing to enforce eight hours. The UCC bitterly rejected Gompers' report as a "lie," adding that he even failed to consult local union officials.[17]

In the wake of the Gompers fiasco, which served to reinforce the Directory's refusal to negotiate a minimum wage, the carpenters again shifted their tactics. As the fair neared its opening date of May 1893, thousands of nonunion carpenters flooded the city to take advantage of the last-minute rush to complete construction. By April fair employment was up threefold and the wages of skilled carpenters rose as high as $.60 an hour; even the wages of nonunion unskilled labor exceeded the minimum. Clearly wages were no longer an issue. The principle issue at stake was the presence of thousands of nonunion tradesmen in the city. Once construction of the fair was completed, these men would be on the street competing with union men for work.[18]

At this juncture, the UCC announced a campaign to "rid the city of scabs" and made a demand on the contractors' assocation for a closed shop, the first such demand since 1887. The union fixed a target date of April 1893 for a strike, recognizing that if it could not secure an agreement with the fair and the contractors before the May opening it might well be unable to secure one afterward.

In March, threatened with a walkout of their skilled carpenters, the contractors' association signed a new two-year agreement. The new contract raised the minimum wage from $.35 to $.40 an hour and, for the first time, committed the employers to hire union labor only. The agreement also formally sanctioned the sympathy strike in exchange for the provision that union carpenters protect their employers' property from damage by other trades during such strikes. In return for these large concessions, the union agreed not to work for those nonassociation contractors who would not pay a fee to the association and sign the contract, a minor concession.[19]

Enforcing the new agreement on the rest of the fair contractors was another matter. On April 3, thirteen hundred carpenters walked off their jobs at the fair for one day to protest the presence of nonunion carpenters on fair construction. Because most fair contractors had already signed the UCC's agreement in March, the bulk of the strikers returned to work. At this point the UCC decided to ask the Building Trades Council to call a sympathy strike. On April 9 most of the building trades quit work, virtually shutting down the fair. Throughout the following day the representatives of the fair and Council haggled over terms of a settlement. At the end of the day an agreement was reached in which the fair conceded a minimum wage—a meaningless concession—but refused to fire the nonunion men. As the president of the World's Fair explained: "We could not grant this demand if we were personally disposed to do so. The World's Columbian Exposition is an institution created and fathered by the U.S. government. The United States have decided that we cannot accede to this demand." As a token, the fair gave union officials free passes to the fair to inspect the work.[20]

Rank and file carpenters were outraged by the minimal concessions gained by Building Trades Council negotiators. UCC President J. B. Cogswell disavowed the pact, explaining somewhat lamely that he was forced to leave the marathon bargaining session because of illness in his family. Just as in 1886, 1887, and 1890, dissension erupted within the union from the more militant carpenters. Led by former UCC President Robert Swallow, they castigated Cogswell for leaving the meeting and permitting a "sellout" for "thirty passes to the World's Fair." Swallow called for another walkout. Other delegates, however, feared that another walkout would be futile since the fair was nearly complete. Moreover, it would be difficult to gain the support of carpenters working overtime at premium wages. Amidst a bedlam of "hisses and protests from all sides," commented the *Tribune*, "as well as the threat of physical violence" the UCC finally authorized another walkout. The strike received lukewarm support and only thirty-six contractors signed the agreement. The fair opened on schedule.[21]

The carpenters' two-year running battle with the World's Fair had brought mixed results. In the beginning, the union had won its first collective bargaining agreement, a substantial wage increase, and later the closed shop. Despite the intransigence of the Directory over the minimum-wage issue and the closed shop, the contractors' association never carried out its threat to cancel the contract, probably because of the dependence of the major contractors on skilled carpenters loyal to the union. Nevertheless, the World's Fair episode highlighted the limits of union power. The Directory, backed by the prestige and authority of the federal government, was able to mobilize local and national resources to give it a decisive edge over the carpenters' union even when backed by other building trades unions. At this time the federal government was not prepared to set a national precedent that would violate laissez-faire dogma by recognizing union agreements. Backed to the hilt by city officials, press, police, and leading businessmen, the fair successfully resisted labor pressure to recognize the closed shop. Within the union, this failure to recognize the closed shop was the first of a series of setbacks for the carpenters' radical leadership.

With the close of the building boom, the carpenters were unable to sustain the momentum of the early 1890s. In the spring of 1893, the union's membership peaked at a level that would not be regained until the second decade of the twentieth century.

The Depression and the High Tide of Carpenter Radicalism

The World's Columbian Exposition opened to the public the same year as the inauguration of the 1893–97 depression. The fair and the depression presented two contrasting images of the new industrial system that had flowered in the post- Civil War years. On the one hand was the glittering "White City" with its landscaped parks and stunning building exteriors: a model utopian city uniting genteel culture, concentrated wealth, and advanced technology. Outside its gates was a grimmer sight, a different testimony to existing industrialism: thousands of able-bodied men languishing in destitution and starvation for lack of work. Under the viaducts and the "El" tracks, in alley ways and vacant lots each night lay the sleeping bodies of thousands of victims of overproduction and what one Populist editor called "intolerable legislative and monopolistic wrongs."[22]

In response to these dire conditions, the carpenters' commitment to labor solidarity and classwide sympathy action reached a peak. Unlike many other un   hich melted away in the depression, the carpenters, though hard   unemployment and wage cuts, were able to survive and maintai   of their previous bargaining gains. This enabled the union to   e lead in three major struggles. By the end of 1893 the union   monstrations demanding jobs and public relief. The following   he union's members voted to strike in sympathy with the Pullm   kers, an action which was stymied by labor's national leadershi   in the fall of 1894 union members formed the backbone of the   -Populist alliance that aimed at a realignment in the nation's p   system.

Chicago's three-year building boom rapidly evaporated with the end of the fair and the financial panic of March 1893. Between 1890 and 1892 a yearly average of 12,177 buildings valued at almost $55 million had been built by Chicago construction workers. Beginning in 1893 the number of buildings erected declined by 37 percent to 8,265, while the total value of new construction fell 50 percent to $28.5 million. In each of the following seven years building activity in Chicago continued to decline, falling to a level in 1900 that had not been equaled since 1882.

Because of the overall decline in employment opportunities, it became impossible for the UCC to prevent its 11,150 members from accepting employment from nonassociation contractors who had refused to sign the new agreement. In May the contractors' association president charged that only 6,150 of the union's members were working for association contractors while over 4,000 men were employed at wages below the agreed-upon minimum. The inability of the union to enforce wage provisions of the contract among its members threatened the larger contractors employing skilled carpenters with being underbid. To prevent this, the association unilaterally lowered the carpenters' minimum wage from $.40 to $.35.[23]

Fearing a conflict that might destroy the union, the UCC after a long debate agreed to submit the wage issue to binding arbitration by a neutral third party. Each side chose an arbitrator. The contractors chose William McHale, while the union chose the nationally famous reformer Henry Demarest Lloyd. These, in turn, selected a third member, banker William Preston. After deliberation, Preston sided with McHale resulting in a two-to-one vote that sanctioned the wage reduction. Bitter resentment reigned within the union at this turn of events. After all, the bosses' association had violated the agreement; legality would seem to dictate a return to the status quo. Instead, the arbitrators had responded to the worsening economic climate by lowering the wage. The experience of that year convinced the union of the dangers of committing itself to binding arbitration by a third party. Never again would the Chicago union tie its hands in that manner.[24]

The $.05 cent wage cut was only the beginning of a series of economic reversals dealt by the depression to the carpenters. By August, UCC business agents reported that few carpenters were receiving the minimum wage, and by late fall many carpenters were working for as little as $.20 an hour. Although the official rate remained at $.35 for the duration of the depression, most carpenters worked for considerably less. Unable to maintain pay rates, the union saw its membership plummet. By the end of the year, union strength had fallen to six thousand. It continued to decline, ebbing at thirty-four hundred in March 1898.[25]

Faced with a stalemate on the collective bargaining front, and with the economy rapidly deteriorating, the union directed its energies toward support of an emerging citywide protest movement against unemployment. On August 15, 1893, three thousand people attended an unemployment rally sponsored by the Allied Wood Workers Trade Council of Chicago, which featured a speech by a carpenter from Local 1. Two days later, when the Knights' District Assembly 24 petitioned City Hall to provide jobs for the unemployed, the UCC endorsed the resolution and appointed a committee to cooperate with the Knights.[26]

In the meantime, carpenters and other labor leaders organized daily marches of unemployed workers. In a typical demonstration, hundreds of idle workers gathered in lakefront parks and marched to City Hall through the central business district carrying crudely made placards or chanting slogans such as "We want work," and "Work or bread." At City Hall, a crowd, often exceeding a thousand workers, would be addressed by local labor leaders and agitators, each offering his own remedy for the depression ranging from the "single tax" to revolutionary anarchism.[27]

Even though the street protests were peaceful, they alarmed business leaders. In late August, after vandalism and street fighting marred several marches, Mayor Carter Harrison gave in to the clamor of businessmen for a ban on demonstrations. In exchange, he appointed one hundred well-known citizens to a special committee to create new jobs; he also appointed a Committee on Food and Drink, consisting of labor leaders, to distribute relief.[28]

These minimal concessions did not satisfy carpenter leaders who forged ahead with plans for a massive parade and lakefront rally on August 30. While the Illinois National Guard, backed by a thousand special police, patrolled the lakefront, the city's main labor organizations mobilized twenty-five thousand marchers to hear Samuel Gompers, P. J. McGuire, T. J. Morgan, Henry Demarest Lloyd, Terence V. Powderly and others who were in Chicago to participate in the World's Fair Labor Congress. Four local carpenter leaders addressed the rally. This impressive show of strength achieved immediate results. Two days later a mayor's committee of top business leaders announced a plan to hire fifteen hundred married men for work on a drainage canal and to provide jobs for another two thousand on future projects in exchange for a promise to halt all protests.[29]

The mutual support that Chicago's unions offered each other during hard times reached a peak in the Pullman strike of 1894. Long aware of the emergent culture of labor solidarity, the conservative *Chicago Tribune* warned its middle-class readers that "if some powerful trade should strike and trouble ensue, all these trades may join in the play. For this reason Chicago may be said to be sitting over a labor volcano. While on the surface all is quiet, [labor's] organization is so close and secret that the magazine may be 'touched off' at any moment."[30]

The town of Pullman, founded in 1880 by the railroad-car magnate George Pullman, like the White City was intended as a model community of the industrial era: architecturally unified, clean and tidy to the point of sterility, and boasting many features, such as parks and a free library, oriented toward the cultural uplift of its residents. Yet, also like the White City with its fences and guards, Pullman was, in the words of economist Richard T. Ely, "a benevolent, well-wishing feudalism, which desires the happiness of the people, but in such a way as shall please the authorities." Whatever was done in the interest of workers was done because it could be justified as profitable; and it was done *for* workers rather than *by* them.[31]

In the summer of 1893 the concealed tensions within the town exploded when George Pullman announced a large wage reduction for his employees while refusing to lower the rents for his company-owned homes and the prices at his company-run store. In May 1894 Pullman fired local union leaders who had led a walkout in protest. At this point the American Railway Union, led by Eugene V. Debs, announced a sympathy boycott of all railroads using Pullman cars. When the federal government intervened on the side of the railroads, the conflict escalated into a call by Debs for Chicago unions to join in a general sympathy strike.

Sentiment for support action was strong among the rank and file of the powerful Chicago building trades unions. German and Bohemian workers in the carpenters and other unions wanted to strike, while most union leaders preferred to rely on their traditional alliance with the local Democratic administration of Mayor Hopkins and Illinois Governor John Peter Altgeld to influence the railroads. But the railroad managers refused to budge and pressured President Grover Cleveland into dispatching thirty-four hundred federal troops to Chicago to keep order. Amid general tumult in the railyards, federal troops, contemptuously called "bluebellies" by the strikers, fired into crowds of workers killing and wounding scores.

With the mood of Chicago and parts of the nation approaching insurrection, the A.F. of L. Executive Board decided to forbid its local affiliates from joining the strike. Samuel Gompers and P. J. McGuire rushed to Chicago to persuade the Building Trades Council to cancel its strike plans. A.F. of L. leaders reasoned that the strike stood little chance of success, and they were fearful that defeat on a national scale would seriously jeopardize the organizational gains made by the Federation in the early 1890s. The fate of the Knights of Labor following Haymarket was fresh in their memory. Faced with the dilemma of choosing between the principle of solidarity and the practical needs of the organization, they opted for the latter. Support for the strike came primarily from the rank and file for whom unionism was more a principle than an institution to be maintained at any cost. This action, along with the imprisonment of Debs and the rest of the ARU leadership, doomed the Pullman strike and put this early industrial union of railroad workers on the road to oblivion.[32]

Meanwhile, as the depression deepened and before the dismal conclusion of the Pullman strike in late July, the radical wing of the carpenters, together with allies in other unions, found increased support for a new labor party, this time in alliance with Illinois farmers in the Populist party. Like farmers, many Chicago carpenters were convinced that public control over the nation's banking system, plus a bimetallic currency based on silver as well as gold, was necessary in order to stimulate a stagnant economy. Many carpenters viewed the collapse of the construction industry as a direct outcome of the tight-money policies of a "government of bondholders." Moreover, like farmers and railroad workers, carpenters tended to be hostile to the powerful railroad corporations and supported the alternative of public ownership.[33]

The labor-Populist coalition that took shape in July 1894 in Chicago appealed to these beliefs among carpenters but also brought to a head a simmering conflict within the union. On the one hand were the radicals who were in favor of political independence and on the other were the conservative "labor Democrats." The latter, led by Robert Swallow and Irishmen J. J. Linehan, James O'Connell, and James

Morahan, were allied with Trade and Labor Assembly leaders and liberal businessmen in the Chicago Civic Federation who supported arbitration of labor disputes. Opposed to the labor Democrats was a loose coalition of Knights, Single-Taxers, and Socialists. Members of this loose coalition among the carpenters were led by James Brennock, Oliver E. Woodbury, Adolph Stamm, and Knights' leaders James G. Ogden and A. W. Simpson. These men were aligned with T. J. Morgan, Henry Demarest Lloyd, and the Central Labor Union.[34]

In July 1894, when the Illinois State Federation of Labor called a convention to organize a labor-Populist coalition, the conflict between the two factions exploded into a public confrontation. The principle issue of contention was T. J. Morgan's "plank 10" calling for "collective ownership of the means of production." When a compromise version of the plank proposed by Lloyd passed the stormy convention, the independent labor faction, with strong support from carpenters' delegates, decided to organize another labor party in Chicago. Meanwhile, the conservatives attempted to salvage their alliance with the Democrats by trying to persuade the new party to endorse Democratic candidates. In August the *Tribune* reported the results of this dispute: "The Socialists and the Populists together with a good many of the delegates representing the carpenters' organization will stick it out for a straight labor ticket. Overtures have been made to a number of carpenters and it's said they have steadfastly refused city jobs."[35]

The inaugural convention of the Cook County People's party held on August 18 quickly dissolved in a shambles, and the city's labor movement split into two camps. The labor Democrats endorsed the Democratic ticket, which slated former Local 1 President O'Connell for County Board president. The bulk of the union, led by District Council President Woodbury, plus the rest of the building trades unions and the cigarmakers, seamen, machine woodworkers, and the remnants of the ARU, supported the People's party. Among other nominees from the labor movement, the new party slated former Knight and UCC President Odgen for county sheriff.

The People's party's platform appealed to Chicago workingmen around Lloyd's modified plank 10, which pledged candidates to the principle of "collective ownership by the people of all such means of production and distribution as the people elect to operate for the commonwealth." In addition, the party endorsed the Populist platform, which, among other things, called for government ownership of the railroads and other monopolies and the free coinage of silver at the ratio of 16 to 1.[36]

The chief architect and spokesman for the new party was Henry

Demarest Lloyd, who, in a major address delivered October 6, 1894, described the Chicago movement as part of a worldwide "counter-revolution" in which workingmen were joining farmers, consumers, and small capitalists to overturn the revolution that had put government in the hands of corporate monopolists, trusts, and bankers. Lloyd argued that the cooperative commonwealth was simply the application to the contemporary social situation of traditional American values of liberty and equality:

> The Declaration of Independence of 1776 declared that the people felt themselves able to manage for themselves the government, all of whose powers sprang from them. This declaration of 1894 is the proclamation of the next step in independence. The people have done so well that they will move forward again and manage for themselves some more departments of the commonwealth all of whose powers spring from them. The democratization of government, the democratization of collective industry—they are parts of one great upward emancipation. The American idea, says Emerson, is emancipation. The co-operative commonwealth is the legitimate offspring and lawful successor of the republic. Our liberties and our wealth are from the people and by the people and both must be for the people. Wealth, like government, is the product of the co-operation of all, and, like government, must be the property of all its creators, not of a privileged few alone.[37]

For a fleeting historical moment in late 1894 Illinois' labor-Populist alliance based in Chicago appeared to be on the verge of flowering into a national alternative to the Democratic party. But Samuel Gompers refused to lend support, citing the fact that many Populist leaders slighted labor's interests. On the local level the coalition received a creditable thirty-one thousand votes in Cook County. But, just as in 1887, the party failed to elect anyone, and independent labor politics faltered. Meanwhile, the rancor generated by the 1894 campaign continued to divide the Chicago labor movement. In 1895 the carpenters joined the cigarmakers and machine woodworkers in splitting from the Trade and Labor Assembly, which had become an adjunct of the Democratic party, in order to found the independent Chicago Federation of Labor.[38]

The defeat of the Pullman sympathy strike and the People's party in 1894 represented critical political setbacks for the radical program of sympathy action in harmony with the struggles of workers and farmers across the nation and advocacy of a cooperative commonwealth. Organizationally, these years witnessed another setback.

Between 1887 and 1894 the carpenters were governed by the United Carpenters Council, an alliance of the various locals of the United Brotherhood of Carpenters and Joiners of America, whose District Council included over 80 percent of all organized carpenters, together with its junior partners, the Knights of Labor and Amalgamated Society of Carpenters. The UCC represented local autonomy from the dictates of the national union within the trade and unity with a major reform-oriented association, the Knights.[39]

Between 1892 and 1894 the national leadership of the Brotherhood began to call into question the local autonomy of the Chicago District Council, not only on such substantive matters as strikes and politics but also on organizational issues as well. As a result, some District Council leaders began to question their adherence to the UCC. They complained that the UCC "has more power than that given to our District Council ... assessments could be levied and strikes ordered without consulting our locals affiliated." Indeed, major trade issues were seldom discussed at District Council meetings. In 1892 the Brotherhood's locals successfully resisted an attempt by the national leadership, along with several Chicago locals, to prevent the UCC from issuing working cards to its locals. But in November 1893 the depression provided the excuse the District Council needed to exert its potential dominance over its locals.[40]

In order to reduce union expenses, the Chicago District Council proposed a reorganization of the UCC that would turn it into an executive council for enforcing decisions legislated within the District Council. When the Brotherhood's delegates were rebuffed, they forced the UCC to adjourn for good on July 1, 1894. This action precipitated a violent conflict with the Knights and the Amalgamated for whom the UCC represented a guarantee of independence from the more powerful Brotherhood. The dispute was marked by a court injunction, the threatened imprisonment of the District Council president, and the murder of Local 28's business agent by Knights of Labor dissidents. The dispute concluded in July 1895 with replacement of the UCC by a body called the Carpenters Executive Council, which continued to function until 1914. Within two years of the dispute, the last Knights' carpenters' assembly had joined the Brotherhood as Local 13, while the Amalgamated dwindled to only 179 members.[41]

In sum, by 1895 the carpenters had pulled back from their commitment to solidarity with the broader labor movement. The Pullman strike had graphically illustrated the limits of sympathy action, while the fate of the People's party had bred cynicism about the prospects for independent politics. With the demise of the UCC, the major organizational link of the Brotherhood to local reform had been severed.

James "Dad" Brennock, one of the founders in 1881 of the United Brotherhood of Carpenters and Joiners of America.—Courtesy United Brotherhood of Carpenters and Joiners of America

The Great Chicago Fire of 1871. In one day four square miles and 18,000 buildings were destroyed, leaving 90,000 people homeless.—From *Harper's Weekly*, October 28, 1871, courtesy Institute of Labor and Industrial Relations, University of Illinois

Membership certificate of the British Amalgamated Society of Carpenters and Joiners, which established a branch in Chicago in August 1870.— Courtesy United Brotherhood of Carpenters and Joiners of America

The labor troubles of 1877, riot at the Halsted Street viaduct. This was one of a series of violent confrontations in which Chicago's predominantly immigrant industrial working class revolted against wage cuts, long hours, and a host of other grievances.—Courtesy Illinois Labor History Society

In July 1877 Chicago police charged into a peaceable meeting of German cabinetmakers at Turner Hall, killing one and wounding dozens.—From *Harper's Weekly,* August 18, 1877, courtesy Chicago Historical Society

P. J. McGuire, founder and first general secretary of the United Brotherhood of Carpenters and Joiners of America.—Courtesy United Brotherhood of Carpenters and Joiners of America

The first Labor Day parade, 1886, a mass demonstration for the eight-hour day.—Courtesy Illinois Labor History Society

William Henry Jackson / Honore Joseph Jaxon. Having been involved with Louis Riel in the Canadian Métis Rebellion, Jackson escaped to the United States, changed his name to Jaxon, and served as "general" routing scabs in the May 1886 strike of carpenters for the eight-hour day.—From *Haymarket Scrapbook* (Chicago: Charles H. Kerr Publishing Co., 1986), courtesy Charles H. Kerr Publishing Company

The World's Columbian Exposition of 1892–93, looking east across the Main Basin, showing the White City.—From R. Reid Badger, *The Great American Fair*, courtesy Chicago Historical Society

National Guardsmen firing into a crowd of workers at Loomis and 49th streets, Chicago, July 7, 1894, during the Pullman strike. Rank and file carpenters supported the railroad strikers, while carpenter union leadership did not, fearing the union would be harmed in the wake of the collapse of the strike.—From *Harper's Weekly*, July 21, 1894, courtesy Chicago Historical Society

HIRAM WORK-AS-LONG-AS-YOU-PLEASE—
"These pesky unions tire me. This is a free country. A man has a right to work for any price. If wages are low let us work longer hours to make up."

Reprinted from the January, 1897, Carpenter

"Hiram Work-as-Long-as-You-Please" (*The Carpenter*, January 1897), cartoon pointing up the need for new carpenter work rules in the face of speed-ups and other contractor abuses.—Courtesy United Brotherhood of Carpenters and Joiners of America

CARPENTERS

ATTENTION

TROUBLE IN CHICAGO

STAY AWAY

Beware of Newspaper articles and advertisements telling of high wages and shortage of carpenters in Chicago,---they are part of the scheme to flood Chicago with carpenters for the purpose of destroying our **UNION.**

Employment agencies are also used for the same purpose.

Carpenters' District Council of Chicago

Chicago District Council poster warning carpenters about the open-shop Landis Award.—Courtesy Chicago and Northeast Illinois District Council, United Brotherhood of Carpenters and Joiners of America

Chicago District Council Building, at 12 E. Erie, constructed in 1925. Refaced, it is still used by the council.—Courtesy Chicago and Northeast Illinois District Council, United Brotherhood of Carpenters and Joiners of America

William L. Hutcheson, general president of the United Brotherhood of Carpenters and Joiners of America, 1915–1951.— Courtesy Chicago and Northeast Illinois District Council, United Brotherhood of Carpenters and Joiners of America

Chicago WPA parade, January 1939. By February 1931, 80 percent of all
Chicago area building trades workers were unemployed, and the situation
was not substantially alleviated until the wartime building boom of the
forties.—Courtesy Chicago Historical Society

The Great Lockout of 1900–1901

The failure of the Pullman strike did not end the carpenters' commitment to sympathy action. It did lead them to confine such action to the construction industry where it was most effective and where unionists, under the tutelage of sober business agents, could most clearly calculate their interests. In fact, the last three years of the century were the heyday of the sympathy strike and the union's power to dictate terms to the contractors. This power led inexorably to a crisis in the relations between the union and the contractors' association, culminating in the Great Lockout of 1900–1901.

Though high unemployment during the 1894–97 depression had significantly reduced membership and undermined the organizational discipline of the carpenters' union, the effect of the downturn on the contractors' association was simply devastating. By 1896 the association controlled only about a third of all Chicago contractors, and turned to the union for relief. To save the closed shop, the carpenters' union finally accepted what the contractors had been demanding since 1891, an exclusive agreement by which they agreed to work only for association contractors. The following year the agreement was broadened to include the organized material manufacturers and millworkers represented by the Amalgamated Woodworkers Union. The expanded agreement required contractors to use only union-labeled woodwork. Millowners were required to confine their sales to contractors' association members and keep their employees from working on outside jobs in competition with carpenters.[42]

In this period similar agreements were adopted by the bricklayers, steamfitters, plumbers, painters, and other building trades. In effect, the unions and employers were applying to the construction industry a fundamental business principle that had been adopted by other industries as a remedy to the depression: cooperate in order to restrict entry into the industry, and thereby stabilize competition and raise the level of prices and profits. The twist was that in construction, weak employers' associations looked to the unions to help them control the market.[43]

This joint effort to stabilize competition was short-lived. In October 1897 the General Executive Board ruled that the exclusive agreement violated the constitution of the national Brotherhood. The District Council did not protest. Many, if not most, Chicago carpenters strongly believed that using strikes or boycotts to compel independent contractors to join the contractors' association was an illegitimate use of union power, a practice that might well boomerang on the union.

Moreover, even under the exclusive agreement, the contractors' association could not employ all union carpenters. Consequently, in March 1898 the union, backed by a ten-to-one vote by the membership, notified the contractors of their withdrawal from the exclusive agreement.[44]

The union's move created a crisis for the contractors' association. Though the nation's economy had recovered from the depression, Chicago's construction industry was still saddled with an oversupply of buildings erected during the World's Fair boom. As late as December 1899 a prominent Chicago architect lamented that "structures of every kind and character are unoccupied, that rents are comparatively low, and that cost of building is high." The end of the exclusive agreement in this context unleashed the fiercest of competitive pressures among the contractors. According to Edward Craig, an official in the Master Steamfitters Association and later secretary of the Builders' Association, "the general run of contractors in the building line [in the late 1890s] appeared to think it was not a good thing to be too well acquainted with your competitors, they looked upon each other as almost enemies. . . . They passed each other on the street without speaking and such a thing as getting together for mutual protection was the last thing they would think of doing."[45]

As competition turned "cutthroat," Chicago contractors attempted to reduce costs by overturning traditional work standards and intensifying the amount of labor they required from their workers. This resort to what was called "rushing" differed from the "sweating" that had resulted from piecework and subcontracting. Rushing had its origins in the union's success in winning the eight-hour day. As one old-time carpenter leader put it, "every time the hours were shortened the bosses made them work just that much harder. . . . When the trades unions increased their demands on the contractors, the contractors increased theirs of the men, and there was no power to make any contractor keep any man who did not turn out a remunerative quantity of work." O. E. Woodbury contended in 1899 that, "I know to my positive knowledge in the carpenter business that men today are doing more than double what they did fifteen or twenty years ago in a ten hour day."[46]

The more acute competition of the 1890s reinforced the tendency to rush and created an intolerable situation for many carpenters. According to James Brennock, contractors often picked athletic, young workers to set a fast pace. They also hired foremen, "not for their ability in superintending, but simply for their brutality and their ability to drive the life out of their workingmen." Woodbury explained: "In our business where a man used to hang eight or ten 1 and 3/8 inch soft pine doors in a day fifteen or twenty years ago, today they are fitting and hanging from sixteen to twenty veneered oak, Georgia pine and in some case 1 and 3/8 inch solid oak. No man lived that can do it and do it right."[47]

Employers lengthened the labor time of carpenters as well as intensifying it. One method was to "steal time" at the beginning or end of the workday or at lunchtime by tampering with the clock. Another method of retrieving the ten-hour day was to insist on daily overtime. Often this meant a head-on clash with customary work standards. For example, some contractors demanded that their employees file and grind their tools on their own time instead of on the job. By the late 1890s many carpenters, particularly the older ones who had been in the forefront of the shorter-hours fight, viewed the great eight-hour victory with mixed feelings. One carpenter leader remarked ruefully that "if we had won seven hours, half of us would be dead."[48]

In early 1898 the union attempted to moderate the work pace by codifying customary work practices in written work rules. According to these new regulations, union foremen could be fined for rushing, using abusive language, or stealing time. Union carpenters were also liable to fines for rushing, sharpening tools off the job, purchasing the heavy and expensive iron mitre box, or failing to leave a job when ordered to by a business agent. Before 1898, carpenter work rules specifying length of working day, overtime pay, and other basic matters were part of the agreement between the contractors and the union and were enforced by the Joint Arbitration Board. In effect, with the collapse of joint efforts—in the form of the exclusive agreement—to stabilize competition and the subsequent disarray among the contractors, the union was attempting unilaterally to regulate the trade and industry in workers' interests.

In the face of contractor criticism, District Council President Woodbury strongly defended this approach:

> It is by curtailing and limiting work that the country is prevented from being destroyed. Even when the work is limited we are doing twice as much work as the workingmen of other countries. Stand out against the non-union men, the rushers, child labor, and labor saving machinery or you will be forced to do the same that the starving men at Pullman were forced to do in 1894.

In January 1898, after the carpenters' union refused to renew the exclusive agreement, the contractors declined to consider the union's new working rules. At this point, the union sent the rules to the Building Trades Council for approval and set up its own Trial Board system along with fines in order to enforce the rules on journeymen and foremen unilaterally.[49]

Carpenter Union Working Rules, 1899–1900

Article 1: No member shall work after the regular weekly payday without receiving his wages in full. Any violation of this rule shall be punishable by a fine of $10, ruled off the job or both.

Article 2: Any member accepting less than the minimum scale of wages or rebating any part of his wages to his employer shall be subject to a fine of not less than $10, ruled off the job and not permitted to work for the same employer again.

Article 3: No member shall be permitted to work with a non-union carpenter or with any member who has an unpaid fine against him in the organization to which he belongs, under penalty of a fine of $5.

Article 4: Any member found filing, grinding or repairing tools in his own time, or who takes his tools home to file, grind or repair when in employment, shall be fined not less than $10 or ruled off the job. Any member who furnishes a patent mitre box shall be subject to a fine of $5.

Article 5: Any member guilty of excessive work or rushing on any job shall be reported and shall be subject to a fine of $5. Any foreman using abusive language to or rushing the men under his supervision shall be fined not less than $10 and ruled off the job.

Article 6: Any foreman or timekeeper who steals time from the workmen by calling time a few minutes before starting time or after quitting time shall be fined not less than $10 and ruled off the job.

Article 7: No member shall work on a job where laborers are permitted to work with carpenter tools of any kind, set up or level up joists on walls. Any violation of this rule must be reported by the steward under penalty of a fine of $5.

Article 8: Any member refusing to give the actual condition of a job when requested by the business agent shall be subject to a fine of not less than $5.

Article 9: Any member refusing to stop work when ordered by the business agent, or treating him with disrespect, or using language unbecoming to a brother workingman shall be subject to a fine of not less than $10.

Article 10: Any member or members going to or remaining at work on a job on a strike, unless authorized by the business agent, shall be fined $25 and ruled off the job.

Article 11: It shall be competent for any carpenter business agent, where he has reason to believe that Article 1 or 2 has been violated to order the carpenters to quit work. They shall be given an immediate hearing before a committee of any five carpenter business agents, three of whom shall form a quorum, and the president of the Carpenters Executive Council to be the chairman, and if the evidence shall seem sufficient to said committee the men shall be ruled off the job pending their trial in their respective organizations.[50]

In March the District Council made another momentus decision. Rather than seek an agreement with the contractors' association, the union drew up individual contracts and prepared for a general strike on April 4. Meanwhile, the contractors met and ordered a heavy fine on any member who signed. James Brennock described the outcome:

Notwithstanding their order our office at 187 Washington Street was too small to accommodate the crowds that came to sign on the first day [of the strike], and two large offices were rented in the Times building. So great was the rush we had to keep two able-bodied men on the doors to protect the crowd from injury. And—wonder of wonders!—the five members of the [contractors'] Arbitration Board came in a body before the week was ended and signed like good little men. After one week the strike was over and peace was established once more, and the Carpenters' conditions were in full force and effect.

Under these conditions the carpenters achieved a $.025 pay increase, and for the first time the weekly payday and Saturday half day holiday during the summer months.[51]

The 1898 victory represented the height of the young carpenters' union's power within the trade, symbolized by Brennock's patronizing reference to the leaders of the contractors' association as "good little men." The union had virtually abandoned collective bargaining and had successfully dictated its demands to employers on an individual basis. This practice was not a tactic to pressure the contractors' association into signing an agreement, as had been the case during the 1887 and 1890 strikes. Rather, the union now treated individual contracts as a matter of settled industrial policy. Though not all building trades unions bypassed their contractors' associations, many rejected exclusive agreements at this time.

Overall, building trades workers, through the use of sympathy strikes, imposed something approaching union control of Chicago's construction industry. Edward Craig later commented that in the 1890s contractors' agreements with unions were hardly more than "scraps of paper," which were "prepared by a committee of the union and handed to the employer with the request that he sign his name on the dotted line . . . which he invariably did." In 1899 British observer Charles Spahr listened to frequent "boasts of power" from building trades leaders of the time, and concluded that "the allied Chicago unions ruled the building trades with an iron hand."[52]

The ability of the unions to bring their collective power to bear so effectively on the contractors in the midst of a severe building slump and the presence of large numbers of unemployed building tradesmen was a remarkable feat. It was due largely to the orchestration of intertrade solidarity through the centralized powers of the Building Trades Council. Though the Council nominally was governed by two hundred union delegates, it was virtually controlled by a Board of Business Agents, operating according to its own bylaws. The Board met three times a week and had the power to call sympathy strikes on any building site without holding a referendum of the unions involved.

Of all the business agents none was more influential than Martin B. (Skinny) Madden of the Steamfitters Helpers Union, who dominated the Board beginning in 1896. Madden was a brilliant labor politician, who was well liked but also feared by his fellow labor leaders. Though allegedly involved in some corrupt schemes by which he secured the personal loyalty of his supporters on the Board, Madden was considered by employers to be "as good as his word" in negotiations. Most importantly, Madden's adroit, two-fisted leadership forged unity among Chicago's building trades unions and enabled them to coordinate their actions to defeat and dominate the contractors, who lacked a centralized city federation comparable to the Building Trades Council.[53]

One measure of the power of the Building Trades Council was

its ability to resolve one of the principal grievances of the carpenters in the late nineteenth century: their inability to collect wages due them from the contractors. James Brennock recalled in 1900 that "the men would come up complaining all the time . . . that [they] could not get their wages—never got it. If there were $5 or $10 or $15 due a man in wages, he could not put up $15 for lawyers." But, said Brennock: "since the building trades council was established, I do not believe the carpenters, with their 5,000 men, for the past three years have spent over $10 to recover wages in court. As soon as they refuse to pay wages, so soon their business ceases."[54]

The unprecedented and almost unbounded power exercised by the unions soon elicited a strong reaction from the contractors as the construction slump continued through the 1899 building season. Contractors began to complain that restrictions on work and machinery by some unions, notably the plumbers, lathers, and stonecutters, and the high cost of material, raised construction prices beyond the reach of builders. Just as vehemently, they claimed that resort to the sympathy strike, "at the drop of a hat," created an intolerable unpredictability in building—the bane of contractors with long-term, high-priced projects. According to one architect, "contractors are going out of business or making no contracts, not knowing how much work will cost nor when it will be finished."[55]

With minimal building activity, many large contractors may have also reasoned that precipitating a crisis around the issue of unionism and labor costs could draw many smaller contractors into their associations. As an added plus, an extended lockout might drive down material prices and ruin their smaller competitors who were operating on a tighter margin. Contractors also may have wanted to force the unions back into exclusive agreements. Or as A. C. Cattermull, president of the Carpenters' General Executive Board, charged, contractors desired "the creation of a monopolistic ring within the building trades; a combination of contractors, architects, material men, and workmen, with the latter at the small end of the horn where he has ever been when his hands were tied with 'arbitration,' especially the kind that the Chicago contractors favor."[56]

Whatever their particular motives, in September 1899 the wealthiest local builders, led by William Behel, president of the Carpenters and Builders Association, and William O'Brien, a mason contractor, created the Building Contractors Council, the first central contractors' association in the United States. On November 17 the new Council passed a series of resolutions—later added to and summarized as the "eight cardinal principles" to be put into effect January 1900.[57]

Eight Cardinal Principles and Comments

1. There shall be no limitation on the amount of work a man may do during a day. Comment: This rule was aimed primarily at unions such as the plumbers and lathers with work rules that specified the amount of daily labor. Carpenter rules against rushing and filing and grinding at home were only sporadically enforced by the union's Trial Board, in part because they were so general.

2. There shall be no restriction on the use of tools or machinery. Comment: Though this rule was not aimed at carpenters, the union in the early twentieth century resisted the introduction of power tools.

3. There shall be no restriction on the use of any raw material or manufactured material except prison made. Comment: This principle was a major source of contention between the carpenters and the contractors as the union had always refused on principle to install nonunion material.

4. No person has the right to interfere with workmen during working hours. Comment: Intended to check the activities of business agents, this principle was never enforced even when adopted as it would completely undermine the union.

5. There shall be no limit on the number of apprentices. Comment: Since the establishment of the apprenticeship program in the twentieth century, the union has not unilaterally limited the number of apprentices. In fact, the union has often had to pressure contractors to take their allotted number of apprentices.

6. The foreman shall be the agent of the employer. Comment: Carpenter agreements always did and still do specify that the foreman must be a union member. However, in the early twentieth century, the foreman was subject to the Joint Arbitration Board, not the union, for rules violations.

7. Workman are at liberty to work for whomever they see fit, but they shall demand and receive wages agreed upon by the Joint Arbitration Board in their trade under all circumstances. Comment: The first part of this principle outlaws the exclusive agreement. The second part, added in 1915, protects Association contractors against competition from independent contractors.

8. *Employers are at liberty to employ and dis-
charge whomever they see fit.* Comment: This principle,
as it turned out, was not interpreted to deny the closed
shop. On the other hand, the union has not questioned
the contractors' right to fire journeymen carpenters, unless they were discharged for upholding union rules.[58]

As the above comments suggest, most of the various restrictions
enumerated by the contractors, while objects of concern, were not
issues of strict principle. The contractors had in the past and would
in the future compromise on these issues with the unions. Most
critical for the contractors was the need to curtail sympathy strikes,
which were the source of the unions' ability to dictate unilaterally
to the employers. Instead, contractors wanted issues of contention
settled by arbitration. Contractors stated that they were not opposed
to "legitimate unionism," by which they meant unions that did not
interfere—other than setting limits on wages and hours—with the
property prerogatives of employers in controlling the way work was
carried on at the jobsite. As Craig put it, the underlying issue from
the contractors' viewpoint was "the right of the employers to have
something to say besides digging up money for the weekly payroll
and passing it around to the men who happened to have their name
upon the time sheets."[59]

Proof that the contractors were more concerned with abolishing
sympathy action than restrictive work practices came with an attempted compromise agreement engineered by material dealer and
United States Congressman Martin Madden (no relation to the business
agent) on December 30, 1899. The agreement substituted trade and
industrywide arbitration for sympathy strikes and prohibited either
party from formulating work rules separately from the trade agreement,
while providing for arbitration of union restrictions on machinery and
allowing restrictions on specified building materials. The Contractors
Council immediately signed the compromise, but the Building Trades
Council, confident in its ability to prevail, refused. This set the stage
for an all-out conflict lasting thirteen months.[60]

On January 6 the Building Trades Council "declared war on the
trusts" by abrogating all monopolistic trade agreements entered into
by the unions. The contractors then locked out the unions, and to
guarantee the end of sympathy strikes demanded the withdrawal of
the unions from the Building Trades Council before they would treat
with them individually. The contractors then advertised for nonunion
men to work under a set of rules that were based on the eight cardinal

principles but also incorporated previous union gains such as eight hours and time and a half for overtime.[61]

The decision by the contractors to employ nonunion men opened the way for a revival of carpenter opposition to the wage system that had been dormant since 1894. In February 1900 a Building Trades Council committee that included Carpenters' Executive Council president Luke Grant inaugurated a cooperative capitalized at $100,000 with the following explanation:

> At the present stage of our industrial development, when capital is being concentrated with the object in view of reducing cost of production, capitalists engaging in the building industry are beginning to realize that the contractor is an unnecessary middleman, that the work can be done directly by the journeyman, thus saving the profits of the contractors, that the work is better done because the incentive to slight is not there, and consequently the contractor is making a last desperate effort to maintain his position, which has no place in the industrial field.[62]

Yet, for various reasons, the cooperative movement, which was backed largely by the carpenters, remained an empty threat. For one thing, Chicago's bankers and wealthy investors, far from switching their contracts to the unions, rallied behind the contractors, whom they viewed as fighting a class battle to rid Chicago of sympathy strikes and union radicalism. Meanwhile, the labor Democrats within the unions returned in this crisis to their time-tested alliance with City Hall. At least twenty-two building trades union leaders held city jobs, generally as building inspectors. This group was principally among the plumbers, painters, stonecutters, ironworkers, and steamfitters. Council President Edward Carroll was president of the Civil Service Board. As part of this relationship, Mayor Carter Harrison II, his police force, and local justices of the peace aided the unions during strikes by taking a hands-off approach. The benefits of this alliance were obvious; but there were drawbacks as well. City Hall Democrats were not about to aid cooperatives by turning over lucrative City Hall contracts to the unions. Moreover, politicking by the labor Democrats of the building trades unions helped alienate the support of the rest of the Chicago labor movement, which at one time was on the verge of a general strike in support of the locked-out men. In short, the cooperative movement was smothered before it started.[63]

The conflict soon turned violent. According to one student of the lockout, the press reported two hundred and fifty cases of assault on strikebreakers during the first five months of the strike, with thirty resulting in serious injuries, and three in death. There were only twenty arrests by police. What was called "slugging" by the press was carried on by two- to three-hundred paid members of the unions' "educational committees." In union parlance slugging a scab was a means of "educating" him into seeing the error of his ways. After the contractors petitioned Mayor Harrison in vain for police support, they hired five hundred special detectives to guard building sites. At one time two hundred nonunion workmen were housed in one of the Marshall Field buildings to avoid encounters with union "educators."[64]

Under intense pressure from business, the Mayor finally departed from his hands-off position. By fall the city banned mass picketing, allowing only two union men per building. Meanwhile, the contractors rejected arbitration offers from the mayor, the Civic Federation, Samuel Gompers, and reformer Graham Taylor and held firm to their demand for the dissolution of the Building Trades Council. In June the unions finally agreed to Congressman Madden's old plan and accepted arbitration boards in place of strikes. When this peace offering was rejected by the contractors, the bricklayers withdrew from the Building Trades Council. The carpenters remained as the Council's bulwark. As a price for remaining and funding the Council nearly alone, the carpenters forced a set of reforms preventing delegates from holding city jobs and giving more voting power to the larger unions. Later Local 1 business agent William Schardt was elected Council president, but was unwilling or unable to break Skinny Madden's hold on the unions.[65]

In August 1900, the carpenters' District Council held a referendum on whether to continue the fight or withdraw from the Building Trades Council. Though the majority voted to stay, Locals 13, 80, and 181 withdrew from the Building Trades Council. The carpenters held out for another six months. Then, under intense pressure from a rival carpenters' union started by the contractors and facing the breakup of the District Council, they capitulated on February 10, 1901. On the union's arbitration board only Brennock and Schardt, both from Local 1, plus one other delegate opposed the agreement.[66]

In their settlement, the carpenters agreed to withdraw from the Building Trades Council, incorporate the eight cardinal principles into their contract, accept the supremacy of the joint agreement over their own working rules, and recognize the authority of an annually elected arbitration board composed of ten members, five from each party, to settle all disputes; there was also provision for an umpire in case of a tie vote. On the other hand, the carpenters won the option of joining a new Building Trades Council and retained almost all the union accomplishments of the 1890s, including the Saturday half-day holiday, which the contractors had tried hard to abolish.[67]

The lockout of 1900–1901 proved to be a major turning point

in the history of the carpenters' union. Throughout the 1890s the trend in labor relations was in the direction of unilateral union control over the conditions on the jobsite through unrestricted sympathy action. The 1901 defeat halted this trend. To be sure, the settlement of that year maintained the gains of "legitimate" unionism, and the union's power in the workplace remained strong. Yet, in the future—with some notable exceptions—that power would be confined within the limits of joint arbitration. The lockout also marked the definitive decline of the late-nineteenth-century inspirational myth that the carpenters' union's ultimate goal was the abolition of the wage system and the establishment of a cooperative commonwealth. Instead, embedded in the preamble of future carpenter contracts, stood the eight cardinal principles, which, however often violated in practice, symbolized the union's ideological acceptance of the supremacy of the contractor in the trade and in the industry.

CHAPTER 4

The New Unionism and the Uniform Agreement, 1901–1929

The recuperative powers of defeated unions is certainly
marvelous, they simply won't stay licked, and become
convalescent quickly after a most serious shock. Union
sympathy is really sympathetic and the union tie is one
that quickly binds men together and draws them closer,
particularly when they are confronted with a common
enemy in a cause which they regard as sacred and
necessary for their protection.
　　　　　　　　　　　—Edward Craig, secretary of the
　　　　Building Construction Employers Association[1]

Fifteen years ago, following a lockout the carpenters,
by force of circumstances were required to sign an
agreement, with what is known as the eight cardinal
principles embodied therein, some of which, no union
man could work under and at the same time retain his
self-respect.
　　　　　　—K. W. Kilson, recording secretary of Local 1367[2]

The 1900–1901 lockout and defeat was for the carpenters and
other Chicago building tradesmen what the 1892 Homestead
strike was to steelworkers, and what the 1894 Pullman strike
was to railroad workers. It was a critical turning point in the
union's history, curtailing dedication to radical goals and broader class
unity and directing future development into more conservative and
trade-conscious channels. After 1900 the power of the business agent
to dictate to individual contractors—a phenomenon called "guerrilla

unionism" by contractors—was replaced in fits and starts by a strong commitment to standardized and centralized bargaining procedures. As a by-product, radical leaders such as O. E. Woodbury, James Brennock, and Luke Grant, who had dominated the District Council during the 1890s, gave way to conservatives such as District Council Presidents James Kirby (1903–5) and John Metz (1905–17). The local tendency was paralleled on the national level by the replacement of General Secretary P. J. McGuire by the conservative Frank Duffy (1901–48) and the ascendancy of conservative General Presidents William D. Huber (1899–1913), James Kirby (1913–15), and William Hutcheson (1915–51). The national trend was the more significant because of a centralizing tendency that gave the general executive board greater power over the conduct of district councils and local unions.

Yet the more conservative direction of the union after the turn of the century cannot be attributed solely to the defeat of 1901. Several other developments reinforced the union's departure from its old policies. First, a continuing series of technological changes in the process of building raised the issue of trade jurisdiction to one of central concern within the union. Increasingly, the use of the sympathy strike became shaped by the goal of maintaining jurisdiction or expanding it into new kinds of work. The effect was to undermine the solidarity among unionists within the construction industry and with the rest of the labor movement.

Second, these same technological innovations facilitated the emergence of the general contractor within the industry operating under the single-bid system and acting as financial coordinator of the various trades. Unlike the millmen-contractors, who dominated the trade in the late nineteenth century, the general contractors were generally opposed to exclusive agreements and to bans on nonunion millwork. They had an overriding interest in long-term stability in labor relations, a goal which they hoped to accomplish through arbitration.[3]

Finally, the post-1900 conservatism was reinforced by a long-term upturn in construction activity in Chicago. Between 1874 and 1900 a yearly average of 5,164 building were begun in the city, costing an average of $32.76 million (in 1913 dollars). Between 1901 and 1929 the yearly average rose to 9,654 buldings costing an average of $87.66 million. This building boom alleviated carpenter unemployment and allowed the contractors financial leeway to accede to union wage demands. This, in turn, deflected the union from guerrilla unionism and from pursuing its more controversial demands.[4]

Despite these developments, it cannot be said that the period between 1901 and 1929 was one of uninterrupted peace. While the union did not strike once between 1901 and 1911, relations with the contractors steadily deteriorated owing to the prevalence of jurisdictional walkouts and boycotts. Between 1912 and 1924, many locals mounted a challenge to the policy of accommodation pursued by the union's leadership. After three major strikes between 1912 and 1919, the resurgence in union militancy climaxed in a fierce counterattack by the contractors in the form of an open-shop movement. With the defeat of the open shop in 1924, the union gradually moved back into accommodation with the contractors, capped by the precedent-setting 1929 agreement.

The Rise of the Jurisdictional Question, 1901–1911

For Chicago carpenters the first eleven years of the twentieth century were characterized by a decline in union power and an unprecedented period of labor peace. Cooperative relations between union leaders and the contractors' association made possible the establishment in 1901 of a jointly operated apprenticeship program designed to maintain the all-around skills of the general carpenter. A novel and nationally acclaimed feature of the "Chicago system" was that apprentices were paid by contractors for attending public school three months a year. Meanwhile, the union settled for small wage increases for the years 1903, 1906, and 1909, in return for which they pledged to adhere to the eight cardinal principles and refrain from boycotts of nonunion materials and sympathy strikes. On the other hand, the union continued to enforce its own work rules through its Trial Board system.[5]

Throughout this period the carpenters remained aloof from the corrupt Skinny Madden group, which attempted to reestablish its influence through the formation of a new Board of Business Agents and a union federation known as the Amalgamated Building Trades League. The course of the union was described by President Metz in 1915 as follows: "The carpenters have had less trouble than any union in the city, I believe. We always have arbitrated our differences. There have been few strikes and the carpenters and contractors have always pulled together."[6]

The union's record of conciliation was, however, gradually and in the end almost completely overturned by major developments in the building process that threatened the carpenters' work jurisdiction. In the late nineteenth century, general contractors adopted structural steel, reinforced concrete, elevators, and caissons in large buildings enabling them to standardize the construction process for floors and rooms. This reinforced the long-standing tendency for the all-purpose carpenter to be replaced by narrow specialists such as millwrights, floor layers, shinglers, and pile drivers. It also accelerated the removal of work done by carpenters on the building site to the woodworking mills where, for example, floors of standardized fixtures could be mass produced by lower-paid woodworkers. By 1908 *The Carpenter* noted that in skyscrapers, "all the doors, the window frames, the wainscotting, the ceiling and the flooring came ready to be put in with the smallest amount of trouble."[7]

This was not the only problem raised by the revolution in building techniques. Wood began to be replaced by cheaper, longer-lasting, and less combustible materials, especially in large commercial and industrial structures. Metal trim replaced wood trim, steel and concrete beams replaced those of timber, steel replaced wood machine parts, and asbestos and asphalt shingles replaced wood shingles. As a result, new unions, such as the Sheetmetal Workers and Structural Iron Workers, sprang up to claim jurisdiction over installing these materials, and older organizations such as the Machinists and Roofers' unions expanded their jurisdictional claims. Faced with the prospect of the gradual strangulation of their craft and the weakening of their union through loss of work, the carpenters in Chicago and other cities responded by becoming the most uncompromising jurisdictional fighters in the industry.[8]

There were two main thrusts to the union's attempt to retain work for its members. Under the motto "all work on material that is made of wood" belongs to Brotherhood members, the carpenters advanced their claim to represent woodworkers in Chicago's mills. Under the corollary to this motto, all work on installations "that was ever made of wood belongs to the Brotherhood," the union fought out its jurisdictional battles with other building trades unions.[9]

The first and most important jurisdictional skirmish was the Brotherhood's bitter conflict with the Amalgamated Woodworkers International Union (AWW) within the woodworking mills. In 1891 there were fifteen hundred independently organized door, sash, and blind men affiliated with the United Carpenters Council. By January 1897, however, most of Chicago's machine woodworkers and cabinetmakers were organized under the banner of the AWW, and the District Council had agreed to recognize the AWW's label on the installation of factory-made woodwork. In return for this, the woodworkers refrained from working on outside jobs The settlement was quickly overturned by the Brotherhood's General Executive Board in October of the same year.[10]

This decision inaugurated the long conflict in Chicago between the carpenters and the millworkers. A similar struggle had begun two

years earlier on the national level when the Brotherhood began ig-
noring A.F. of L. awards of jurisdiction to the AWW. From the carpenters' viewpoint, there were several motivations for taking a hard
line in this rivalry. Because of their lower wages and longer hours
than the carpenters, the millworkers were often used by employers
on outside jobs to install fixtures or trim, work that was usually done
by carpenters. At times millworkers were used as scabs during strikes.
The Brotherhod thus hoped that by assuming jurisidiction over the
mills it could minimize the incentive to turn carpenter work over to
the millworkers. Finally, absorption of the millworkers would prevent
the threatened decline in the union's membership and power within
the construction industry.[11]

At the beginning of the century, the Brotherhood tried to woo
the AWW with the offer of high union benefits and the ability to mount
effective boycotts of nonunion materials. When that failed, each side
employed more forceful tactics. Both unions attempted to get mill
employers to refuse employment to the others' members. Then, the
Brotherhood began a boycott of AWW-made materials. In 1904 the
Chicago District Council welcomed its first pure millworkers' local,
1367, followed in 1906 by the accession of the furniture workers as
1786. By 1907 over twenty-five hundred local AWW'ers had joined
the District Council allowing the Brotherhood to argue that the AWW
was too weak to maintain viable collective bargaining. When the 1909
AWW convention refused the Brotherhood's offer to amalgamate, they
were expelled from the Chicago Federation of Labor at the behest of
the District Council. Finally, in 1911 and 1912, the remnants of the
Chicago AWW, including two of its business agents, joined the District
Council, and the struggle was over.[12]

In effect, the Chicago millworkers had exchanged membership
in a fledgling national industrial union for an alliance with the carpenters based on the expectation that outside men could enforce a
local monopoly in the Chicago material market through a boycott of
out-of-town, nonunion material. The immediate result of this alliance
was the District Council's attempt to delete article 3 of the eight cardinal principles—prohibiting boycotts of nonunion materials—from
the agreement with the contractors. Notwithstanding this solidarity,
historians have charged that the Brotherhood subordinated the interests of the "inside men" to that of the "outside men." The Brotherhood,
it is alleged, refused to organize more than a small segment of the
woodworking industry, as its interests were limited to "policing" its
own industry rather than in unionizing the woodworking industry.
As a result, critics allege that wages and conditions of millworkers
stagnated.[13]

It is true that the number of organized millworkers in Chicago declined, from ten to twelve thousand under the AWW to six to seven thousand under the Brotherhood. By the 1920s the District Council had less than four thousand inside men. But those millworkers who were members of the Brotherhood significantly improved their well-being. By 1911 a strike by door, sash, and blind workers gained the eight-hour day; other millmen won the eight-hour day in 1918. By 1920 Chicago millworkers received $1.10 an hour, only $.15 less than the outside men who faced seasonal unemployment. In 1915 mill-owners complained that high wages had driven half of the industry out of Chicago in the previous decade, a fact which tends to refute charges that wages stayed low and also may account for much of the decline in the number of unionized millworkers in the city. Mean-while, the union maintained strong opposition to "time and motion" studies and divisive pay classifications of millworkers. In sum, while the union may have lagged in organizing millworkers, those who did become members of the Brotherhood enjoyed improved benefits.[14]

In the other main jurisdictional thrust of the union, the revo-lution in building methods and materials led to a never-ending series of skirmishes with other building trades unions. By 1913 fully 75 percent of all work stoppages in the industry were due to jurisdictional disputes, many of them involving sympathy walkouts undertaken by coalitions of unions. The carpenters were involved in more of these disputes than any other union. In 1908, for example, the carpenters were involved in forty-five of sixty-eight jurisdictional cases.[15]

Beginning in 1905, such disputes grew intolerable to contrac-tors. They were also a problem for rank and file building trades work-men, who found themselves idled as entire projects shut down because of obscure conflicts between two unions over the apportionment of work. Even worse, jurisdictional shutdowns undermined the legiti-macy of the sympathy strike and the reputation of the union movement in the eyes of the public. Nonetheless, they continued because juris-dictional questions crucially affected the amount of work available to the average building trades workman.

Unfortunately for the carpenters and other building trades unions, such disputes could not be resolved within the labor move-ment. By the turn of the century strong national unions had emerged within each of the building trades, overshadowing local building trades councils. Indeed, between 1900 and 1910 the carpenters had become the second largest national union in the A.F. of L. and the largest in the building trades. Each of the national building trades unions was dedicated, above all other considerations, to protecting its jurisdic-tional interests. The industrial interests of the combined trades found representation mainly in the Building Trades Council. Yet, at the very time that the national unions were becoming more powerful, in Chicago the Building Trades Council had suffered a catastrophic defeat followed by continuing factionalism. Even when the Building Trades Council was reestablished in 1911 it was dominated by the smaller and weaker unions and lacked the legitimacy and power to impose settlements in jurisdictional matters.[16]

Increasing resort to jurisdictional walkouts disturbed what was otherwise a period of peace in the first decade of the twentieth century. At the same time the unions' inablity to resolve these disputes internally pushed the question into the laps of the contractors, who attempted to substitute a system of arbitration. This issue, compounded by the carpenters' new insistence on resuming their boycott of non-union materials to protect their millworker members, set the stage for a new period of conflict between the carpenters and the contractors.

Article 3 and the New Unionism, 1912–1918

By the end of the first decade of the twentieth century, labor relations in the Chicago building trades were in chaos. On the contractors' side, the Building Contractors' Council began to disintegrate, leaving a leadership vacuum. Into the breech stepped the city's Loop-based general contractors. In 1906, sixty of these contractors organized a select club known as the Builders Association. Their goal was to take collective bargaining away from the building sites and to regularize and centralize the process so that they could exert more control over it. Ultimately they hoped to change Chicago from what a prominent banker called "labor's storm center" to what Edward Craig termed "a strikeless city."[17] When the Building Trades Council was reorganized in 1911, the Builders Association responded the same year by creating the Building Construction Employers Association (BCEA), a more centralized and financially stable version of the old BCC. In 1913 the BCEA brought to fruition the long discussed idea of an industry-wide arbitration committee in the form of the Joint Arbitration Board. Two years later the Board wrote the industry's first uniform contract and imposed it on the various unions and contractors' associations.[18]

At first, union leaders cooperated with the BCEA. The president of the new Building Trades Council, plumber Simon O'Donnell, backed by bricklayer President Peter Shaughnessey and carpenters' President John Metz, wanted to replace the tradition of "guerrilla unionism" with labor statesmanship. By 1915 it appeared that a consensus had emerged within the industry on upholding the eight cardinal principles and abolishing sympathy strikes.[19]

Yet below the top levels of union leadership, there was considerable dissatisfaction with the proposed system of labor relations. Within the carpenters' union, an increased restiveness and militancy emerged in this period based on two developments. First, the entrance of millworkers into the union along with their radical business agents such as Anton Johannsen, militated against conservative craft exclusivism. Indeed, the carpenters were no longer a craft union, but rather a craft-industrial union. The logic of this transformation compelled many outside men to advocate class solidarity with industrial workers over the issue of boycotting nonunion-made materials.

The second development directly affected the outside men. Between 1890 and 1910 construction activity as measured by the distribution of land values had shifted to the central portion of the city where large contractors were powerful. After 1910 there was a reverse, decentralizing shift to residential home and apartment building construction in Chicago's outlying areas. The small-scale, less-organized contractors were at a bargaining disadvantage with the union locals in these areas. As a result, there was a dramatic increase in union membership after 1910 from eight to eleven thousand to twenty-one thousand in 1915. At the same time there was an increase in the percentage of carpenters organized by the union from 29 percent in 1900, to 33–35 percent in 1910, to 64–77 percent in 1920. It seems that most of these new members were foreign born carpenters who flooded into fast-growing Locals 58 (Scots), 181 and 62 (Danes and Norwegians), and 504 (Jews).[20]

The growing strength of dissent in the union stemmed from the addition of these fast-growing locals to the millmen and to older power centers in the union such as Local 1. It is safe to say that the motivations of the dissenters were diverse. Some were socialists, some were labor militants, some were both; still others were strong advocates of jurisdictional fights. Most, however, were opposed to the restrictions on sympathy strikes and material boycotts embodied in the new system of arbitration championed by Metz and the contractors. The result was a powerful movement within the union corresponding to a larger development within the trade union world during this period that labor historian David Montgomery has termed the "New Unionism."[21]

That new movement was evident in 1912 in the first confrontation of the carpenters with the new structure of collective bargaining. The 1912 strike was very reluctantly led by President Metz. During the previous five years Metz had dragged his feet in the chartering of

millworkers' locals as their presence complicated his amicable relationship with the contractors. Meanwhile, the millworkers had found
a staunch champion of their position in Secretary Treasurer Daniel
Galvin. According to an "inside story" based on an interview with
Metz published in the *Chicago Tribune*, the contractors were disturbed
to find that "with the advent of the millmen and the election of Daniel
Galvin . . . Metz has been crowded somewhat into the background."
The article claimed: "The millmen are classed as radicals. They were
taken into the union mainly to keep them from doing outside work
and from poaching on the carpenters' reserves. It is understood that
Metz opposed their affiliation with the district council without success. Immediately, close observers saw the attempt of Galvin to climb
to the top."[22]

Metz was able to keep the lid on until local millowners began
complaining to the District Council that the influx of cheap nonunion
material threatened to undermine the wages of unionized millworkers.
Conservatives' qualms about the explosiveness of fighting against article 3 also seem to have been overridden by an upswell of solidarity
in the ranks of the union. Said one carpenter leader: "We are not
fighting for ourselves. It won't do us any good to have union-milled
lumber to work, because I don't think there is any difference between
it and other lumber but we are working to help out the men in the
mills who are paid starvation wages."[23]

The result was that on April 1, 1912, fourteen thousand outside
men struck for a $.05 wage increase and the removal of article 3. Within
ten days of the strike the union had enough of its men employed by
independent contractors to pay ample benefits to out-of-work members. The Loop general contractors soon split from the diehard medium-sized contractors, and on April 11 agreed to a compromise. The
carpenters gained a $.05 wage increase, but rather than removal of
article 3, the union received the pledge that, should price and quality
be equal, the contractors would give preference to Chicago material.
Millworkers were not impressed. On the eve of the ratification vote,
a District Council leader tried to explain the position of the leadership:
"No doubt, some of the radicals will send up a howl at the meeting
of the District Council tonight, but we feel sure that the vast majority
of the organization favors the agreement. We tried to get as much as
possible for the greatest number possible." He was right, for the outside
men approved the agreement 7,555–636.[24]

The issue of nonunion material in the industry was raised again
in January 1913 when several unions shut down construction of the
Field Museum over the use of nonunion-cut marble. When Building
Trades Council President O'Donnell proved unable to get the men to

return to work, the BCEA locked out twenty-seven thousand union men. Faced with a loss of public support, O'Donnell caved in. In 1915 he accepted, on behalf of the unions, an industrywide conciliation and arbitration committee, soon renamed the Joint Conference Board, which functions to this day. Together with the arbitration committee, the unions agreed to a no-strike provision forbidding walkouts while committee decisions were pending.[25]

In 1915 the Joint Conference Board, on which O'Donnell and Metz served, extended its power to the various trades by drafting a "uniform form of agreement." This was a standard agreement for all trades embodying the eight cardinal principles and providing for universal recognition of the Joint Conference Board as the final arbiter of jurisdictional disputes, and a uniform expiration date for all contracts. For the first time the unions had voluntarily accepted what had been imposed upon them in 1901. According to historian Royal Montgomery, writing in 1927, it was "the great compromise in the history of the Chicago building trades."[26]

The Building Trades Council defended its acceptance of the plan in a remarkable document in union annals, which conceded that restrictions on basic union practices—strikes and sympathy action—were necessary to counteract the public's belief that construction unions were corrupt. "The business agent," said the document, "who has forgotten how to live within an honest salary must now entrench. . . . The unions will be free from the unnecessary strike curse which has stamped them as a menace to the city." This acquiescence in the common stereotype of the business agent does not seem to have been warranted. Royal Montgomery, an impartial observer of the building trades unions, thought that only a handful of well-known leaders were actually corrupt. Meanwhile, those militants opposed to the agreement of 1915 and the existing Council leadership were tarred with the brush of corruption.[27]

Among the carpenters a large faction, led by Metz, supported the uniform agreement as a realistic compromise with the contractors, one that would reduce time lost to unnecessary work stoppages. But opposition increased, both to Metz within the union and to O'Donnell within the Building Trades Council. This was expressed forcefully by a carpenter business agent:

> The unions cannot expect to win their fights against the bosses unless they stick together. They put scab lathers to work in place of union men. The bosses would do the same with every other union if they could. That's why they want to tie our hands with that uniform agreement, which they say will prevent sympathetic strikes. That's the unions' strongest weapon.[28]

Despite the carpenters' formal support for the uniform agreement, the union became involved in a fight against it. Smaller contractors had opposed the general contractors' policy of offering a wage increase to the unions to ensure compliance with the new agreement. This forced the carpenters out on strike on April 16, 1915. In addition to the demand for a wage increase, the union asked for elimination of article 3, an earlier contract expiration date to make the contractors more vulnerable to a strike, and recognition in the contract of independent contractors who belonged to the union. With these demands the carpenters joined the lathers and plasterers in what was generally interpreted as a strike against the uniform agreement.[29]

By this time the union was badly divided between the militants led by Secretary-Treasurer Galvin and President Metz. During negotiations Galvin was accused of witholding from the membership a letter from the contractors offering a $.025 wage increase because it might undercut support for other issues in the strike. Though this charge was denied and its accuracy is impossible to assess, the incident was symptomatic of the seriousness of the rift within the union. Led by Galvin, many outside men wanted to stay out, not only for the abolition of article 3, but to do something about issues such as excessive rushing on the job, the lack of appliances on the job to sharpen tools, and the discharge of men early in the morning. This meant, of course, opposition to the uniform agreement.

Yet, it soon became obvious that much of the carpenters' leadership had never intended to challenge the uniform agreement. According to Local 434's business agent, writing in *The Carpenter*, "if the arbitration board of the contractors had at any time before or during the strike offered us the wage of $.70 per hour, which we have now established, the strike would either not have occurred or would have ended quickly." Once started, however, the strike was extraordinarily successful. Over 11,000 carpenters found work with independent contractors, leaving only 4,480 members to support. Not one union carpenter was brought before the Trial Board for strikebreaking. Their bargaining hand strengthened, the union membership in June overwhelmingly rejected Mayor William ("Big Bill") Thompson's arbitration offer.[30]

With independent contractors controlling two-thirds of existing construction, the Carpenter Contractors Association turned to the BCEA, with which it was not affiliated, for assistance. The BCEA responded by arranging a material manufacturers' boycott of independents. The tide quickly turned, and on July 9 the union accepted the uniform agreement and in return received its wage demands; article 3 and the old expiration date remained in the contract. All independent contractors signed the new agreement.[31]

Dissension within the union over article 3 and the uniform agreement was only temporarily quieted. In 1917, American entry into World War I diverted funds from construction activity and led to a precipitous decline in building. Millowners, seeking to escape ruinous competition, turned to the union for help. They proposed to the District Council that it get contractors to remove article 3 from their agreement, in return for which contractors would receive a discount on material, and millmen would receive a wage increase and shorter hours. The union, now led by William Brims, who had succeeded the retired Metz, jumped at this opportunity. In April 1918 the carpenters joined with the contractors in a secret four-cornered deal. Carpenters were allowed to boycott nonunion sashes, doors, and interior trim, and received a wage increase to $.80, plus a Saturday payday; inside men received an increase to $.50 plus an eight-hour day; contractors received a $.15–$.25 discount and greater leverage over independents; and millowners gained relief from competition. The agreement was a critical breach in the seventeen year old record of union compliance with the eight cardinal principles and opened a period of industrial war within the trade.[32]

The Landis Award and the Open Shop Movement

Between 1921 and 1924 contractors and a committee representing Chicago's largest industrial, commercial, and banking firms combined in an attempt to impose the open shop on the Chicago building trades. Perhaps no other struggle in the history of the Chicago building trades, certainly none in the history of the carpenters, was fought with more tenacity, bitterness, and violence. Past antiunion drives by employers had come as responses to periods of extraordinary union strength. In 1887 builders vainly attempted to destroy the fledgling building trades unions following the eight-hour upsurge. In 1900–1901 the contractors took on and defeated the Building Trades Council over the widespread use of the sympathy strike. The open shop movement of the early 1920s was, in essense, a reaction to the breaching by the unions of the 1913–15 system of arbitration and the uniform agreement. Because it was the carpenters' union that led in this reassertion of union independence and militancy, it was the carpenters who bore the brunt of the employers' counterattack.

The year 1919 was a critical year in the history of the labor movement and more generally for class relations. Among American working people the months following the armistice of November 1918

that ended World War I were ones of enormous expectation and op-
timism. Throughout the country the catchphrase "industrial democracy" came to symbolize the hope that the cooperation of labor and
capital in the successful war effort had ushered in a new era in labor
relations. As an editorial in the A.F. of L.'s *Federationist* reprinted in
the *The Carpenter* expressed it: "the great social fact of our time is
this declaration of independence by labor from its previous status as
an inferior class. It is asking for a place of complete equality in industry
and society."[33]

In the spring of 1919 President Woodrow Wilson asked representatives of labor and capital to meet in Washington, D.C., to reorder
industrial relations in postwar America, a prospect which the *Chicago
Tribune* heralded as a "Radical Revolution in the Wage System." To
many conservative A.F. of L. leaders, equality in industrial relations
simply meant the legitimization of collective bargaining. To other
union men, however, the prospect of reordering opened the way for
workers' control of industry. The most striking example was the plan
of the railroad brotherhoods for public ownership of the nation's railroads, the operation of the lines to be governed by a tripartite board
representing labor, management, and the public. Meanwhile, American workers struck in unprecedented numbers to win collective bargaining rights, improved work rules, and to stay abreast of the soaring
postwar inflation. In Chicago railroad workers wildcatted in April,
and stockyard workers struck in July and August; city streetcar employees and International Harvester workers also walked out.[34]

When it became clear that employers, backed by the courts and
state governments, were determined to crush rather than cooperate
with the labor movement, unions in America's urban-industrial heart-
land began to turn to labor parties. In the spring of 1919 the Chicago
Federation of Labor created a Cook County Labor party and slated its
president, John Fitzpatrick, for mayor. In February and March the
District Council endorsed Fitzpatrick and donated to the new party
the names and addresses of its members to act as poll watchers. The
District Council adopted a special committee's report stating that:

> History in the last two years shows that injunction after in-
> junction has been used against labor, state militia and even
> United States soldiers used against strikes. We, your committee,
> believe that this great force which is used against organized
> labor should be used in the interest of all the people. Therefore,
> We Recommend, That all unions under the jurisdiction of the
> Chicago Carpenters District Council affiliate with the Labor
> Party, assist in nominating candidates for office from the ranks
> of labor, and boost the Labor Party and work for the election
> of all Labor Party candidates.

During the campaign the C.F. of L.'s *New Majority* reported that "some of the very best efforts of the whole campaign were put forth by various members of the Carpenters' Union. Several of them ran for office on the Labor Party ticket, and in many wards the organizers belonged to this trade." This occurred without the support of General President William Hutcheson, a staunch supporter of free-enterprise capitalism and Republican presidential candidate Warren G. Harding.[35]

Meanwhile, carpenters began to forge their own vision for reconstructing postwar labor relations. Many unionists wanted to restore some version of the old 1890s policy of offering only individual contracts to the contractors. A large segment of this group, led by Harry Jensen, president of Local 181, opposed all restraint on carpenter jurisdictional claims and the union's freedom to defend them. They tended to pursue a go-it-alone policy, which ultimately meant withdrawal from the Building Trades Council and the Joint Conference Board, just as General President William Hutcheson, an uncompromising jurisdictional fighter, had withdrawn from the newly established National Board for Jurisdictional Awards and the Building Trades Department of the A.F. of L.[36]

In addition to the jurisdictional militants, there existed a wing of socialists and other "progressives"—more prominent in the union in 1919–20 than at any other time in the twentieth century. As an alternative to the policy of jurisdictional advantage, they advocated solidarity among the building trades. This group, based mainly in Locals 1, 62, 181, and 504, initiated the demand for a uniform industrial wage for all skilled trades. One carpenter local even proposed a unified industrial agreement to replace bargaining by individual unions. The long-term goal of this group was "amalgamation" of all building trades unions in one big construction workers' union.[37]

Who Were the Carpenter Progressives?

Despite the growth of business unionism during this period, a variety of self-described "Progressives"—revolutionary syndicalists, municipal socialists, and revolutionary communists (1920s)—flourished in union leadership positions. Charles Sand (secretary-treasurer of the District Council, 1922–48): Born in Sweden in 1873, Sand was apprenticed as a piano-maker and arrived in America in 1895. After he joined the Socialist party in 1899, he became an active unionist. A resident of Lakeview, he was one of the leading Scandinavian socialists in Chicago during the first two decades of the century. In 1911, while serving as editor of the Swedish socialist paper, *Svenska Socialisten*, he was nominated by the Socialist party as an aldermanic candidate from the 25th Ward. A longtime member of Local 58, Sand seems to have subordinated his politics to union concerns once in office.

Knute Torkelson (longtime officer of Local 181 and District Council secretary-treasurer, 1903–7): Another Scandinavian socialist, Torkelson was an important leader in the Chicago Federation of Labor and in the Chicago Public Ownership League. In 1919 he served as the candidate of the Cook County Labor party for treasurer.

Daniel Galvin (secretary-treasurer, 1907–22): A leading Irish radical, Galvin was a strong advocate of abolishing article 3 in the second decade of the twentieth century and in 1919 served on the Executive Council of the Cook County Labor party.

Roy Lee Wolfe (president of Local 141 beginning in 1916): Wolfe ran on the Labor party ticket in 1919 as an aldermanic candidate and in 1924 ran on the Farmer-Labor party ticket.

Anton Johannsen (former business agent in the AWW; later president of Local 1367): The German-born Johannsen was a leading anarcho-syndicalist, believing that organized workers should own and operate all industry. A strong advocate of labor solidarity, he was a leader in the McNamara defense campaign (a labor cause in the second decade of the twentieth century) and in "Wobbly" (Industrial Workers of the World) free-speech fights. In 1907 Hutchins Hapgood wrote a book on the labor movement based on Johannsen's early life entitled *The Spirit of Labor.*

C. M. DeGroot (leading union activist in Local 62): The Dutch-born DeGroot was a member of the Communist-run Trade Union Educational League in the 1920s. In 1928 he ran for District Council president on a militant, antiadministration platform and received 28 percent of the total vote of almost twenty thousand.

Nels Kjar (leading 181 activist in the 1918–28 period): Along with DeGroot, the Danish-born Kjar led the

Progressive Carpenter caucus that opposed Jensen and later the 1929 contract endorsed by the Flynn administration. A member of the Communist party, he was expelled from the Brotherhood at the behest of President Hutcheson in 1928 and later deported by federal authorities.[38]

In the 1919–20 period the progressives and the jurisdictional militants formed two powerful opposition blocs within the carpenters' union. Though diverging in their long-term goals, most could give assent to a program that included the following four points: 1) support for a uniform wage and for a uniform expiration date for contracts in the basic trades so as to discourage jurisdictional conflict and encourage solidarity; 2) opposition to arbitration and umpiring of trade disputes; 3) a return to the mass organizing campaigns that had typified the union in the late nineteenth century (for example, Local 181 proposed to lower the initiation fee to draw in new members and urged the District Council to join the C.F. of L.'s organizing campaign in basic industry); 4) politically, opposition locals opposed the "Red Scare" of the period and were active in the Labor party and the C.F. of L..[39]

The carpenters' participation in the events of 1919 stemmed from two sources: the uniquely favorable bargaining climate created by the shortage of skilled labor during the war and the consequent shift of contractors to cost-plus contracts, combined with the need to keep up with the postwar explosion in inflation. In mid-July nineteen thousand Chicago carpenters struck for a $.20 an hour increase to $1.00, a demand designed to give carpenters parity with the highest paid building trades. Building Trades Council President O'Donnell immediately charged that the walkout emanated from the "impulse of the mob." Contractors in the BCEA and millowners responded with a lockout and a material boycott to shut down the union's allies among the independent contractors.[40]

Throughout the long summer, the union stuck to its demands and refused arbitration offers from O'Donnell, Mayor Thompson, and the United States secretary of labor. On September 19, the contractors, weakened by a building slump, completely capitulated. On the heels of this victory came a favorable court decision finding the material manufacturers guilty of criminal conspiracy and enjoining them from engaging in future boycotts of contractors employing union men. Altogether, 1919 had brought the most unequivocal victory achieved by the union since the late 1890s.

When inflation continued into 1920, the union resorted to a wage reopener clause to claim successfully a $.25 wage increase. At this point, all Chicago building trades workers, with the exception of laborers and helpers, received a uniform wage. In May 1920 the millworkers, who had been demanding wage parity with the outside men, received a $.30 an hour increase to $1.10.[41]

The union's strength had reached high tide. In May a major recession and rapidly falling prices hit the nation, and employers launched a stunning counteroffensive. The "take-back" movement began with wage-cutting and quickly extended into an assault on union work rules. In March 1921 the Illinois legislature set up the Dailey Commission to investigate the high cost of building. Its highly sensationalized findings attributed the building slump to high construction costs, which in turn were blamed on monopolistic agreements among unions, contractors, and employers and inefficient union work rules that allegedly contributed to a "productivity crisis." In this climate, indictments rained down on the unions, including District Council leaders William Brims and William Schardt for violating the Sherman Anti-Trust Act in the boycotting of nonunion materials.[42]

Meanwhile, national employers, led by United States Steel— soon followed by the National Association of Manufacturers and the United States Chamber of Commerce—thrust aside the Progressives' embryonic vision of industrial democracy and inaugurated an antiunion drive dubbed the "American Plan." In Chicago, banker John O'Leary of the Chicago Association of Commerce and nonunion printer Thomas E. Donnelley of the Employers' Association convened leading businessmen in closed-door meetings during the last half of 1920 to plan a campaign to undercut the strength of the Chicago labor movement. The movement was joined by the large woodworking mills led by the Edward Hines Lumber Company and a new, antiunion group of carpenter general contractors, the Associated Builders, which favored wage cuts and the restoration of article 3.[43]

Mr. Dooley on the Open Shop

"What is all this talk in the papers about the open shop?" asked Mr. Hennessey.

"Why, don't you know?" said Mr. Dooley. "Really I'm surprised at yer ignorance, Hinnessey. What is th' open shop? Sure, 'tis a shop where they kape th' door open t' accomerdate the constant stream of min comin' in t' take jobs cheaper thin th' men that has th' jobs. 'Tis

like this, Hinnessey, Suppose wan of these freeborn
Amerycan citizens is wurkin' in an open shop for th'
princely wages of one large iron dollar a day for tin hours.
Along comes another free-born son-of-a-gun an' sez t' th'
boss, 'I think I could handle th' job for 90 cints.' 'Sure!,'
sez the boss, an the wan dollar man goes out into th'
crool world t' exercise his inalienable rights as a free-
born Amerycan citizen and scab on some other poor devil.
An' so it goes on, Hinnessey. An' who gets th' benefit?
Thrue, it saves th' boss money, but he don't care no more
for money than he does fer his right eye, It's all principle
with him. He hates t' see min robbed of their indipend-
ence regardless of inything ilse."

"But," said Mr. Hinnessey, "these open ship min
ye minshun say they are for the unions, if properly conducted."

"Shore," said Mr. Dooley, "if properly conducted.
An' there ye are. An' how wud they have them conducted? No strikes; no rules, no contracts; no scales; barely
iny wages, an' damn few mimbers."

—Finley Peter Dunne[44]

In January 1921, with approximately 75 percent of all construction workers unemployed, the Associated Builders and the BCEA asked
for a 20 percent wage reduction for the skilled trades and 30 percent
for laborers. Tom Kearney, the new Building Trades Council president,
reasoning that a tactical retreat was in order, favored a compromise.
He was rebuffed in a referendum of the Council's constituent unions.
Within the carpenters' union, the employers' demands strengthened
the position of the insurgents. At this point the militant locals challenged Brims for the presidency. They were led by Local 181 President
Harry Jensen, an ambitious labor politician who represented the protest of these locals without sharing in their outlook. In June 1920 Brims
had won a narrow election victory over Jensen, which set off a series
of rancorous disputes within the District Council. It began when Jensen
questioned the fairness of the election in an appeal to General President
Hutcheson. Following this, a Local 58 business agent allied with the
administration, and later accused of selling the union label for personal
gain, slugged a Jensen poll watcher and attacked Secretary-Treasurer
Daniel Galvin during a Council meeting. As tensions mounted, Local
181 introduced a hotly debated resolution to withdraw from the Building Trades Council, which was deemed too accommodating to the

contractors. "The carpenters," said the resolution, "have been the fight-ers and stood the brunt of battle not only for themselves but for all other trades as well in the years that have gone by, and received nothing in return, so we believe it is time to make one good fight for the carpenters."[45]

The insurgent locals got their fight. On April 15, 1921, the contractors locked out all building tradesmen over the wage dispute. The District Council replied by offering contractors individual agree-ments. But the Brims administration—for reasons that are not clear—did not adequately enforce the rules preventing carpenters from work-ing for contractors who had not signed the agreement. Local 504 spoke for the insurgents in protesting that "this Local is of the opinion that the District Council has lost control of the carpenters in the present lockout." By June, so general was the perception of a vacuum in lead-ership that Jensen won a substantial victory over Brims in the general election.[46]

The new administration faced a mammoth crisis. On June 11 the Building Trades Council had accepted Judge Kenesaw Mountain Landis as an "impartial umpire" in the lockout, and submitted all wages, and even work rules—an unprecedented and controversial move—to binding arbitration. The carpenters, in accordance with tra-dition, rejected participation in such arbitration, causing dissension within the Building Trades Council. Yet, with little or no support from other unions, the Jensen administration had no choice but to continue the Brims policy of seeking a stopgap agreement with the Associated Builders to forestall mounting public pressure to accept Judge Landis as an arbitrator. On June 29 the two parties compromised by restoring article 3, in return for which contractors agreed to maintain the old wage rate and the freedom of the union from the decisions of the National Board of Jurisdictional Awards. But the compromise was not acceptable, either to the rank and file or to Judge Landis. In a vote, the carpenters rejected the proposed agreement; meanwhile, Judge Landis stated that the agreement violated his guidelines. At this point the union informally agreed with the contractors to work under the old contract until the Landis Award was announced.[47]

All eyes were now on Judge Landis. Certainly both parties ex-pected that the widely respected judge would work out a compromise solution to the dispute. Instead, Landis decided to constitute himself a virtual dictator in the name of the public, basing his conception of the public interest on the findings of the Dailey Commission. Using this approach, he decided to revise the work rules of each trade using a new version of the eight cardinal principles as a yardstick. Landis also created a new standard contract that differed from the old in two important ways. The old agreement had allowed nonunion men to be employed by contractors if the local and international union could not supply union men within ninety-six hours, with these substitute workers being subject to union rules. Landis stipulated that substitutes could be used as the contractor saw fit. Second, Landis abolished that part of the uniform agreement that had given unions the right to strike should nonunion men of another trade be employed.[48]

With these principles in mind, Landis objected to a series of provisions of the carpenters' union contract: those that allowed double-time for overtime, eight-hour pay for seven hours' shift time, and, most importantly, provisions that defined jurisdiction and allowed the union to strike if the contractor violated these rules. To enforce these proposed changes in the carpenters' and other trades' contracts, Landis decreed wage penalties for unions that refused to accept them. He also ended the recently won uniform wage scale and unilaterally set different wages for each trade. The overall result was a drastic lowering of real wages for all trades, on an average of 25 percent below those of 1914. Landis added insult to injury by decreeing these wages maximum rather than minimum.[49]

Chicago building trades workers greeted the announcement of the Landis Award on September 7, 1921, by spontaneously walking off their jobs. For unions other than the carpenters, painters, and several smaller unions, this was equivalent to a revolt against their leadership. Building Trades Council President Kearney candidly admitted: "The situation is one we cannot control." Yet, despite the fact that the unions opposed to the Landis Award represented 70 percent of all affiliated construction workers, the Council—dominated by the small unions—endorsed the award. At a raucous Council ratification meeting many unions were swayed by Kearney's charge that opposition stemmed from IWW propaganda; other delegates may have had their votes miscounted.[50]

With the carpenters vowing all-out defiance, the Associated Builders began in September to import nonunion carpenters. Already, however, the city was in the midst of a building boomlet. As a result, many contractors, especially those on the outskirts of the city where speculative builders were strong, would not limit themselves to the Landis wage. Nor could most contractors bear the cost of recruiting, housing, and guarding their strikebreakers. So carpenter contractors appealed to Chicago's open-shop businessmen in the Association of Commerce and the Employers' Association. On November 21, led by Donnelley and O'Leary, Chicago's American Plan advocates established the "Citizens Committee to Enforce the Landis Award," a group of 176 leading businessmen representing the city's major downtown department stores, manufacturers, and utilities.[51]

In return for financing the contractors, the Citizens Committee required them to sign an open-shop pledge. According to Donnelley, it stipulated: "That in those trades where unions refused to accept the Landis Award . . . they be permanently on an open shop basis, that foremen would be non-union, and that never again would negotiations be entered into with these unions to give them control of the trade, also that the Citizens Committee would permanently have a voice in the labor policies of the contractors' association." In addition, contractors had to pledge not to allow the business agents of "outlaw" unions to visit the jobsite, nor to allow more than 50 percent of the workmen on any particular job to be union members.[52]

Of the eleven unionized trades—later fifteen—declared "outlaw," the carpenters, as the largest and most militant of the unions, was the Committee's principal target. By December 1921 hundreds of scab carpenters were entering the city each week and other unions refrained from striking in solidarity with the carpenters. Meanwhile, the struggling millworkers had been compelled to accept a $.20 wage reduction "to preserve our organization in this city at the present time." On December 14, Joseph Noel, president of the Commerce Association, declared optimistically, "the carpenters union is dead as a labor power."[53]

This was no idle boast. The Citizens Committee established an employment bureau with offices in twenty-three cities throughout the United States, and by September 1922 had placed twenty thousand nonunion men in jobs in Chicago, over eight thousand of them carpenters. The Committee inaugurated a trade school with an enrollment of 250. To protect contractors and scabs from the wrath of unionists, the Committee hired 700 guards under the direction of an ex-army officer and subscribed to $800 million in insurance to cover nonunion construction work. At the peak of its success in August 1922, 1,250 contractors, 85 percent of all BCEA members, had signed the Committee's pledge. Meanwhile, 500 architects had signed a pledge to confine their work to Landis Award contractors.[54]

In stemming the onslaught of the Citizens' Committee, the carpenters' union faced two problems: reaching unity with other building trades; and gaining control over their own membership and nonunion newcomers. The two were closely related, for to gain control of the trade the union needed sympathy action from other trades. Yet, other trades, even other anti-Landis trades, refused to support the carpenters as long as they claimed their old wage of $1.25 and the freedom to engage in jurisdictional disputes, thus flouting the authority of the National Board for Jurisdictional Awards. In the absence of a unified Building Trades Council, the union turned toward an alliance with the Painters and other anti-Landis trades. To cement the alliance, the union agreed to settle with the contractors for the highest existing construction wage, $1.10.[55]

Even this concession could not prevent carpenters from accepting work under Landis conditions. In the fall of 1922, Local 242 complained that "over half the scabs in the city are union men, and when asked for their cards they say they do not belong to the union." Even men working for contractors approved by the union often got their pay in two envelopes: $.90 in a Landis envelope and $.35 as a bonus to meet union scale. In this case there was no incentive for nonunion contractors to come to terms with the union.[56]

Another option for the union was violence and intimidation. According to one source, in the three years following the Landis Award there were eleven deaths directly traceable to the anti-Landis struggle, plus many more instances of altercations and damage to property of nonunion workmen. As early as 1915 an ex-business agent of the union, Luke Grant, wrote that:

> In recent years there has been a marked change in the nature of violence committed in the building trades and in the methods used. The ordinary workman who in former days was apt to use his fists on the head of the "scab" for the sake of "the cause," seldom does so now. His place has been taken by the professional thug and gunman. Violence has become commercialized and made more brutal.

Labor racketeering, in short, had become widespread in Chicago even before Prohibition and the rise of bootlegging. By the early 1920s there were approximately fifty to sixty gangster-related bombings a year in Chicago, about half labor-related. Landis Award violence came to a head on May 9, 1922, when two policemen were assassinated gangland style in connection with a bombing of an open-shop glazier's firm. According to the magazine of the Association of Commerce, the killings "aroused the law abiding element in Chicago to a level of indignation unequaled since the Haymarket riots." In retaliation Chicago police raided building trades union headquarters and arrested 163 union leaders including one carpenter business agent. Eventually, three of the most unsavory leaders were indicted: "Big Tim" Murphy of the gas workers, Cornelius "Con" Shea of the theater janitors, and Fred Mader, president of the Building Trades Council. None were convicted. But, according to one informed report, by the late 1920s over thirty Chicago unions, mainly in the building trades, were partly or completely under the control of gangsters, principally the Capone gang.

There is no evidence that any carpenter leader employed the

services of local gangsters, nor were any charged in connection with Landis Award violence. This does not mean that the union opposed the bombings. As Luke Grant put it:

> Ask any ordinary union man in any building trade if he ap-
> proves of violence and he probably will answer that he does
> not. He would not think of assaulting a nonunion man himself.
> He would not destroy property under any circumstances. If he
> hears or reads, however, of a building that is being erected by
> nonunion men in his particular craft having been destroyed by
> dynamite and that the employer as a result has decided to
> employ union men, he does not feel overwhelmed with grief
> at the outrage.[57]

Nonetheless, neither bombings nor the kind of organized intimidation the union's educational committees employed in the 1890s would work in the face of the widespread decline in union loyalty of carpenter members. By early February 1922 the union was obliged to choose among three courses of action. The union could, as conservative Local 58 advocated, "appoint a special committee to meet with the contractors' association to try and formulate an agreement before we are thoroughly licked." Such a course was never seriously considered in the District Council for it would have raised a revolt by many locals, even before President Hutcheson would have vetoed it. A different course, advocated by Locals 1, 242, and 504, was to resurrect the tactic of the nineteenth century German socialists in calling for a general strike to "keep the union scab at home." When this course was rejected—predictably—by the Building Trades Council, the only way to organize a general walkout would have been to hold mass meetings at the jobsites to attract the rank and file of the pro-Landis unions. This tactic was proposed and explicitly rejected by the Jensen administration.[58]

Rather than "allow an element of discontented men to hold meetings," the District Council adopted a moderate policy. The union decided to "man all jobs with our men with a thorough understanding that union conditions [be maintained]"; and that "the advisory board be empowered to put men on any jobs [including Landis jobs] they deem advisable for the purpose of unionizing said jobs and report daily to this office the conditions of the jobs." This was nothing other than the nineteenth century tactic known as "missionary work" employed effectively during the 1890 strike.[59]

The great drawback of this approach was that the union's $60 initiation fee discouraged many prospective members from joining. This problem was intensified by the accleration of the building boom in the spring, which found the union unable to supply all the men needed by contractors, even by the minority of union contractors. To encourage Landis men to join the union, the Council finally adopted a "permit system" whereby prospective members received weekly working cards while paying their initiation fee in installments over a five-week period. This was potentially a dangerous move, for the union was taking in strikebreakers and making them secure in their jobs. Yet, the labor shortage was likely to continue, leaving jobs in abundance for scabs. Another justification for this policy in Jensen's words was that "a very effective method of warfare is to be able to use the enemy's ammunition."[60]

To supplement the union's new approach, the carpenters turned toward the C.F. of L. Under John Fitzpatrick's leadership the anti-Landis unions held mass meetings throughout Chicago to get out the union side of the story that the press would not report. Slowly the spirits of the Chicago labor movement began to revive. Labor's citywide campaign against the open shop culminated on April 29, 1922, in a grand march down Michigan Avenue of between fifty- and one-hundred-thousand workingmen. Union men carried signs reading, "Did Judge Land-us? No"; one from a war veteran read, "We Are Out To Fight the 'Hun'-dred Per Cent 'Pay'-triots of the Citizens(?) Committee." The Carpenters' District Council declared the day a holiday and turned out ten thousand men, 70 per cent of its membership, led by a forty-piece band.[61]

Following the parade, the carpenters withdrew from the pro-Landis Building Trades Council. When conciliation efforts by A.F. of L. President Gompers failed to reconcile the two factions, the carpenters and five other "outlaw" unions formed a new council in December 1922. Three months later the carpenters and painters agreed to strike jobs where nonunion men in each others' trade were employed.[62]

There was little pressure for the union to return to the old council. Within four months of the new missionary policy almost 2,000 new members joined the union. Though the installment plan ended in March 1923, the District Council's membership continued to sky-rocket as a result of the greatest building boom in Chicago's history. By August 1925, when the carpenters dedicated their new Council building at 12 E. Erie, membership had increased to 29,480, double that during the bleak winter of 1921–22. Membership peaked in September 1927 at 32,239.[63]

Most of the rise in membership was attributable to the shortage of skilled construction labor. According to one general contractor, "It got so that any man who turned up with both a rip and cross cut saw along with his hammer was welcomed as a master carpenter." In this environment, speculative builders, operating outside the Loop, undermined the open-shop policy of the contractors' associations by refusing to require that work be done by Landis contractors.[64]

With the Associated Builders "practically broken up" in the words of Jensen, the union turned its attention in the spring to the large intercity general contractors. On April 27, 1923, President Hutcheson announced that after June 1 any intercity contractor running nonunion in Chicago would be struck by carpenters in other cities. Soon, job after job was "straightened up" including the construction of a Commonwealth Edison plant and even the *Tribune* Building (though the newspaper remained verbally pro-Landis, privately it assured the District Council that it would employ only union men). In September 1923, the three largest intercity contractors, Griffiths, Thompson-Starrett, and Fuller, announced their withdrawal from the Citizens Committee and their return to union hiring. By 1924, only 94 of the 400 to 500 general and carpenter contractors who had signed the Committee's pledge remained. Only 20 percent of Chicago's building was done under the Landis Award and less than 25 percent of the Committee's original contractor membership remained.[65]

In June 1924, in the presence of President Hutcheson, the five largest general contractors signed up with the District Council for a closed shop at $1.25 an hour with doubletime for overtime. The same contractors pledged to influence BCEA members to employ union men. But the two-year contract did not allow for a union-label boycott, causing considerable opposition within the Council. It was not submitted to the membership for approval. In the meantime, the Building Trades Council settled with the BCEA in March 1923 on the basis of the old uniform agreement, the uniform scale, and acceptance of the decisions of the Joint Arbitration Board. Only in 1926 did the BCEA accept the closed shop.[66]

Credit for the defeat of the Citizens Committee's open-shop drive often has been attributed in union literature to a court injunction secured by the carpenters against the Citizens Committee for a criminal conspiracy to take control of the construction industry. In fact, the injunction was not issued until *after* the large general contractors had accepted the union's terms. More crucial to the union's victory was the conspiracy suit that had been won in 1919 by carpenters' attorney Hope Thompson outlawing the boycotting practices of the material manufacturers. The inability of the Citizens Committee to mount a material boycott severely curtailed its ability to discipline independent contractors. In San Francisco, where contractors were backed by a material boycott, a similar open-shop fight during the same period was lost by the building trades unions.[67]

The open-shop movement in the Chicago building trades had been an attempt by big business to dictate the labor policies of the contractors in light of their inability to resist militant unionism of building trades workers, led by the carpenters and painters. To these businessmen, the open shop was part of a national policy of ridding their industrial plants of unions and creating a more docile brand of unionism where it could not be destroyed. According to this strategy, even those trades not operating under the open shop should be made to feel the presence of a sword hanging over their heads as T. E. Donnelley put it in 1924:

> As long as we maintain 15 trades on the open shop basis the 18 trades operating closed shop will be good and live up to their agreements as they know they will be placed on the open shop if they do not; and the same condition exists in the national way. As long as Chicago, Duluth, St. Paul, San Francisco, and Minneapolis are on an open shop basis you will have good conditions in the building industry.[68]

No doubt, if the open shop had been established in all trades, the "citizens" would have attempted to impose on the construction industry some version of the antilabor policies they were implementing in factories like Chicago's International Harvester—where Donnelley served as a director—during this period. These included company unions, paternalistic welfare plans, and scientific management to replace union work rules. The defeat of the Chicago Citizens Committee by the carpenters and the painters prevented such a fate and played an important role in the preservation of building trades unionism nationally as well. And yet, the victory of the carpenters had been accomplished using traditional craft union policies, without resort to the alternatives proposed by the left opposition within the union. This would have significant consequences for the future of the new unionism.

Restoration of the Uniform Agreement, 1924–1929

The 1924 agreement obtained by Jensen did not completely remove the problem of the Landis Award contractors. Almost 20 percent of all Chicago construction work remained Landis, including much of the Loop work carried out by large contractors. Moreover, as long as the carpenters lacked support from the Building Trades Council and an agreement with the BCEA, the open shop would remain an ever-present threat, weakening the union's bargaining position.

The union began to recognize this in the months following the 1924 agreement, which Jensen had relied on to get reelected. When it became known that Jensen had allowed restoration of article 3, the socialists and other progressives, along with millworkers generally, expressed strong opposition to the settlement. This group was joined by a larger group in Locals 13, 58, and 80 who criticized Jensen for failing to rejoin the Building Trades Council.[69]

The basic issue separating the carpenters from the Building Trades Council was the union's national policy regarding jurisdiction. When the Council had been reorganized in 1924 under the auspices of the Building Trades Department, the carpenters were denied entry because President Hutcheson had withdrawn from the Department when it had awarded the Sheetmetal Workers Union jurisdiction over hollow metal trim. Meanwhile, Chicago carpenters had come to the realization that to secure aid from other trades in "straightening up" Landis jobs, they would have to affiliate with the Council. When they tried this in March 1925, the bid was rejected because the carpenters attached the condition that "we reserve the right to pursue the policies of our general organization, and that we cannot relinquish any of our rights or jurisdictional claims."

In May, after Hutcheson had settled with the Sheetmetal Workers and the union had signed a three-year agreement with nine general contractors accepting arbitration in all but jursditional disputes, as well as the decisions of the Joint Arbitration Board, the union again applied for membership in the Council. Again the bid was rejected, this time because the carpenters failed to accept the authority of the National Board for Jurisdictional Awards.[70]

Finally, dissent within the District Council reached a boiling point in July 1926 with charges that Jensen had stolen the votes of millmen's Local 1786 that would have given his opponent the presidency of the District Council. The following year Thomas Flynn of Local 13 challenged Jensen for the presidency. Flynn, who represented a less militant coalition of Locals 13, 58, and 80, advocated affiliation with the Council and the Chicago Federation of Labor and promised fair play and honesty in District Council elections. Solidarity with the millworkers was implied by the presence on his ticket of vice presidential candidate Ted Kenney, business agent from millmen's Local 1922. In the election of June 1927, Flynn defeated Jensen, thus ending the power of a group of locals centered around Local 181.

Following Flynn's election, the last obstacle to membership in the Building Trades Council disappeared when President Hutcheson succeeded in having the National Board for Jurisdictional Awards abolished, thus paving the way for the union to rejoin the A.F. of L.'s Building Trades Department. In November 1927 the carpenters were seated by unamimous vote in the Building Trades Council. Flynn optimistically reported to the District Council that, "we expect within a short time to make the Landis Award and the Citizens Committee a thing of the past." Nonetheless, the problem of creating an acceptable procedure for settling jurisdictional disputes among national unions continued to fester through 1929, hindering attempts to rid the trades of nonunion workers.[71]

As the the issue of unity against Landis contractors faded in importance, a new issue gained prominence within the union. Beginning in 1927 there was a steady decline in construction activity. Yet, the influx of carpenters into Chicago continued, turning an undersupply of labor into an oversupply. Piecework was soon on the rise, and complaints of rushing—"throwing older and slower carpenters out of work"—multiplied. When some rank and file members demanded that the union enforce its antirushing rule, the District Council replied that:

> From the earliest times our Organization has had its agreements based upon several cardinal principles, one of which states that "there shall be no limitation as to the amount of work a man shall perform during the working day." We cannot see how it could be otherwise owing to the endless variety of the work upon which the carpenter is engaged, together with the fact that our work is continually changing as new materials come into use.

Rather than work through the trial board or attempt to alter the contract, the union would rely on the common sense of carpenters on the job to determine and enforce a standard of what constituted a fair day's work.[72]

The union did attempt to deal with the problem of oversupply. In March 1927 the District Council established a Central Examining Board for prospective carpenters to prevent locals from initiating members rejected by other locals just to gain the $100 initiation fee. Throughout the next two years locals continued to clamor for further measures. They opposed acceptance of clearance cards from out-of-town members—a right guaranteed by the Brotherhood's constitution—and advocated reducing both overtime and the issuance of special work permits for Saturday and Sunday work. By 1928, however, these restrictive measures had failed, and the most prominent issue became the proposed five-day week, a measure intended to increase employment opportunities.[73]

Judging from the resolutions presented to the District Council by the locals during the 1929 bargaining for the new contract, the most important issues were the five-day week and removal of article 3. But the union's leadership was willing to slight these issues in order to forge unity with other building trades and local contractors in order to defeat the remaining Landis contractors. In February 1929 Flynn accepted a new uniform agreement stipulating the closed shop but also recognizing the eight cardinal principles; the union also agreed to recognize the authority of a new National Board for Jurisdictional Awards should it be reestablished, and to give up the option of striking over jurisdictional issues under the penalty of other trades allowing nonunion carpenters to be employed. The contract was of five years' duration and included a small wage increase to $1.5625 and eight hours' pay for seven-hour shift time. There was no provision for the five-day week or the removal of article 3.[74]

Strong opposition to the settlement was immediately voiced by an unlikely combination of elements. Millmen concerned about the union label lobbied outside men's locals to reject the contract. President Hutcheson wrote the District Council opposing the recognition of the authority of any future National Board for Jurisdictional Awards. Hutcheson's mortal enemies, the Communists, organized in the small "Progressive Carpenters" caucus, also opposed the agreement. In a leaflet passed out to members, the caucus claimed that the agreement included clauses "that are a complete abandonment of certain fundamental rights that our union has won only after years of fighting for them." It singled out for special attack the tough compulsory arbitration clause that prohibited strikes. In March the District Council voted down Flynn's proposed agreement 5,696 to 3,832.[75]

Forced to renegotiate, Flynn returned to the District Council with a wage reopener clause for 1931. Secretly, he had also secured a verbal agreement to a wage increase to $1.6250 beginning October 1929. Meanwhile, the union leadership could argue to its rank and file that the "good will" of the contractors would prevent the use of nonunion materials just as the common sense of carpenters on the jobs would prevent rushing. With substantially the same agreement, Flynn blamed the previous vote of rejection on "lying unsigned literature" from the Communists and called for a new ratification vote. This time the contract was overwhelmingly approved.[76]

There were two major reasons for the membership's new stand. Most important, was the worsening building slump and the increased strength of the general contractors in the Loop. On the eve of the vote Flynn candidly assessed the situation in an address to the locals: "In the past we had in the event of a strike the flats and bungalows; in other words the contractors of such buildings were always in the past available and our friends, and when approached would employ our men and sign our individual agreement." But, "with unemployment at a peak" and "no indication of boom" this favorable climate had disappeared: "with very few prairie contractors operating, a strike at this time . . . might be disastrous to our organization."[77]

Second, the opposition within the District Council was weaker, more isolated, and thus more vulnerable to attack. By the late 1920s the left opposition had been greatly diluted by the entrance into the union of thousands of former Landis Award men and other nonapprenticed carpenters who had little knowledge of or concern for craft traditions. Meanwhile, the old eclectic group of socialists, union militants, and political radicals had given way to the leadership supplied by members of the Communist party. Though as late as 1928 a Communist running as a protest candidate could receive 28 percent of the vote for District Council president, the Communists' uncompromising attacks on the District Council's leadership and their unwillingness to make coalitions, as had the socialists, served to isolate them within the union. Moreover, the Communists did not recognize the importance of the jurisdictional issue. In 1925 five members of Locals 62 and 181 were suspended and later reinstated because of ties to the Communist-run Trade Union Educational League. Three years later President Hutcheson, backed by a compliant national convention, succeeded in suspending and expelling the two principal Communist leaders of the Progressives.[78]

The 1929 agreement was a major watershed in the union's history. Beginning in 1912, strong pressure from the millmen and a large segment of outside men had reasserted a commitment to class unity and to carpenters' autonomy and militancy in the workplace. This carpenter unity and militancy, combined with the national leadership's policy of jurisdictional warfare, had steadily undermined local arbitration agreements and unity within the less militant Building Trades Council. In 1920 the "new unionism" was countered by the employers' open-shop campaign. Victory over the Citizens Committee in Chicago and settlement of key jurisdictional disputes nationally opened the way for reaffiliation of the union with the Building Trades Council and acceptance of a new uniform agreement governing jurisdictional disputes and strikes. By the late 1920s the opposition forces were weaker and more isolated, and the District Council, under the leadership of Thomas Flynn, consolidated conservative policies. The struggle to revise the uniform agreement was abandoned in return for wage concessions.

In his willingness to arbitrate all conflicts with the contractors, and in his cooperative stance with other building trades, Flynn represented a return to the sober, conservative policies of John Metz before the war. Indeed, in the twenty-nine years since the Great Lockout the union had come full circle. With this difference: in 1915 the union's acceptance of the uniform agreement under Metz' leadership had lasted only three years; under Flynn's leadership the 1929 agreement established the conditions for a half century of labor peace.

CHAPTER 5

The Carpenters and the Federal Government

From the New Deal

to Taft-Hartley,

1929–1947

If the Federal Government can establish a six-hour day
there is no reason in the world why some future
Congress cannot establish a ten-hour day. What they
give us they can take from us.
  William Hutcheson, general president of the United
  Brotherhood of Carpenters and Joiners of America[1]

In the first third of the twentieth century, the carpenters, along
with other A.F. of L. unions, had abandoned their original goal
of replacing capitalist-run industry with a cooperative order operated by the trade unions. With the defeat of 1901 and the adoption of the eight cardinal principles, the carpenters accepted the
legitimacy of the contractor in the trade—his right to a fair profit and
his right to manage—subject of course to the limits imposed by a
collectively bargained trade agreement. The new ideal became the
mutual accommodation of business and labor—cooperation or self-
government in industry—within the confines of capitalism.

In this vision the state was to play a minimal role. Having signed
the Standard Agreement, accepted the Joint Conference Board, and
reached a gentlemen's agreement with the Builders Association over
the boycotting of nonunion materials, the carpenters in 1929 felt quite
satisfied with their capacity to resolve their differences with the con-

tractors with no outside interference. Little wonder that the union both locally and nationally was a staunch proponent of the American Federation of Labor's philosophy of voluntarism in which the state would leave workers, particularly skilled craftsmen, free to bargain according to their strength. General President William Hutcheson stated this philosophy succinctly in opposing a shorter-hours bill in 1936: "I say, establish your hours by negotiation and not by law. If the Federal Government can establish a six-hour day there is no reason in the world why some future Congress cannot establish a ten-hour day. What they give us they can take from us."[2]

The union, in short, viewed with suspicion government intervention in collective bargaining matters to protect the public interest. Indeed, in Chicago the union could point to the actions taken by Judge Landis in the name of the public as proof of the partiality of "neutral" arbiters.

Nonetheless, A.F. of L. unions, including the carpenters, did advocate certain kinds of government intervention. At the 1919 industrial conference, staunch employer opposition to unionism had prevented a genuine cooperation in industry based on collective bargaining. In the ensuing years employers had resorted to a virulent open-shop campaign and the widespread use of injunctions to defeat unions. Despite many court decisions in the 1920s tending to validate the claim of unions that they were legal entities, the status in law of collective bargaining was still highly uncertain. From the District Council's point of view the union's satisfactory relationship with the Associated Builders in Chicago was balanced by threats to the bargaining position of millworkers and the continuing, though marginal, threat of Landis Award contractors. For these reasons the carpenters and other unions welcomed many labor measures of the New Deal beginning with the National Industry Recovery Act, which promised to compel employers to recognize and bargain with unions.

Yet by 1937 the carpenters found themselves embroiled in a series of bitter disputes with the federal government. In the course of these conflicts the union found to its dismay that in return for legalizing collective bargaining the state would demand much in return. With some misgivings the carpenters were ultimately compelled to recognize and accept a far more activist role for the state than their voluntarist philosophy had allowed for.[3]

The Carpenters' Response to the Great Depression: "To Build Fences" or "To Cultivate the Friendship Among the Craft"

In the Chicago construction industry serious economic problems were evident several years before the Great Depression. By the late 1920s speculative building based on the issuance of real estate bonds had led to an oversupply of residential homes. Consequently, the building industry had already sustained small declines in 1927 and 1928 before the bottom fell out of the industry in 1929 and 1930. By the end of 1930 almost all of Chicago's mortgage bankers were bankrupt, as were most of the second-mortgage holders. The building market hit rock bottom between 1932 and 1934 when the yearly value of new construction averaged $3.2 million. In contrast to the 1922–29 boom years when the yearly adjusted value (1913 = 100) averaged $138.78 million, the 1930–45 period averaged a paltry $15.2 million.[4]

Employment fell just as precipitously. According to a District Council survey of its members in October 1930, only 23 percent of the eighty-five hundred respondents were employed at the trade. In February 1931 the C.F. of L.'s *Federation News* reported that 80 percent of all Chicago area building trades workers were unemployed. But statistics pale against the human suffering, the atrophy of talent and skill, and the loss of personal dreams, even of hope, that were realities for those who lived through the Depression. In September 1930 Local 1 referred to "a condition of distress and want among various members and their families to the extent that some have lost their homes, pawned their trinkets of jewelry, even their tools." Even worse, recalled one local official, many out of work carpenters became "embittered and depressed" at their plight and cynically cursed all institutions of society including the labor movement.[5]

Union membership during the early years of the Depression fell sharply and steadily from the 1927 high of 32,239 to 29,328 in December 1929, to 26,965 in October 1930, to 23,496 in October 1931, then to a low point of 11,066 in 1933.[6] The pre–1933 figures understate the steepness of the decline because members in arrears for their dues could be carried on the books of their locals for a period of twelve months before being dropped. In December 1932, for example, Secretary Charles Sand reported that 50 percent of all members were in arrears; almost all these men were dropped when the 1933 figures were reported. Many carpenters left Chicago in search of work or left the trade altogether as indicated by the 1940 United States Census, which reported 14,810 fewer carpenters in Chicago than in 1930, a 53 percent decline.[7]

The consequent decline in union dues caused severe financial and organizational problems for locals and the District Council. Many locals, notably the mill locals and the Du Page County locals, were unable to support their business agents, yet refused District Council proposals to submerge their organizational identities by consolidating with other locals. On the District Council level the number of business agents for both inside and outside men was reduced from three to two, and Council officers voluntarily reduced their salaries. President Flynn, who had traveled regally in a chauffered automobile during the prosperous 1920s, was reduced to driving himself.[8]

In an attempt to limit the severe decline in members, the District Council cooperated with General President Hutcheson's "dispensation plan" offered in March 1931. This plan authorized the District Council to readmit members who had been dropped for nonpayment of dues during the October 1930-July 1931 period by allowing them to pay back dues and "dispense" with the constitutionally mandated initiation fee. The period during which the dispensation applied was regularly extended until October 1937. Hutcheson's plan was a realistic compromise between the need to maintain a flow of funds to maintain union officials and the need of impoverished members to retain their working cards.[9]

But the way the union implemented the plan revealed a deep streak of exclusivity that had pervaded the union since the late 1920s. In effect, many carpenters wanted the union to monopolize scarce work for the dwindling minority of paid-up members, who were generally the highly skilled men. Thus the Council set up a special committee to pass on the skill qualifications of all applicants availing themselves of the dispensation. According to the Organization Committee's rationale:

> During the peak of the building boom [incompetent tradesmen] could find work to do which required little skill, but when the depression set in they could no longer make the grade, and probably concluded they had better give up trying to follow carpentry for an occupation. . . . The weeding out of the incompetent so-called carpenters who should never have been permitted to become members will tend to strengthen our organization.[10]

In short, there was a strong conviction that the entrance into the union of lesser skilled and unapprenticed men during the boom— many of whom had come to Chicago as Landis Award workmen— had diluted the strong union and craft traditions of the Brotherhood. As early as 1928 a carpenter delegate to the Chicago Federation of Labor had explained that "in the last eight years the membership of [my] organization has tripled [and] practically two-thirds of the members in that local union . . . had never been taught anything beyond being good [working] card men." He charged that the approach to unionism of these men was "to leave all responsibility to the [union's] delegates." One carpenter recalls that during the late 1920s there was considerable animosty on the job between former Landis Award men and veteran unionists. The latter distrusted the Landis men and often referrred to them as "scabs." When layoffs began, they charged that the boss would let the union man go first rather than the Landis man.[11]

Yet, if the goal of giving preference to the skilled and general carpenters, who were the backbone of the union, was understandable and in some ways defensible, there was little justification under union principles for the District Council to retain its $150 initiation fee— which Local 1 had proposed raising to $200 in April 1927. In April 1931 the General Executive Board, over District Council protests, forced Chicago to lower the fee to $100, charging that the high levy kept out legitimate carpenters and hurt the organization.[12]

This was hardly the only instance of what veteran unionist Stanley Johnson, later president of the Illinois State Federation of Labor, recalls as the tendency toward "fence-building" during the Depression. Some business agents used their influence to put men from their locals on the job in preference to other carpenters, a violation of the union's constitution. As late as 1938, Local 62 requested the officers to take steps to stop business agents from "discriminating against members belonging to local unions other than their own." In 1939 North Shore and Chicago Heights locals unsuccessfully proposed to set a ceiling on the percentage of Chicago men who could be employed in their areas.[13]

Beginning in November 1930, after the Builders Association granted the union the five-day week, there was a perceptible shift in the direction of the union's energies toward devising a system of work sharing or job rotation. From the start of the Depression many large contractors had adopted rotation schemes voluntarily. Many other building trades unions, at the urging of Building Trades Council President Patrick Sullivan, did the same. The carpenters' basic difficulty in implementing a rotation plan of their own lay in the fact that they did not have a hiring hall. Unlike craftsmen in the closed trades such as plumbing and electrical work, carpentry had always been an "open trade" with a strong tradition of hiring off the street. To police a rotation system required that a central employment registration service keep track of all unemployed members, a partial break from the union's past.[14]

In the proposal of Local 62 in July 1930, no member would be permitted to change jobs until the waiting list of unemployed members was exhausted. There were other proposals as well, the most popular one being that all contractors be compelled to institute shifts—for example, two six-hour daily shifts or forty hours every two weeks. All, however, involved some limited form of hiring hall. But old traditions died hard. In December 1930 the District Council, after considerable discussion, defeated a rotation proposal by Local 1, concluding that "no one should be allowed to dictate who should be employed." It was decided instead to cooperate with contractors who voluntarily agreed to rotate. Eventually, members were allowed to work a week with each cooperating contractor. By September 1932 President Flynn reported that rotation was being carried out everywhere where "practical."[15]

The traditional freedom of the carpenter to seek work wherever he could find it was not the only reason for opposition to a union registration system. The union was divided between those with and those without jobs. While those without work were understandably sympathetic to the registration system, those holding full-time jobs were disinclined to give them up without strong protest. In fact, despite Flynn's report to the District Council that a voluntary approach to work sharing had been successful, it was common knowledge that many employed carpenters were not rotating. Some of these men, it was charged, were friends of the incumbent administration.[16]

The issue within the union of equitably sharing available work became most serious during construction of Chicago's Century of Progress Exposition world's fair of 1933–34. Conceived during the boom years of the 1920s by Chicago's unofficial government of downtown businessmen, the world's fair, unlike the 1892–93 exposition, was organized and financed as a private project. By the early 1930s it was widely viewed as a means of attracting business and employment to the depressed city. It was symptomatic of the times that when the fair's building contracts were let, huge throngs of contractors and workmen vied with each other for the privilege of building. Unfortunately, the Century of Progress Exposition, unlike the 1892–93 exposition, did not stimulate even a minor building boom in Chicago, but it did become the focus of rank and file efforts to establish job rotation.[17]

On December 8, 1932, Local 58 called for rotation at the fair, where, "it seems impossible for anyone but the regular gang employed there for a long time to get a job." Three weeks later another Local 58 communication summed up the feelings of many out of work carpenters:

> Other trades in our district have adopted and work under rotation systems. It is folly indeed to have some members work practically all the time, while a great majority are and have been looking for work for a year or more and many of them are reduced to a state of pauperism. . . . At no time in our history

have the objects of the District Council, "to cultivate the friend-
ship among the craft and to assist each other to procure employment" been put to a more severe test than at the present
time.[18]

The question at issue was whether the union would uphold its
principles of equity and solidarity amidst the worst depression in
American history, and the voluntaristic approach of the Flynn administration was clearly inadequate. Within a month this issue had opened
up a serious breach of trust between unemployed rank and file members and the District Council leadership. The initiative of Local 58
gathered support from a host of other locals, representing perhaps a
majority of the union, all asking that jobs be rotated. Local 1's resolution on January 12, 1933, calling for a strike at the fair brought the
issue to a head. At the District Council, Flynn spoke vehemently
against the resolution arguing that rotation was a "failure" and that:
"where rotation is taking effect . . . the men on the jobs are protesting;
they want to stay on the job. Some of them have been out of work a
long time and after finding a job and getting a few days work they
complain that it is unfair to be taken off." The following week, after
Flynn initiated negotiations with the fair, he reported that fair officials
had agreed to establish a central employment office to allow applicants
to register for work, but were "absolutely opposed" to job rotation.
Meanwhile, fair officials had erected a fence around the fairgrounds,
and the union was unsure whether or not union men were being
employed at union scale.[19]

At this point a group of rank and file activists took an extraordinary step. Acting outside the union's regular channels, which they
felt were useless, approximately three hundred unemployed carpenters, many of whom wanted jobs at the fair, organized a protest on
February 1 at District Council headquarters. To these men leaders like
Charles Sand had grown out of touch with the membership's concerns.
A committee of five including Joseph McAlinden, Jack McLennon,
William Shand, William Mitchell, and Michael J. Connolly met with
the District Council leadership. After being refused admittance to a
meeting of business agents, they confronted Sand and other officers
in an angry exchange of words. Then they left, but not before they
had presented demands for world's fair job rotation, for policing of
the fair by the union, the exemption of unemployed carpenters from
dues payments, and the reinstatement of carpenters put on probation
or expelled for their political views. The latter referred to action taken
by the Council against the organizers and participants of a Communist-
sponsored public meeting held November 27, 1931, at Imperial Hall

protesting the inaction of the Flynn administration on the issue of unemployment. Though the committee of five had no affiliation with the Communists, they supported their right to air the grievances of carpenters.[20]

At the next Council meeting Flynn warned the dissenters against violating union procedures: "If there is any group attempting to form an organization or committee outside of the union without authority from the union they had better think twice." But in the next breath he announced strikes on three world's fair projects. By March 30 Flynn could report to the District Council that 96 percent of all world's fair work was being rotated.[21]

Though the issue of rotation faded, it was hardly the end of opposition to Flynn. Several months later the same group of activists nominated an opposition slate headed by the popular president of the millwrights local, Harry Kirby, son of the former general president. Michael J. Connolly of Flynn's Local 13 opposed Sand for secretary-treasurer. A year earlier Flynn had received only 43 percent of the presidential vote, a bare plurality, after running unopposed the four years previously. On the eve of the 1933 election Flynn acted to consolidate his hold on the presidency. Kirby and Connolly were disqualified by the Council on technicalities. A week after the election each was expelled from the union by the Trial Board—Connolly for participating in the February 1 "insurrection" (he was finally reinstated in 1941). In the election itself Flynn narrowly defeated challenger Fred Weaver who had replaced Kirby at the last minute on the opposition slate, by a vote of 2,693 to 2,475. A number of irregularities marred the election, including the disqualification of the votes of Local 62, a large Scandinavian local opposed to Flynn. It was nothing short of an election coup, similar to the one Flynn had charged Harry Jensen with perpetrating in 1926 (Jensen had been expelled from the union for this and other transgressions in July 1931). The 1933 election set an important precedent in discouraging future organized opposition to the existing District Council leadership.[22]

Cornering employment versus work sharing was not the only major issue that challenged the union by 1932. Many members "put their cards in their shoe," as it was termed, to work below union scale. Others rebated part of their wages to get around union rules. The situation was worsened by a widespread practice known as "scalping," whereby contractors would skim the legitimate profits from a contract and then "sub" the job out, forcing the subcontractor to speed up his men, or work them below scale to make any money. The problem became so serious that beginning in December 1932 the District Council authorized the Trial Board to expel any member caught working below scale. Hundreds of carpenters lost their working cards before Hutcheson voided the penalty in April 1933 as being too severe.[23]

The decline in the union's hold over its membership could also be measured by the fact that Landis Award construction in the city increased from 10 percent of the total in 1928 to over 20 percent in 1933. Up to half the Loop construction was Landis Award during the early years of the Depression. Meanwhile, citywide contractors' federations called for a 25 percent wage reduction as part of a national movement of building employers to stimulate construction. Doubtless remembering how the unions' refusal to accept a wage reduction had been used during the 1920–21 depression as an opening wedge for the open shop movement, Building Trades Council President Patrick Sullivan decided to recommend a 19 percent wage reduction to all building trades unions. In February 1932 the carpenters agreed to reduce their wage to $1.3150, a level which lasted through 1936.[24]

The millworkers faced the same wage-cutting pressures earlier than the outside men. The mill locals had not completely recovered from the shock they had received in 1920–21. Nonetheless, they had won a $1.20 wage in 1926 and had defeated an open-shop lockout in 1927. In August 1930 the Millwork and Cabinet Manufacturers Association proposed to reduce wages to $.90 citing competition from low-wage manufacturers outside the city. In April 1931 they increased their reduction demand to $.70. The union refused to go along, arguing that a wage cut would merely accelerate a downward spiral of wages for millworkers both in and outside Chicago. The union wanted to retain the existing wage and adopt a five-day week plus work-sharing to combat layoffs. Faced with a refusal to compromise, the union's Arbitration Board formulated individual agreements that jettisoned the five-day week demand and voluntarily reduced wages to $1.00. By the end of July the union had signed up most of the mills.[25]

With the Depression worsening a year later, the Millwork Association demanded a wage reduction to $.65. The mill locals refused to accept this, instead demanding the six-hour day. Negotiations soon broke down resulting in a strike, July 1932. With virtually no market for millwork, the employers could afford to wait. Over half the 119 shops in the city simply shut down and 9 shops employing 410 men operated nonunion. By this time there were fewer than 2,500 millmen in the union, only 1,400 in good standing.[26]

Despite their weak bargaining position, the mill locals, in a vote held six weeks into the strike, refused to lower their wage demand to $.65. Flynn blamed the rank and file's intransigence on "Communist literature of the rankest kind." He then convened a meeting of mill local presidents, who issued an appeal stating "that to preserve our organization we must sacrifice wages." In a new referendum held in September the millworkers relented and revised their wages to $.85.[27]

But the millowners, sensing complete victory, refused to negotiate. Only solidarity by the outside men of the District Council brought them back to the bargaining table. In October 1932, carpenters working on the Marshall Field and Mandel Brothers' jobs struck because the Fuller Company had sublet the trim contract to a large Chicago mill firm that had locked out its union millworkers. With work tied up, the large general contractors agreed to act as intermediaries in the mill dispute. On November 2 the mill locals reluctantly agreed to a highly disadvantageous five-year contract providing for an eight-hour day, five-and-a-half-day week (though Saturday was paid doubletime), and a scale 15 percent higher than the average wage for all millworkers within a radius of five hundred miles of Chicago. In March 1933 an arbitrator provided for in the settlement set the Chicago wage at $.75. The contract also stipulated that the union work only for Millwork Association members.[28]

By the end of 1932 the Brotherhood in Chicago was reeling from loss of membership, wage cuts, and internal dissension.[29] That year fewer buildings were built than in any year in the city's recorded history. But in November 1932, the same month in which the millworkers had barely salvaged their organization, the nation elected a new president, Franklin Delano Roosevelt. Along with millions of other American workers, carpenters took heart.

The Carpenters and the Early New Deal, 1933–1935

In the first four years of the Depression, the carpenters had seen their union steadily contract. Lacking the ability to remedy their economic predicament, they had begun to turn inward, squabbling among themselves over the dwindling quantity of available work. The flurry of New Deal legislation during Roosevelt's first "hundred days" created a new climate of hope in the country. Along with this came the new belief that it was possible and legitimate for the federal government to assume responsibility for raising and maintaining the level of national income and social welfare in the country. Beginning in 1933 the union externalized its energies, regained much of its strength by reaching out to ex-members, and soon moved onto the offensive in struggles with employers and the government.

The centerpiece of the early New Deal was the National Industrial Recovery Act (NIRA), passed by Congress in June 1933. The act set up the National Recovery Administration (NRA), which was authorized to approve codes of "fair competition" for the nation's industries, each code to be negotiated by employers' trade associations with representatives of organized labor. According to the official goals of the act and federal guidelines, the codes would legalize various noncompetitive practices by business firms so as to allow them to raise prices, reduce hours, and restore wages and employment. In return, labor received guarantees of an industrywide minimum wage, maximum hours, child-labor prohibitions, and the right of workers to organize unions of their own choosing and to bargain collectively. The guarantee of collective bargaining, written into the well-known section 7(a) of the act, set an important precedent, being the first time other than in war that the federal government had given legal sanction to collective bargaining.[30]

For the carpenters, still another precedent was set by the Public Works Administration (PWA), also established by the NIRA. Headed by Secretary of the Interior Harold Ickes, the PWA was mandated to finance a massive public works drive to provide immediate employment in the construction industry and to stimulate the economy. Previous to this the carpenters had pinned their hopes for a revival of employment on private investment, most notably a joint plan of the Building Trades Council, the Builders' Association, and Building Construction Employers Association known as the "Rosenthal Plan" (named after the president of both contractors' associations). Under this plan a $1 million investment trust would be established by selling shares in installments to unions and construction investors. But by 1932 financial stringency had compelled the carpenters to withdraw from the Rosenthal Plan. By 1933 the union was ready to turn to the federal government as a source of construction investment.[31]

The labor movement enthusiastically approved of the NRA. President William Hutcheson, a supporter of Herbert Hoover, endorsed the act as did the A.F. of L. In Chicago the *Federation News* proclaimed, "labor has been plunged into a new relationship with both employers and government, and a new type of state is rising amid the ashes left from the great fire of 1929." In August the Chicago District Council also voted to lend its support to the NRA, and in November endorsed Roosevelt's New Deal.[32]

The millworkers were the first in the union to take advantage of the NRA. In July and August the mill locals lowered their initiation fee from $25 to $5 and inaugurated a fruitful organizing drive. President Flynn then approached the Millwork Association with a demand for a thirty-five-hour work week based on the NRA's model industrial code guidelines. In October the District Council endorsed a call for a conference of all union millworkers within a five-hundred-mile radius of Chicago in order to create a consensus preparatory to code bargaining with the millowners. The conference decided on a maximum number of eight hours a day and a minimum wage of $.95, the scale not to vary by more than 25 percent within the region. But the final codes affecting the mills proved to be far closer to the millowners' views. They provided for a uniform forty-hour week and no change in the hours and wages applicable to Chicago that had been previously negotiated. The results were disappointing, but at least the employers' take-back movement had been stopped.[33]

The District Council's outside men, who had just begun negotiations with the Builders' Association for a renewal of the five-year standard agreement, faced similar difficulties. Five months before the NRA, the contractors had proposed a forty-eight-hour week. The union, led by Local 58, countered with a demand, then quite popular among Chicago unionists, for a six-hour day and thirty-hour week. For the carpenters the six-hour day was more than a temporary measure to spread out existing work. According to Local 58's adopted resolution, it was a response to the expected loss of carpenter jobs through advanced methods of construction, such as the increased use of Skilsaws and other machinery on the job and the much-feared shift to prefabricated housing.[34]

When the contractors were first told of the six-hour day demand, "they threw up their hands" according to the report of the union's Arbitration Board. Meanwhile, the six-hour day movement gathered in force from 1933 into 1934 fueled by the NRA's stated goal of reducing hours and by continuing negotiations between the national building trades unions and contractors' federations. In 1933 the A.F. of L. gave voice to the movement by proposing a six-hour day bill in the United States Congress.[35]

In May 1934, after more than four months of negotiating, the two sides deadlocked. The union demanded the thirty-hour week at $1.75 with a ban on subcontracting by Builders' Assocation members to prevent "scalping." The contractors offered in return only a forty-hour week at $1.315, plus an "emergency" one-year provision that provided for two six-hour shifts each day. To prevent wages and hours from being governed by the regional NRA "blanket" codes, which provided for $1.20 an hour at eight hours for northern building tradesmen without collective bargaining, the two sides agreed to extend the old contract indefinitely.[36]

By this time every other Chicago construction trade had signed up for eight hours, with the exception of the painters who had earlier won six hours, thus leaving the carpenters virtually isolated. As had happened so often in the past, lack of unity among the building trades critically hampered the carpenters. The contractors claimed that it was impractical to grant the carpenters six hours while other trades worked eight. When it became clear that the contractors were adamant, the

union leadership submitted three proposals to a membership referendum vote along with a recommendation that the six-hour day demand be abandoned. Government work, said the accompanying letter,
now comprised 80 percent of all construction work in the city: "Our
experience in past strikes proves that the private work done by small
contractors who employed our members enabled them to win. At the
present time there is not sufficient private work to give us the advantage
afforded us by the small contractors in previous strikes."[37]

Despite Flynn's recommendation, a solid majority of the 4163
votes cast in the election supported the six-hour day, and of these
votes a plurality supported the alternative of six hours at $1.3125. The
six-hour stand was reaffirmed by the membership in a second vote in
September 1934. An analysis of the votes reveals that the Scandinavian
locals and Jewish Local 504 lent overwhelming backing to the six-
hour day demand. Under rank and file pressure, the union leadership
reluctantly formulated individual agreements and announced that the
six-hour day would go into effect October 15. Chicago carpenters had
earned the distinction of being the only District Council in the Brotherhood to fight for six hours.[38]

Jewish Carpenters in Local 504

Local 504 (now merged into Local 1539) is one of
the most striking examples of the carpenters' tradition of
ethnic locals. The local was founded by Jews who emi-
grated to America from the Pale of Settlement of Russia
in the last twenty years of the nineteenth century. About
100 of the union's first members originated in the tiny
town of Motele in the Russian state of Grodno. Among
these Motele immigrants was Morris Holzman, whose
surname described his Russian occupation, woodsman.
Since the local's early years the Holzman family, beginning with Morris' son Charles, dominated the affairs of
the local. In part, this happened because the family cultivated a tradition of loyalty and service to the union.
The family also contributed a large number of the local's
active members. Morris had four brothers, all carpenters;
of his nine sons, eight became carpenters, all union men;
seven of their sons also became staunch Brotherhood
members.

The first Jewish carpenters encountered job
discrimination, and often were only able to work for Jew-

ish contractors. They may also have been denied entry into the Brotherhood during this period. In 1900 Jewish carpenters revolted against the long hours offered by their employers, and were given a charter as Local 504 in the Chicago District Council. Since 1905, when "progressive" Jews under Sam Ostreitsky overthrew the conservative local leadership, 504 could be counted on the political left of the union. By the 1930s the local numbered in its ranks a host of socialists, IWW members, and Communists. Union meetings during this period were occasions for fraternizing and for expressing and debating political opinions. Old-timers recalled animated discussions that lasted until 2:00 A.M., several concluding in fistfights.

Of all locals, 504 had the highest percentage of contractor members; these were journeymen who had gone into business for themselves yet retained their union and class loyalties. Since 1945 the local has been the home of at least one hundred European Jewish carpenters fleeing the Holocaust. These men have been among the most active of the local's members. Despite the local's Jewish heritage, usually about one-third of the membership have been Gentiles.[39]

Unfortunately the six-hour day had only limited applicability to the trade. Most carpenters, as the Flynn administration had pointed out, were working under government contracts governed by eight-hour codes. In the private sector, despite the fact that many general contractors had informally adopted six-hour shifts, the Builders' Association refused to set a precedent by signing a six-hour agreement at whatever wage. In December 1934 the NRA announced its policy of area agreements. Since Chicago would set the standard for the Midwest, the adoption of a local collective bargaining agreement became necessary to forestall adoption of a nonunion code. In April 1935, over many protests, the outside locals narrowly approved a new one-year agreement for eight hours at $1.3125.[40]

For both inside and outside men the NRA, after raising high expectations, had proven a disappointment. Meanwhile, the promise of a massive public works program, which the District Council had lobbied for since 1930, also went unfulfilled. Carpenters had expected that the PWA would inaugurate investment in construction of schools, post offices, waterfront and sanitary facilities, and low cost public housing. But, under Ickes, the PWA was too slow in planning the details of building and too conservative in disbursing funds to have much impact on unemployment. As a stopgap measure, Roosevelt established the Civil Works Administration (CWA) in October 1933 to provide employment in the winter of 1933–34.[41]

According to its rules each CWA-funded project— principally school construction—drew 50 percent of its employees from relief rolls, and 50 percent from the unemployed. Workers were allowed a maximum of twenty-three days of employment. These and other rules caused immediate difficulties for the Brotherhood. For example, CWA work lasted six days a week, and carpenters on relief were often sent to work by local authorities at wages below scale. Even worse, ex-members, now on relief, were hired to work side by side with union men. Rather than take the unpopular step of striking these jobs, the District Council allowed ex-members to work for two weeks before paying the initiation fee to rejoin the union.[42]

When the CWA ended March 31, 1934, the carpenters returned to vigorous lobbying for the funding of PWA projects to restore private employment. But as important as employment was, the union also had to straighten out various PWA rules that conflicted with standard union practices. For example, the government rule that gave first priority in employment to ex-servicemen threatened to divide the union into two hostile camps in early 1934. Then there was the continuing problem of enforcing jurisdiction and getting the government to live up to the Bacon-Davis Act of 1930 mandating the prevailing wage.[43]

Most of these difficulties were cleared up after the District Council signed its contract with the Builders' Association in 1935, at which time the PWA reverted to its standard policy of requiring contractors to adhere to union work rules. The positive results led Secretary-Treasurer Sand to twit the noses of the six-hour militants: "This should cause [those within the union] who are prone to argue that agreements are not important, to stop and reflect upon the question of what might be the consequences if we were without an agreement."[44]

The problems encountered with the new government-sponsored projects plus the pending six-hour dispute with the contractors, ultimately led the District Council to abandon its early Depression policy of attempting to retain scarce work for its remaining members. Instead, the District Council, following the precedent of the Jensen administration during the 1920s open-shop conflict, moved to open up the union. In September 1934 the Council substituted an initiation fee of $25 for accumulated back dues as a requirement for suspended members rejoining the union. It was a pragmatic aquiescence in the necessity of preserving the organization. The low fee lasted until June 1936 when it was replaced by a $60 fee. Two years later, when the dispensation ended, the fee reverted to $100.[45]

The six-hour day fight and the "straightening up" (making sure work was done by union labor under union rules) of CWA and PWA work were temporary difficulties. By contrast, the NRA had a lasting impact on the carpenters in the area of jurisdictional policy. When the District Council signed the Standard Agreement in 1929 accepting the decisions of the Joint Conference Board, the bad feeling between the carpenters and other building trades unions had largely disappeared. Subsequently, most jurisdictional disputes had been settled on the local level through the Board with little or no interference from the national office (the jurisdiction of carpenters varied from locale to locale depending largely on custom).[46]

However, there were certain jurisdictional quarrels that were decided on the national level, notably the wide-ranging, longstanding dispute between carpenter millwrights and the Machinists Union. On this level the Brotherhood's policy of jurisdictional laissez-faire continued from the 1929 to 1934 at which time the NRA banned jurisdictional strikes and, at Roosevelt's direction, set up a new National Board for Jurisdictional Awards as a court of final appeal. To avoid government dictation, Hutcheson was forced to rejoin the Building Trades Department, from which he had withdrawn in 1929, so that he would be free to influence jurisdictional settlements.[47]

The effects of the government's clampdown on the Brotherhood's "no holds barred" jurisdictional policy could be seen in the carpenters' dispute with the cement finishers over who would install mastic tile. The carpenters, who had walked out at several sites in 1934, were forced back to work in January 1935 "due to threats that the government might put in non-union men." Though scattered and short-lasting jurisdictional disputes continued to plague the industry, mainly after 1936, the principle of negotiated settlements was now firmly established on the national as well as the local level.[48]

The carpenters' experience with the NRA was hardly unique. By 1934 many American workers had renamed it the "National Run Around." Section 7(a) guaranteeing collective bargaining was practically a dead letter. Except for well-organized industries such as construction, few workers had participated in codemaking and, where the codes protected labor, they weren't rigorously enforced. Meanwhile, the United States Supreme Court had ruled that company unions fulfilled NRA requirements. Finally, the PWA had alleviated building trades unemployment only slightly. Not surprisingly, there was little mourning in the labor movement when the Supreme Court declared the NRA unconstitutional in May 1935.

The Union and the Second New Deal, 1935–1940

The first phase of the New Deal had relied on the principle of cooperation of all organized parties in industry to restore prosperity. By 1935 it was clear that the principle of self-government in industry, which the union had contended for since 1919, had proven a failure, even when promoted and sanctioned by the government. To facilitate economic recovery, to forestall the growth of radical solutions such as Senator Huey Long's "Share Our Wealth" plan, and to contain the national strike wave of 1934, President Roosevelt backed what has been called the "Second New Deal." In this new phase of federal legislation there was significantly increased reliance on government supervision of private economic activity.

In July 1935 Congress passed the National Labor Relations or Wagner Act to put teeth behind federal guarantees of collective bargaining. It provided for the establishment of a National Labor Relations Board (NLRB), which would define and enforce fair labor practices and conduct elections to certify unions as bargaining agents. The purpose of the act was to use unions to raise the consumption power in the economy. But—what was not fully recognized at the time of its passage—the Wagner Act also embodied a new approach to unions. Instead of accepting existing unions as legal entities, the act was based on the principle that unions had legal rights only as agents of workers. It followed that federal regulations were justified not only to ensure collective bargaining but to ensure that unions adequately represented workers. It was an approach that ultimately would lead to a confrontation between the NLRB and those unions, such as the carpenters, which sought to preserve their traditional jurisdiction.[49]

Meanwhile, Congress passed another recovery act that also led to a confrontation with the carpenters. Abandoning the expensive and slow-moving policy of federally sponsored public works as a means of creating jobs, the New Deal turned to federal work relief under the authority of the Works Progress Administration (WPA) headed by Harry Hopkins.

"Americans don't like charity," Hopkins had said arguing against the dole. Workingmen receiving relief were not idlers and deserved a job—a means of contributing to and participating in society—even if it had to be provided by the government. For millions of American workers the WPA restored the dignity and self-worth that had been sapped by years of unemployment and charity. But for the carpenters and other building trades unions the WPA created a series of headaches as well. With the government acting as direct employer of men on relief, rather than letting contracts to private employers, the WPA threatened with its rules to undermine the entire structure of collective bargaining built up by the carpenters and contractors over half a century. Building trades unions became particularly suspicious when Congress rejected the prevailing wage principle and authorized payment of the "security wage"—a monthly rate above that of a welfare check but far below union scale.[50]

In September 1935 Hopkins, after meeting with national union presidents from the A.F. of L. Building Trades Department, agreed to pay the prevailing wage by reducing the number of required hours union men would put in on WPA projects to get their monthly checks. Thus, a unionized WPA worker would work only 56 hours a month for his check, while a nonunion man had to labor 130 hours.[51]

But no sooner had this difficulty been overcome when the union was confronted by another WPA rule according to which only 10 percent of the workmen on a project would be paid prevailing scale. With as many as seven hundred carpenters about to be hired on a series of WPA projects for the Chicago Board of Education, the 10 percent rule threatened to undercut the wage scale of carpenters and other building trades in the private sector. In December 1935 the Building Trades Council authorized a general strike on all WPA projects in Cook, Lake, Du Page, and Kane counties. After a week of negotiations the government relented. In a letter to the District Council the WPA agreed to pay scale to every union carpenter and to work these men on two-week shifts with four days of work each week.[52]

Though relatively few carpenters were hired on the Board of Education projects, massive federal spending created a significant recovery in construction activity in Chicago, both in the private and public sectors. The value of construction work in the city more than doubled between 1934 and 1935 and rose again in 1936 though it remained far below the 1929 level. The number of residential units built in the metropolitan area in 1936 was more than nine times greater than in 1934 and 39 percent of it was PWA-financed public housing: Jane Addams Homes, Julia Lathrop Homes, and Trumbull Park Homes. In 1937 Congress established the Federal Housing Authority, and the local Chicago Housing Authority replaced the PWA in making home loans and supervising construction of public housing.[53]

The resurgence of economic activity after 1934 and the more favorable collective bargaining climate created by the Wagner Act helped the carpenters expand their membership, not only by recovering ex-members but also by expanding into new areas. In July 1936 the union, led by Local 1's business agent, Barney Braakman, began to organize carpenter maintenance men working for large downtown hotels, factories, and office buildings—a major preserve of open-shop strength. Though Braakman operated in a dictatorial and high-handed manner and was accused several times in the District Council of "building a fence" around the Loop to corral jobs for his local, he was an effective organizer. By July 1937, using a reduced scale of $1.00 and several strikes, Braakman had "straightened up" Marshall Field's. The Hotel Owners Association had also agreed to employ union men.[54]

During the same period, Local 504's business agent Charles Holzman, organized the floor sanders in Local 1509 and in 1937 signed up the bowling alley workers. That year the independent union of installers of asbestos, shingling, and composition siding joined the District Council as Local 2094. By the end of 1937 the District Council's membership had increased to approximately sixteen thousand.[55]

The new climate contributed to the virtual demise of the remaining Landis Award contractors. The Associated Builders had been given a body blow in 1934 when the NRA's construction code outlawed company unions and the yellow dog contract. In August 1936 the final seven open-shop contractors, including the influential Gerhardt Meyne, signed up with the union. The Landis Award Employers Association limped on until 1944 when it merged with the Employers Association of Chicago.[56]

When the 1937 contract came up for renewal, Local 504, encouraged by the Brotherhood's General Convention's endorsement of six hours, and the Supreme Court's validation of the Wagner Act in April, called on the District Council to stand firm for shorter hours. This proved impossible because of lack of support from other trades, but the carpenters did win a wage increase to $1.615, and a revision of the joint working rules, including penalties against employers paying subscale wages, increased wages for foremen, and payment by the contractor for lost tools. The same year millmen, after revolting against a proposed three-year contract at $1.00, signed a one-year agreement for $1.05.[57]

The gains of 1937 were soon overshadowed by the gathering storms of 1938 and 1939. In 1935 John L. Lewis, president of the United Mine Workers, led industrial union advocates out of the American Federation of Labor to form the Congress of Industrial Organizations (CIO). The immediate issue was the refusal of the Federation to allow craft workers in basic industry to be organized in industrial unions along with mass production workers. The subsequent rise of the CIO and its rivalry with the A.F. of L. has been popularly termed a dispute between craft and industrial forms of organization. For the carpenters this was not true. Since the turn of the century, the Brotherhood had been a craft-industrial union, a more inclusive category than craft, and in that lay the root of the conflict. The craft versus industrial issue was, by itself, compromisable. The issue of organizational power was not. Hutcheson and the United Brotherhood wanted to maintain the hegemony of the conservative craft unions within the A.F. of L. by integrating newly organized industrial workers into the existing unions rather than allow them to create new ones that might afford power to left wing groups.[58]

In 1937 the CIO chartered the International Woodworkers of America (IWA) to organize Pacific Northwest lumber workers, a group whose jurisdiction was claimed by the Brotherhood. Then the National Labor Relations Board, implementing its mandate to decide jurisdictional questions, allowed lumber workers to vote on whether they wanted to stay in the Brotherhood or join the IWA. The lumbermen deserted the Brotherhood in droves, and in August 1937 Hutcheson responded with a national boycott call against mills with CIO agreements. According to the directive: "Let the watchword be: 'No CIO lumber or millwork in your District.' "[59]

The boycott campaign had two immediate and unintended consequences in Chicago. As the jurisdictional boycott heated up in 1938, Chicago millworkers began to ask: if outside men can boycott CIO material so effectively, why can they not do the same for nonunion material? The millworkers also criticized the national union for chartering new mill locals in the surrounding area at wages far below the Chicago scale. In April 1938 the District Council responded by inaugurating a massive drive to rid Chicago of nonunion millwork, something the leadership had dragged its feet on since the early 1920s. It began with an internal educational campaign heralded by the words "demand the UB label on all manufactured material" attached to the first page of the District Council's proceedings distributed to each local. To builders and architects the union issued a letter threatening work stoppages unless union material was used. Then, reviving a 1912 slogan, carpenters began a "patronize home industry" campaign with the Board of Education and the city government.[60]

In January 1939 John R. Stevenson, who had replaced Flynn as president after the latter's death in April 1937, boldly announced, "I take the position that this organization shall never again sign an agreement containing Article 3 [banning material boycotts] in its present form." But the climate in the country had changed since the NRA days, when the government had sanctioned restraints of trade enjoined under the Sherman Anti-Trust Act to facilitate recovery. In December 1938 the New Deal had inaugurated an attack on monopoly in industry, and in November 1939 Attorney General Thurman Arnold announced a drive against anticompetitive practices in the constructon industry. The following February, Hutcheson, Stevenson, and other Chicago officers were indicted under the Sherman Act for boycotting CIO and nonunion materials. The drive against article 3 was dead for the moment.

But in February 1941 the United States Supreme Court handed down a decision in favor of the carpenters. This, plus another favorable settlement of an antimonopolistic practices suit brought by Arnold in St. Louis, represented a major victory for the Brotherhood by establishing the right of union boycott and all other activities designed to enforce jurisdiction. These decisions restricted the NLRB's authority, which had been one of Hutcheson's goals.[61]

The break between the Brotherhood and the New Deal over jurisdiction in the mills and material boycotting was paralleled by a widening rift between carpenters in the construction industry and the WPA. In June, fearful that government deficits and inflation would inhibit private investment, Roosevelt cut back on PWA investment and WPA funding in order to balance the budget. The result was a nationwide depression in 1937 and 1938. In Chicago relief rolls jumped from 50,000 to 120,000 in the first five months of 1938.[62]

To make matters worse, in May the WPA violated its 1935 pledge to use only union men for skilled work and to pay the monthly equivalent of the prevailing wage. Despite the WPA's frequently stated position that there could be "no strike against the government," the Building Trades Council called a general strike. President Stevenson protested the call, noting that with relief stations closed stopping WPA work would deprive hundreds of carpenters of all livelihood. Rather than a general walkout, which he called "ridiculous," he advocated walkouts by individual unions. On May 24, 1938, one thousand building tradesmen struck fifteen WPA projects, mainly in the suburbs. The WPA relented, and by the end of June the strike was over on most jobs. Meanwhile, the Depression continued, and outside men signed a five-year extension of the standard agreement providing for the status quo on hours and a $1.6250 wage with a reopener clause.[63]

Relations with Congress worsened in 1939 when a more conservative Congress confirmed the worst fears of building tradesmen by replacing the prevailing wage with the "security wage" for skilled WPA positions. In addition, Congress set an eighteen-month limit on employment and enacted the "25 percent rule" requiring local sponsors to pay 25 percent of the cost of the project. In Chicago the ax fell in July when the WPA announced the lowering of union wages and the dismissal of twenty-two thousand men, one-quarter of all those employed by the WPA in Chicago. In mid-July the Building Trades Council called on its 212 affiliated unions to strike. At the same time, A.F. of L. President Green met with President Roosevelt to request a return to the prevailing wage rates. But nothing could be done until the next congressional session, and the government responded by discharging 1,566 strikers. The demands were lost.[64]

The dispute with the WPA and the Thurman Arnold suits of 1940 led to an open break between the carpenters and Roosevelt's New Deal. In fact, the union's rapprochement with Roosevelt's Democratic party had been tenuous from the start. In Chicago the carpenters' leadership had been solidly pro-Republican since the advent of Mayor Bill Thompson in the second decade of the century. As late as 1931 the District Council endorsed Thompson for reelection over Democrat Anton Cermak. Following passage of the NRA, the District Council endorsed the Democratic mayoral regime of Edward Kelley, which took over control of contracts and city jobs. By the end of 1939, however, many local carpenters were returning to their earlier political moorings and the union joined other building trades in preventing the 1940 convention of the Illinois State Federation of Labor from directly endorsing Roosevelt. Thoughout this period, General President Hutcheson maintained a highly visible anti-Roosevelt stance during national elections. The union's unequivocal support for the New Deal was at an end.[65]

World War II and Postwar Reaction, 1941–1947

Just as the union's conflict with the Roosevelt administration was heating up in 1940, New Deal reform began to give way to a program of national rearmament. In October 1940 after Adolph Hitler's armies overran France, Congress authorized a $17 billion defense buildup. The New Deal had done much to reduce unemployment and alleviate poverty, but there were still 8.5 million out of work in June 1940. Only the war economy wiped out the remaining unemployment.[66]

Together with defense work, housing construction increased in Chicago from 1939 to 1941. But, after 1940, the diversion of materials and labor from the private sector to the war effort led District Council members to turn to defense construction for employment, principally outside of Chicago. Chicago carpenters built new facilities at Fort Sheridan and at Camp Grant near Rockford. By April 1941, twenty-three hundred carpenters, eighteen hundred from Chicago, were helping build munitions works at Wilmington, near Joliet. Less than a year later thirty-eight hundred carpenters were employed at the Great Lakes Naval Training Center. Throughout 1944 between six hundred and one thousand carpenters were engaged in building ships at the Pullman Company's yards.[67]

The defense boom and the union's support of the war effort did not alleviate the tensions and outright disputes that had arisen between the union and the federal government since the advent of the New Deal. At first, carpenters publicly voiced their concern that defense construction would be carried out under WPA auspices with first priority in hiring given to carpenters on relief, and pay rates reduced to the security wage. They were also concerned about the government's age limit of fifty-five for workers. When this was relaxed and when the WPA was quickly phased out, the principal issue facing the union became how to respond to the burgeoning strain on exisiting manpower created by the war.[68]

The issue was first faced over the question of pay rates for daily overtime. In violation of the union contract, which stipulated doubletime for overtime, the government refused to pay more than time and a half. The union protested this ruling vociferously. Doubletime was not primarily a money issue; it had originally been adopted in the 1890s to prevent employers from reinstating the ten-hour day in the guise of required overtime. Ultimately, the Brotherhood, together with other national building trades unions, compromised the issue. In August 1941 the union agreed to forego doubletime in return for a closed shop at the prevailing wage and nonrecognition of "dual unions." This latter provision froze out the CIO, which had been making feeble attempts to organized Chicago building tradesmen on an industrial basis since 1937.[69]

The manpower shortage intensified after Pearl Harbor as building workers on defense construction were pushed to the frenzied pace of seven days a week labor. The shortage of labor combined with high union wages led to a flood of new carpenters entering the metropolitan area. The problem of the early 1890s and 1920s revived: how to regulate the influx of labor into the city in order to prevent a surplus of labor after the boom. Though these newcomers were union men, there was still a consensus within the union that some means had to be found of "preventing a large oversupply of carpenters in our District in order that our regular membership might be assured the best possible employment." The answer was a special permit system—which lasted through 1945—whereby incoming carpenters would purchase monthly work permits instead of depositing their clearance cards, which would have entitled them to become permanent members.[70]

With the beginning of the war, General President Hutcheson and other union leaders offered Roosevelt a no-strike pledge. An overall policy of cooperation was soon formalized with the establishment of the War Labor Board designed to resolve disputes without strikes. Then in June 1942 the government and the Building Trades Department agreed to stabilize wages on all construction beginning in July.

In Chicago the District Council stepped up its negotiations with the Builders' Association and signed an agreement just before the deadline giving the carpenters a $.0750-cent wage increase.[71]

The outside men were satisfied with the agreement, but the millmen were positively outraged at the retention of article 3, which, according to one millworker "enslaves all millmen in Chicago." After all, the Supreme Court had just legalized material boycotting in 1941. In August the millmen received support from Hutcheson, who refused to approve the settlement. The union went back to the negotiating table, and in November the contractors agreed to an addendum to the eight cardinal principles stating that carpenters were not required "install mill and cabinet work not manufactured by members of the United Brotherhood of Carpenters and Joiners when same is available." It was the first time since 1918 that the union had a contract sanctioning the union label.[72]

By the winter of 1942–43 defense construction was nearly complete. Thousands of carpenters began leaving Chicago in the spring, many for West Coast shipbuilding yards. Even with this outflow, the union was faced with the prospect of renewed unemployment. In response, the District Council turned in two directions. First, it supported Mayor Kelley's request to the government to lift its October 1942 ban on home building in Chicago. On March 23 the National Housing Administration announced a quota of three thousand new homes and two thousand remodeled units, largely on the city's Southwest Side and in the southwest suburbs surrounding the newly built warplants.[73]

But, according to Patrick Sullivan, who addressed the carpenters in July, this was a mere "drop in the bucket." Instead, both he and Stevenson (now second general vice-president) recommended another course, that the outside men go into the warplants and obtain collective bargaining under the jurisdiction of the Brotherhood. This would mean a higher wage rate than that offered by the government as well as opening up a new employment niche for District Council members. For the first time since the early 1920s, when the District Council had chartered a short-lived Stockyards local, the carpenters were organizing large-scale industry. But this meant a head-on clash with the rival CIO.

To compete, the District Council decided to organize industrial carpenters separately instead of recruiting them into existing locals. This had been the policy in 1941 when the shipbuilders were given a charter for a new local (980), rather than being required to join waterfront workers Local 643. Similarly, in 1943 the union chartered Local 1954, with a $5 initiation fee, in order to organize millwrights and maintenance men at the Douglas Aircraft plant, Dodge-Chrysler plant, Burch Baking Company, and the Aluminum Company of America. The new local found immediate success. The turning point for Local 1954, which at one point was holding nightly meetings, came when it soundly defeated the CIO in a NLRB election at Chrysler. By March 1944 it had over three hundred members.[74]

Meanwhile, the District Council came up against the government's manpower and price-setting mechanisms in two important disputes. In the spring of 1943 Roosevelt ordered defense industries to institute a forty-eight-hour week. To prevent a shift of labor into more desirable private work, the War Manpower Commission, over labor's strong protests, began enforcing an executive order freezing workers in their jobs in Chicago and other designated labor-short areas. All labor recruitment was centralized through the United States Employment Service. Finally, in April 1944, the Building Trades Department concluded an agreement with the government to place all private construction on time and a half—a measure to reduce the incentive for skilled tradesmen to leave defense work. Chicago carpenters defiantly refused to go along, authorizing President Michael Sexton to refuse overtime permits to contractors paying time and a half. However, the union was isolated among the building trades and, under pressure from the national union, capitulated under protest in August. The District Council's stubborn defense of doubletime was not in vain. In December the Building Trades Department was able to get the government to rescind its order.[75]

The carpenters' difficulties with the war bureaucracy continued in a dispute over wages. In 1943 and 1944 price increases far outstripped wage increases granted by the War Labor Board. The millmen presented a sorry case. In 1943 millowners had granted them a $.0250 hourly increase, which was denied by the War Labor Board. In July 1944, after mill rank and file rebelled against accepting the same $.0250, the union negotiated a $.0750 increase, which was again denied. With higher paid work available, some millmen simply quit their jobs in disgust. Only after the war, in a two-day strike in September 1945, were wages increased $.10. A portion of that increase was then made retroactive to June 1944. During this same time, outside men asked for a wage increase to $1.85 to equal the highest wage paid in the building trades. This increase was refused by the Wage Adjustment Board. Finally, a joint protest together with the Builders' Association led the Board to grant the wage increase in July 1945.[76]

Despite constant friction with the government and the sacrifices entailed in foregoing wage increases and giving up highly prized contract provisions, the carpenters and other American unions emerged from the war in a comparatively strong position. The District Council had maintained and extended the jurisdictional boundaries that defined the work available to its members, even in the face of CIO competition. With overtime, union members' income had been augmented. On the debit side the union leadership found itself again and again playing a mediatory role between a rebellious membership and the federal government, whose decisions the union was compelled ultimately to accept.

Difficulties with the government did not cease in the period immediately following the war. Wage-price controls were lifted after June 30, 1946, setting off skyrocketing consumer prices. In Chicago the carpenters received an increase to $2.15 without a strike, but across the country many unionists struck to catch up. The strike wave set the stage for a much feared postwar reaction. Employers had not reconciled themselves to the newfound power of organized labor, whose membership had grown from 3.7 million when the Wagner Act was passed in 1935 to 14.6 million in 1947. But business leaders knew that they could not completely roll back the gains of unions as they had done following World War I. In the face of widespread public acceptance of the idea of collective bargaining, they sought to amend the Wagner Act in various ways in order to use the authority of the federal government to contain and hamstring the freedom of action of unions.

In 1947 a Republican-dominated Congress passed the Taft-Hartley Act over President Harry S. Truman's veto. Taft-Hartley was a comprehensive revision of labor law shifting the legal balance in favor of employers. The entire labor movement was shocked and embittered. The new law opened up unions to federal injunctions and damage suits by employers, and it allowed the president to proclaim a "cooling off" period during a strike that created a national emergency. It required union leaders to file financial disclosure and anti-Communist affidavits, and it allowed states to outlaw the union shop. Aimed at the building trades were provisions that outlawed the closed shop and made illegal all strikes and boycotts aimed at enforcing jurisdiction or preventing the use of nonunion materials. This, in turn, led to the establishment in 1948 of the National Joint Board for the Settlement of Jurisdictional Disputes as a final court for settling jurisdictional conflicts.[77]

Claiming that everything labor had won in the last half century was in jeopardy, the Brotherhood set up carpenters' "nonpartisan" committees to educate, organize, and register members to vote out antilabor politicians. In practice, this meant opposition to Republican candidates and support for Democratic ones. On the national level the Brotherhood abandoned, in effect, its nonpartisan policy and funded Democratic party candidates in 1948.[78]

But the practical effect of Taft-Hartley on the day-to-day operation of the carpenters' union was far less drastic than anticipated. Rather than a major counterrevolution, Taft-Hartley, for the most part, confirmed and extended existing trends in Wagner Act jurisprudence. An officer in the union at the time recalls that shortly after its passage a leading local labor lawyer advised the union that Taft-Hartley would be a serious blow to the carpenters' union. The union leadership chose to disregard this pessimistic view and to continue discretely its existing course of action. Relying on its post–1929 tradition of cooperation with contractors in the Builders' Association, the status quo was preserved. Facilitating this tacit understanding was the fact that key practices banned by Taft-Hartley—notably, the right to engage in jurisditional and sympathetic strikes and material boycotts—had already been voluntarily limited by the union in the course of its bargaining relationship with the contractors.[79]

In the eighteen years under consideration, the carpenters had confronted a troublesome dilemma regarding the federal government's intervention in society. Having suffered greatly during the Depression from lack of work, they were strongly supportive of federal legislation setting up the modern Social Security system and funding public as well as private employment. Along with other A.F. of L. unions, they also endorsed the National Industrial Recovery Act, which seemed to offer federal support for the extension of collective bargaining beyond the narrow bounds to which it had been confined during the 1920s. There can be little doubt that rank and file carpenters rallied overwhelmingly behind F.D.R.'s New Deal.

Yet, to union officials, issues such as jurisdiction and prevailing union standards loomed almost as large as the issue of immediate employment. In this respect, the extension of federal authority created as many problems as it solved. Federal programs such as the WPA undermined the union's prevailing wage and union standards through job regulations legislated by Congress. Meanwhile, under the Wagner Act, unions gave up their role as collective bodies with specific rights in exchange for a role as agents for employees. It was the rights of employees rather than of unions that were to be validated and enforced by the National Labor Relations Board. Consequently, the New Deal launched an assault on standard union practices such as the maintenance of exclusive jurisdiction through use of the boycott and strikes. By the late 1930s the NLRB gave crucial aid in establishing a union in the Pacific Northwest inside the Brotherhood's jurisdiction. The Justice Department also filed suit against the carpenters for monopolistic practices stemming from their policy of boycotting nonunion materials. Each of these developments tended to counterbalance the legitimization of collective bargaining and independent unionism offered by the Wagner Act. From the 1933 through 1945 nearly all conflicts engaged in by the union were with the government rather than private contractors.

Not surprisingly, despite strong rank and file support for the New Deal, many carpenters' leaders had remained officially nonpartisan and some, such as District Council President John R. Stevenson (1937–41) remained Republican, a legacy of the 1920s. But passage of the Taft-Hartley Act made it clear that federal intervention was inescapable. With the state now a major terrain for class conflict, the carpenters broke with nonpartisanship—despite retaining their verbal commitment to it—and used their financial and organizational resources to defeat antilabor candidates and aid prolabor candidates. The new policy was most obvious not on the local level of government, where the union had always made pragmatic alliances with city administrations of either party, but on the federal and state levels. When Democratic Senator Paul Douglas addressed the District Council in 1950, the political leanings of the union were clear.

Underlying this shift was the fact that the carpenters' voluntarist philosophy had been irrevocably undermined. Henceforth, the federal government would be at least a silent partner in all collective bargaining matters. Having accepted the embrace of the state in 1933, it was too late to withdraw in 1947.

CHAPTER 6

The Era of Union-Contractor Cooperation, 1948–1987

Jurisdiction is a constant job. Jurisdiction is the
lifeblood of the construction industry. You blow your
jurisdiction, you blow your industry. It isn't the dollar,
it isn't the fringe benefit; it's jurisdiction. If you don't
have the work, you don't have an organization. If you
work with the employer, be part of his business,
support him for his support, you can survive in the
industry. But, if you want to go out there and fight that
employer every time he turns around, and do not
recognize his problems and help him resolve them,
then you're dead because they're going to beat you.
　　　　　—George Vest, Jr., president of the
　　　　　Chicago District Council of Carpenters.[1]

With the Depression, World War II, and wartime controls behind them, the carpenters' union and the Builders' Association cooperated in opening a new era of conciliation and prosperity, finally realizing fully the promise of the 1929 settlement. On the employers' side, the new era was characterized by the absence of any challenge by open-shop advocates to the principle of collective bargaining. In return for this acquiescence in union standards, the carpenters and other building trades unions offered contractors a commitment to avoid jurisdictional walkouts and strikes.

Yet it is doubtful whether such a mutual understanding could have been sustained had not a massive and long-lasting demand for construction work in the Chicago area afforded employers the ability to pass on the costs of unionism to the building public. Beginning in 1945 the city enjoyed a steady increase in home and apartment building, culminating in 1950 when total residential units built in the metropolitan area approached 1920s levels. Fueled by a housing shortage inherited from the 1930s and early 1940s combined with a generally properous economy, this boom market continued through the mid–1970s when it began to falter. The recession years of the early 1980s concluded the boom.

Between 1950 and 1978 a yearly average of forty-three thousand residential units were built in the metropolitan area, compared to a yearly average of almost 46,000 between 1922 and 1929. Beginning in the early 1950s the local market became sharply divided, with Chicago construction being largely limited to high-rise office and apartment construction, while the suburbs and small towns on the outskirts of the city became the sites for an explosion of home building plus industrial, commercial, and highway construction. The growing distinctions between the two markets and the overall shift of work to areas outside of the city would have important consequences for the union. Nonetheless, the central fact of the postwar era was an abiding prosperity that carried the union to 1972 without a strike, an era of peace lasting fifty-three years.

Jurisdiction: A New Emphasis

The postwar construction boom and friendly relations with the contractors accelerated several important trends present since the turn of the century affecting union policy and the nature of the union itself. Perhaps the most obvious fruit of the favorable collective bargaining climate was the steady increase in the carpenters' compensation in wages and fringe benefits. Between 1948 and 1981, carpenter wages rose from $2.35 an hour to $15.40 an hour, a 555 percent increase, far outstripping the rise in consumer prices, but trailing the 687 percent increase in the average cost of a Chicago area home during the same period.[2]

Rank and file carpenters also benefited from the creation of a union-contractor operated health and welfare plan in 1952. Five years later the union won a pension plan to supplement the much more modest union-run plan, which in 1978 afforded retirees only $14 a month. Both funds are administered by a joint Board of Trustees. Union business agents have the responsibility of policing the industry to ensure that regular contributions to the fund are made by all contractors.

Notwithstanding these advances, the carpenters have not been the pacesetters in the Chicago building trades in compensation. Since the turn of the century, no trade has been more affected by the introduction of new materials and new methods of construction—resulting in threats to employment—than have the carpenters. The union, therefore, has traditionally considered the goal of keeping its members at work a far more vital issue than compensation. One salient example of the union's emphasis came in its response to the Depression in the late 1920s and early 1930s. Along with the painters, the carpenters pressed for a shorter work week and the six-hour day, while other trades held back, fearing the inevitable sacrifice in wages. In the postwar period the emphasis of union policy has continued to be maximizing employment opportunities, but the means has shifted away from reducing hours and become almost exclusively that of maintaining and extending jurisdiction. Although jurisdiction has been of paramount concern since the turn of the century, new circumstances have given this old goal added importance and have compelled the union to pursue it in new ways.

The most important new development has been the increased willingness and ability of contractors to cut costs by introducing new building materials and methods. From plastic trim to interior wall systems, new technology has presented substantial new threats to the carpenters' traditional ways of working. But the union can no longer protect its jurisdiction using Bill Hutcheson's old "go-it-alone, fight-it-out-to-the-finish" tactics, an approach last taken in Chicago in the 1920s by the administration of Harry Jensen. Stable contractual relations with the contractors and the ever-lurking shadow of federal law and NLRB action provide ample inducements for the union to abide by the framework of interunion mediation, and the awards of the Joint Conference Board locally and the Joint Board for the Settlement of Jurisdictional Disputes nationally.[3]

Commitment to conciliation and arbitration has led the union to marshal an entire array of policies to serve the cause of jurisdictional advantage vis-à-vis other unions. Most importantly, the union's wage policy has undergone a subtle transformation. While the carpenters continue to press for and achieve high wages, a wage equal to that of the highest paid building trade is no longer one of its goals. Instead, the union has allowed the wages of other trades to forge ahead in order to avoid pricing itself out of the labor market. This is a policy that closely reflects rank and file sentiment, for even in the best of times, the average carpenter works only thirty-seven to forty-five weeks a year.

By not asking for high wage settlements, the carpenters have signficantly reduced the incentive for contractors to encroach upon their jurisdiction with new materials and lower paid workmen. The most striking illustration of how this policy benefits the union is the dispute between the carpenters and the structural ironworkers. In 1956 the total wages of carpenters—wages plus welfare, pension, and other fringes—contributed by employers were 95 percent of those of the structural ironworkers. By 1970 that percentage had fallen to 79. That widening differential gradually induced cost-conscious architects and builders to replace structural steel in high-rise construction with reinforced concrete, a material on which carpenters do much of the work—setting the forms.[4]

In 1982, among the nineteen basic building trades the carpenters were in the lower half in total wages, a stark contrast to 1919 when the carpenters climaxed a half century of struggle to reach parity with the bricklayers, then the highest paid trade. The union's wage policy does not necessarily mean a lower standard of living for carpenters relative to other trades. Carpenter leaders reason that the increased hours of work for their members yield a yearly income that more than compensates for whatever hourly wages are foregone at the bargaining table.

The union has also relaxed its already permissive attitude toward the introduction of new, often factory-made materials. Rather than wage a futile, rearguard battle against the introduction of new building technology as have many other building trades unions, the carpenters have taken the pragmatic position that they will work on any material as long as it is union made. While this position has ratified the progressive deterioration of traditional wood craftsmanship, particularly in high-rise construction, and multiplied the number of specialty crafts within the union, it has enabled the union to retain and even expand the amount of work available for its members. Thus, despite the steady decline in the use of wood in all kinds of construction, the carpenters remain the largest building trades union in the Building Trades Council. Over the last eighty years they have maintained a constant one-fifth proportion among unionized building trades workers. In the last quarter of 1981 the carpenters bought 27,000 working cards from the 120,000-member Cook County Building and Construction Trades Council.

There is no more dramatic illustration of the success of the union's policy toward new materials than the dispute, beginning in the 1940s, over who would install drywall. Because drywall replaced both lath and plaster, the lathers' and plasterers' unions attempted to prevent its adoption by contractors. Had they merely claimed jurisdiction over its installation, they would have probably retained the work for their members. Instead, the resulting jurisdictional dispute culminated in a decision by the Joint Conference Board to award the work to the carpenters. The Wood, Wire, and Lather International Union was so depleted in membership and finances by the dispute that it eventually relinquished its identity by merging with the Brotherhood.[5]

The union's focus on jurisdiction also explains a key revision in one of its customary work rules. Traditionally, the steward was either the first man on the job or was to be elected by union carpenters on the job. Under the operation of this rule, it was often the case that company favorites became stewards, usually because they were the first hired. To enforce its jurisdiction and other union standards more stringently, union negotiators spent eight years at the bargaining table to win the right of the business agent (BA) to appoint the steward. On most jobs stewards are still elected, but the result of the election must be approved by the BA. Where repeated contract violations are found, the BA retains the option of appointing a committed union man.[6]

Finally, the union has put new emphasis on its apprenticeship training program at Washburne Trade School run in cooperation with contractors and the Chicago Board of Education. Unlike other trades, the carpenters have never been able to use apprenticeship regulations to limit the supply of skilled craftsmen in the trade or to stand in the way of new materials. Rather, they have used apprenticeship simply to preserve the integrity of general carpentry skills while at the same time keeping young carpenters abreast of new building technology affecting jurisdiction. For example, when plastic trim came into use for a period before the energy price hike of 1974, the apprenticeship program quickly introduced this skill into its curriculum. The existing apprenticeship program attempts to train journeyman carpenters in three main areas of competency: framing for residential home building; installation of interior systems for all kinds of building; and the setting of concrete forms, mainly for commercial and industrial construction. In maintaining a high skill level, the union not only intends to win the confidence of contractors when it comes to jurisdictional disputes but also to give them an incentive to employ union rather than cheaper nonunion labor. Today, approximately a quarter of all journeymen working at their trade have been apprenticed.[7]

Internal Developments in the Union

In addition to an increased emphasis on all that relates to jurisdiction, important developments in the postwar period have affected the nature of the union. The grass-roots foundation of the carpenters' union in Chicago has always been the many neighborhood-based, ethnic locals that together comprised the Chicago District Council. As the reader will recall, the first carpenters' unions in the city, during and after the Civil War, were based on nationality and language. Citywide unions were loosely joined amalgams of ethnic branches. The Brotherhood's multilocal system established in 1884 was itself a concession to the potential divisiveness of ethnic loyalties.

But, on balance, ethnic ties reinforced rather than undermined labor solidarity. The typical carpenter local with its neighborhood hall, its weekly meetings, and its self-administered benefit system securely bound the immigrant carpenter to the broader union. The old union hall was a place for carpenters to socialize with fellow members between jobs. Many locals had small libraries and reading rooms and loaned money to members in need. The fact that carpenter locals were numerous and small enough to be immediately responsive to the rank and file carpenter—unlike the centralized and unwieldy citywide locals of most other building trades unions—afforded the carpenters a healthy balance between local democracy and necessary centralism across the city as a whole.

The late nineteenth-century trend was away from ethnic loyalty toward broader forms of trade unity. With the founding of Locals 1 and 28 (now 10), between one-third and one-half of all Chicago carpenters in the 1890s were in mixed or multi-ethnic locals with memberships of over a thousand. Into the early twentieth century these large locals provided leadership to the United Carpenters Council and later the District Council.

By the second decade of the century the trend changed from amalgamation of ethnic locals back to an ethnic resurgence. By World War I the locus of power in the union had shifted to a half dozen ethnic locals, notably 13, 58, 80, 141, 181, and 504. This period through the end of World War II may be called the heyday of the ethnic local. As late as 1930, when figures on nationality are last available, 64 percent of all Chicago carpenters were foreign-born.

With the end of massive immigration from Europe in the 1920s, and the dearth of new members during the Depression, the carpenters of Chicago began to age. In 1940 almost two-thirds of Chicago carpenters were over forty-five years old; in contrast in 1890 only one-quarter had been over forty-five. During the postwar boom this situation was transformed as the last generation of ethnic carpenters retired, giving way to a much younger wave of American-born journeymen. By 1960 the percentage of members over forty-five had declined to 40 percent, reaching 34 percent in 1980. It was also during this period that many of Chicago's closely knit ethnic communities broke up under the strains of urban renewal, the movement of Southern blacks into the city, and the lure for well-paid journeymen carpenters of plentiful jobs and cheap homes in the suburbs. With suburban lifestyles and a decaying inner city, many members ceased to attend weekly meetings at their old meeting halls, still located in Chicago. Many joined the new and fast-growing suburban locals, which lack the ethnic/neighborhood flavor of most of the old locals. The culmination of this trend came in 1983 when the General Executive Board used the authority given it in 1974 to mandate a merger of a host of Chicago locals. For example, Jewish Local 504 went out of existence; while Czech Local 54 became just another mixed local. Today, apart from the fact that some locals still are dominated by a small ethnic clique, ethnicity is confined to the millworkers locals.[8]

At the same time that the ethnic local was in precipitous decline, the importance of the local in general was being called into question as the District Council became more centralized and bureaucratized in its operation. As with other American unions, bureaucratization of union functions was actually a continuation of developments that began in the early 1890s with the first successes of the District Council in collective bargaining. As the union transformed itself from a tenuous social movement into an accepted institution, the charismatic orator and organizer of the late nineteenth century typified by a William Kliver or a William Henry Jaxon in Chicago or a Peter J. McGuire on the national level gave way to the union functionary skilled in administration such as a John Metz (1905–17) in Chicago or a Frank Duffy nationally. The twentieth century leader is less an exhorter to action and more a negotiator of contracts and enforcer of work rules.[9]

In the postwar period this trend has been reinforced as a result in large part of the professionalizing of collective bargaining. The old-line general contractor who employed his own tradesmen is being replaced by the "broker" who subcontracts his work and knows little of the complexities of each trade. Today in the city there are only a dozen general contractors who employ all the basic trades. Many of these new type general contractors are college-educated and want everything spelled out in the contract. Another influence has been the necessity of complying with federal guidelines, particularly those guaranteeing equal opportunity. As a result, the days of the one-page agreement consummated by a handshake across the bargaining table are over. No longer can substantive matters be left to a softly spoken gentleman's agreement. Every detail must be translated into legally enforceable language by professional negotiators and approved by lawyers. The 1981 contract is forty-six pages long.

The trend toward professionalization has also been furthered by the shift to areawide bargaining. Since 1972 the union has negotiated its standard contract with an employers' federation of large industrial, commercial, high-rise, and road-building general contractors, known as the Mid-America Regional Bargaining Association

(MARBA). The bargaining region now covers an area stretching from southern Wisconsin to northern Indiana. Meanwhile, the District Council extended its jurisdiction beyond the boundaries of Cook County into Lake and DuPage counties, and presently includes Grundy, Kane, Kankakee, Kendall, Iroquois, McHenry, and Will counties (and LaPorte County, Indiana, for waterfront and pile-driving work). One result of the broadened scope of negotiations is that local unions are more than ever before dependent on the District Council and the national union for information and legal guidance.

Still another professionalizing influence has been the responsibility of the District Council to police and help administer a several-hundred-million-dollar fringe benefit fund, one of the top ten multiple-employer funds in the nation.

In general, the decline of the local, the detailed contract, area-wide bargaining, and the administration of fringe benefit funds have combined to exalt the role of professionals in the day to day running of the union. According to George Vest, Jr., the president of the District Council since 1966: "We have sought out the most knowledgeable people in professional life to handle our affairs: be it the administrators, the managers of our various departments, our program analysts, our C.P.A.'s, our actuaries, and our attorneys."[10]

While this approach has afforded the union efficient administrative operation, the running of much of its affairs as a business has contributed to the decline in rank and file participation. There can be little doubt that the decline in membership participation has accelerated since the 1930s. In that decade prolonged unemployment decimated membership and undermined faith in the efficacy of unionism. The much-disputed 1933 election of Thomas Flynn and the subsequent expulsion from the union of opposition candidates may also have been a turning point in the discouragement of a sustained, open opposition to the existing District Council administration. Old-timers, with roots in the prewar period, universally decry the decline in commitment and participation in union affairs exhibited by most present-day carpenters. The contemporary carpenter is more likely to view the union in pragmatic terms as a valuable service instead of a movement to which he can devote himself.

The decay in the union's internal life first became obvious in 1948 when the Mike Sexton administration succeeded in lengthening the terms of Council officers from one to three years, thus bringing to fruition a proposal that had been debated by District Council delegates and defeated several times since the 1920s. In 1957 the term was lengthened to four years. During this period the Council also reduced the frequency of its meetings from weekly to biweekly. The same changes have occurred on the level of the local unions.[11]

Another measure of the same phenomenon has been the steady increase in the length of time served by union officers. In the 1880s and 1890s the length of time served did not extend beyond two years; during the first third of the twentieth century (after 1905) the longest time a president served was twelve years and the average time was eight years; in the second third of the century three presidents served an average of ten years, none longer than fifteen years; in the last third of the century George Vest, Jr., has been the only president, serving over twenty-one years since his election in 1966. Again, similar trends are evident within most locals.

One result of these trends has been the decline in the autonomy and policy-making function of the District Council's Board of Delegates. In contrast to the prewar period when most issues were the subject of debate and discussion by local delegates, it appears from published Council proceedings that delegates have informally ceded much of their initiative to District Council officers.

In sum, increasing centralization, bureaucratization, professionalization, and the decline of membership and local union participation have been the predominant trends in the postwar period. And yet, carpenter union officials have generally performed their duties efficiently, honestly, and fairly; knowledgeable observers point to the carpenters as the best governed of the Chicago building trades unions. It is significant that, since the Jensen administration in the early 1920s, there has not been even the hint of corruption in top union leadership. Perhaps this is a result of the fact that carpenter leaders have generally been apprenticed and take pride in their craft and their union. President Vest, for example, came from a union family, went through the carpenters' apprenticeship program after serving in the navy during the war, never missed a meeting of his local (141), and served as a business agent before becoming president. Meanwhile, he was working his way up from journeyman carpenter to general superintendent of construction for several large industrial firms. Despite the decline in unionism among much of the rank and file, as long as the commitment to unionism remains strong among a minority of skilled, apprenticed journeymen, it will be possible for the union to field high-quality leadership.

The Business Agent: Myth and Reality

Not the union official, but the business agent—known in the nineteenth century as the "walking delegate"—is the heart of the carpenters' union. More than anyone, he is the "policeman" of the trade, with the power to shut down instantly a job site by calling out the contractors' union work force.

Though the first carpenters' walking delegate dated to 1884, it was only during the 1887 strike and lockout that the public took notice. Then, the *Chicago Tribune* called him "the most unique product of modern trades unionism." Indeed, the walking delegate quickly became the symbol of trades unionism. The 1887 and 1900–1901 lockouts took on the nature of class vendettas, specifically aimed at "crushing out the walking delegate." But the walking delegate survived and prospered for two simple reasons. To the employer he was a labor contractor delivering the right number of men possessing the requisite skills at a stated price. During the 1890s heyday of "guerrilla unionism," the walking delegate did most of the negotiating with individual contractors. Union members also recognized the necessity of delegating union authority to a roving agent. Only by concentrating power in the hands of the walking delegate could the union maintain uniform standards among workmen with widely varying degrees of union commitment at scattered work sites. As the functions and authority of the walking delegate became established, the name was soon replaced by the term "business agent."[12]

Since the 1890s a pervasive mystique has been built up around the business agent. Many were able to build powerful "machines" within their locals based on their control over employment. In the first quarter of the twentieth century, it was widely believed that many business agents would accept bribes in return for overlooking rule violations. Labor militants and critics of "business unionism" have assailed them for their "narrow" outlook limited to trade issues and their resistance to class consciousness. The historian of the carpenters, Robert Christie, argued that business agents supplied the ranks of the new conservatives who replaced socialist and radical leaders like McGuire in the early twentieth century.[13]

This view exaggerates the influence to the business agent. Actually, the everyday practices of business agents have ambiguous implications. In the authority they exercise over journeymen and in their day-to-day business dealings with contractors, there may be a tendency to adopt a businessman's mental outlook of small businessmen. Yet it is not always realized that the business agent, as the principal organizer of the union, must often bring newcomers into the union against the wishes of existing members who fear that there will not be work enough for all. Because of their role as union organizers, business agents retain an appreciation of the need for labor solidarity. Also militating against a business unionist outlook is the fact that business agents have been the target of open-shop advocates who consider work rules to be an intolerable invasion of property rights and the closed shop to be the equivalent of tyranny. All this helps explain how it was possible for radicals and militants like James Brennock and Anton Johannsen to serve as business agents. Today there are two kinds of carpenter BA's: those selected by the locals and those by the District Council. Both must be elected and tend to reflect—for better or worse—the temper and standards of the union's membership.

The primary task of today's BA remains checking to see that carpenters on the job are union men with paid-up union cards, and that the contractors do not violate the union's "area standards." Since the advent of federal and industry safety rules, he is also responsible for scrutinizing the workplace for unsafe scaffolding and ladders, power saws without safety guards, and other violations. His most difficult task is to identify and root out subcontractors who try to avoid payment of fringe benefits and violate work rules.

When the carpenter on the job has a grievance that cannot be handled by the steward, it is the business agent who intervenes on his behalf. At first, the BA tries to mediate, for the union does not want to drive contractors, particularly smaller union contractors, out of business by calling a strike. His next step may be to compel the contractor to take on a special union steward to check on rule violations and report back to him. Only as a last resort does he call the carpenters off the job.[14]

The business agent remains central to carpenter unionism. Indeed, should the membership decide to dispense with every other elected official, the union could still survive with its core of business agents.

Problems in Residential Construction

The successes of the union and the lack of the kind of intermittent warfare with contractors that characterized the late nineteenth century and 1912–24 periods does not mean that there have not been important areas of dispute since the war. In contrast to the Landis Award period, however, when the union used its friendly relations with small residential builders to pressure the open-shop general contractors in the Loop, the union in the postwar era has faced its most stubborn open-shop threat from among home builders. Since these employers give work to 60 to 65 percent of the Council's membership, this is a problem of considerable concern to the union.

The genesis of the problem occurred during the post-war housing boom that attracted large-scale developers of "tract housing" to the outlying areas of the city and the suburbs. The largest developers, such as U.S. Homes, were able to override the union's traditional resistence to specialization within the craft. On projects calling for hundreds of units of identical homes, the developers cut costs by assembling crews of carpenters, each one specializing in a task such as rough framing, or the laying of concrete foundations, or the installing of decks, doors, joints, or rafters. Instead of working on one job site until the home was completed, the specialist carpenter learned only a small part of the general craft and repeated this well-honed skill on a different site each day. Some developers supplemented this by specifying how many hours each task was to take.

Specialization was reinforced by the union's relaxation of its long-standing opposition to factory-made materials. Prehung doors, plastic trim, and truss roofs could be installed easily by men with a minimum of skill. Finally, the decline in the all-around general contractor, who employed his own men, decreased the number of carpenters with experience in all aspects of the trade. By the mid-1960s, when the market for tract housing gave way to the demand for high-quality single dwellings, the union found itself hard pressed to supply old-style general carpenters to contractors.[15]

Though the union deplored specialization, since a wide variety of skills has always been necessary for promoting year-round employment and a sustained commitment to the trade and the union, little was done about it in the immediate postwar years. In the meantime, the general decrease in skill of the bulk of the new carpenters who entered the trade during the building boom, and the steady growth during the twentieth century of specialty areas—shingling, carpeting, insulating, resilient floor building, component building, and lathing, to name only a few of twenty-six specialty areas covered by the union—opened the door for piecework and the employment of nonunion labor in residential construction. Aside from specialty areas, these developments occurred mainly in the suburbs, where small- to medium-sized home-building firms have sought to evade what the union calls "area standards." By the 1970s piecework was rife in the installation of drywall, an easily learned task that could be paid by the square foot. Some of these pieceworkers were Chicago union men migrating to the suburbs in search of work; more of them were nonunion Mexican immigrants, many of them illegals, who received less than scale for their labor. Even when they received the full wage, the nonunion subcontractors who employed them tried mightily to evade payment of fringe benefits contributions, thus threatening the integrity of the union's health, welfare, and pension funds. The growing trickle of nonunion work also threatened the union's hard-won jurisdiction.

Policing of nonunion work by carpenter business agents has become steadily more difficult in the postwar period as general contractors have increased the practice of subcontracting work. A typical project may be fronted by a legitimate general contractor with the bulk of the work done by scores of subcontractors, many of whom cannot be trusted to adhere to union standards. In carpentry this problem is made more difficult because, unlike the mechanical trades contractors, who work out of shops and must hold licenses, carpenter contractors are unlicensed, require little capital to start up, and can work out of the trunks of their cars. With as many as a dozen carpenter contractors on a job, it is difficult for the union to keep track of who is employing its members.[16]

Since the early 1930s the union has demanded a "subcontracting clause" from the Builders' Association to control the small subcontractor. After decades of saying that this was "none of the union's business," the Builders Association agreed to an article in the contract in the late 1960s making employers responsible for the subcontractors' adherence to union standards. All subcontractors must now be signatories to the basic agreement and possess the same legal credentials as general contractors. This provision was the union's single most important contract victory in the postwar era. Even with this provision, the District Council often resorts to "task forces" consisting of several business agents to police large pojects in outlying areas.

Despite these difficulties, the Chicago District Council of Carpenters, supported by other strongly unionized building trades, has done significantly better than the rest of the Brotherhood in maintaining union strength in residential work. In the nation as a whole, less than a quarter of all home building is done by union labor. Even in large metropolitan areas, where unions are relatively strong, there are commonly two wage rates: an industrial and commercial rate and a lower residential rate. In 1957 the Metropolitan Home Builders Association attempted to establish a dual wage rate in the Chicago area by asking the NLRB to force the union to negotiate a separate agreement with it. The union fought this in the courts and won. For many years the Chicago District Council could boast of having the nation's only single wage rate for all carpenters.

Meanwhile, the union began to search for a cooperative employers' spokesman to bring some stability into residential building. In 1972 President Vest helped residential builders set up the Residential Construction Employers' Council. Though wages and other contract provisions were "rolled over" from the areawide agreement, the union conceded several work rule changes in an attempt to stimulate home building. Nonetheless, by the late 1970s it was becoming more difficult to enforce union standards among the growing ranks of small residential subcontractors. In 1979 the union was able to defeat RCEC's attempt to establish a dual wage rate by selectively picketing its Executive Board members. But the severe building slump of the early 1980s finally forced the union to concede a second and lower wage rate in 1982.[17]

Developments in Nonresidential Construction and Millwork

Notwithstanding the problems in residential construction, relations with Chicago's industrial and commercial general contractors, represented by the Builders' Association, remained cordial until 1972. In that year the actions of the Mid-America Regional Bargaining Association undermined a record fifty-three years of labor peace. MARBA, an outgrowth of the conservative "Business Roundtable," was the latest in a long series of corporate attempts to rationalize the construction industry by breaking the power of the unions. Representing fourteen regional employers' associations, MARBA's basic goal was to end what it called "whipsawing," that is, the pacesetting influence that the strongly unionized Chicago building trades unions exerted on contract negotiations within the region. It therefore called for the contracts for all the basic trades in the region to end on the same date.[18]

The Chicago District Council did not have a major quarrel with the concept of regional bargaining. It did, however, steadfastly oppose sixty-two work rule changes that MARBA proposed that the union accept in return for a large wage settlement. According to President Vest, the proposed agreement "would have allowed the contractors to own the union." Given the long absence of strikes, MARBA did not expect that the carpenters would authorize a strike. Confidently they refused to compromise. In reply the District Council authorized on June 23, 1972, its first strike since 1919.[19]

Within three days the union virtually shut down all building within Lake, Cook, and Du Page counties with the help of sympathy action by other trades. Then the union returned to its traditional policy of seeking employment for its members with the area's approximately three thousand small, independent contractors, the bulk of whom have union roots and continue to hold cards. This latter group, Vest calls "the backbone of the union" because of its commitment to union standards on the job.

With most of its members employed, Vest went to leading members of the Builders' Association and persuaded them to sign an interim agreement based on the status quo for work rules. The union continued selective picketing of the prime contractors of each of MARBA's associations. When the 1973 building season began, MARBA capitulated and retracted all of its proposed work rule changes. Though the District Council now negotiates its contract with MARBA rather than the Builders' Association, MARBA's membership has declined to nine associations and its goal of a uniform contract termination date remains frustrated.

Chicago's millworkers have not enjoyed the success of the union's outside men. Indeed, they never fully recovered their strength in the city following the assault of open shop employers in the 1920s and severe unemployment during the 1930s. These traumatic events caused the millmen's leadership to take a conservative turn, particularly business agents Ted Kenney and Emil Johnson. Though they were able to sustain opposition to pay classifications proposed by the mill employers, wages lagged considerably.

In 1966, following the death of Kenney, Charles Svec was elected as the mill division's business agent. Svec restored democratic procedures, which had fallen into disuse in many locals under Kenney, and along with Warren Burdeau and Stanley Jourowsky he helped lead the millmen in their first major strike in three decades. After two weeks they won a $.97 increase. This was followed in 1970 by a four-week strike in which millmen won another major pay increase plus a yearly vacation of up to four weeks. On the heels of this victory, the millmen won a unique stewards' clause that put the burden of proof for the firing of a steward on the employer, a work rule superior to that of the outside men.

In the meantime the Vest administration created the long-sought "universal working card" that allows inside men and outside men to switch jobs without fomenting rivalry among local unions for membership. In 1975, under Vest's direction, the millmen established an employer-funded plan that supplemented the welfare plan established for millmen in 1959.

Despite the fact that the Chicago mill division is recognized as the pacesetter in union conditions in the country, the city's millmen face a problematic future. Unlike the outside men the cabinetmakers have not been able to trade a traditional skill for jurisdiction over new work. Once the nation's center for the production of window, sash, door and trim work, by 1975 Chicago had lost almost all the manufacturers of this work to localities with lower wage rates. The city is left with approximately two hundred small shops, each employing an average of eight to ten highly skilled men, the vast majority of whom manufacture office fixtures. By far the largest shop is Woodwork Corporation of America, which employs one hundred and fifty union cabinetmakers and thirty union finishers. The bulk of the production of these shops—highly customized and expensive architectural woodwork—has faced competition from cheaper products produced outside the city. The steady drain of employment left Chicago mill locals with less than twenty-two hundred members in 1981, compared to well over three thousand in 1970. The effect on the union of these trends became evident in 1985. After a long and bitter strike, the union, for the first time, accepted a job classification scheme that resulted in a drastic wage cut for many union members.

Chicago mill members have traditionally been of Germanic and Slavic descent, with a scattering of other European nationalities, and this continues to be the case today. In contrast to the outside men's locals, the mill locals retain a strong ethnic complexion because of a continuing trickle of immigration. They have not, however, been immune to the trend of declining participation in union affairs, a result in large part of the dispersion of members to the suburbs.[20]

Blacks, Hispanics, and Women in the Union

In addition to challenges stemming from the union's continuing battles over jurisdiction, piecework, and the enforcement of union work rules, the carpenters face a major test as a result of demands for increased participation by minority groups and women. At bottom, this is the same issue that the union confronted and resolved in the late nineteenth century, when it assimilated a variety of ethnic and religious groups into the Brotherhood through the local system. Since the 1960s, when blacks and Hispanics replaced European immigrants as the city's low-wage labor force, the union has been put to a similar test. The major difference is that social prejudices against blacks and women are deeper and far harder to uproot than the old prejudices against the Czechs or the Jews. But the cost of failure to overcome these prejudices is the same: the undermining of union standards by piecework and nonunion labor.

Unlike some old-line A.F. of L. unions, the carpenters both nationally and in Chicago have never barred blacks from membership nor given official sanction to racial discrimination. Peter J. McGuire in the nineteenth century and Frank Duffy in the twentieth were strong advocates of organizing black carpenters—to the extent of appointing black organizers in the South. Throughout the union's history its leaders have realized that to leave blacks or any other group unorganized could undercut the wages of already unionized carpenters.[21]

This is not to say that black carpenters did not meet with harsh discrimination in the trade. The bulk of it, however, came from employers and the informal networks that have governed hiring in the carpentry trade. The carpenters' union has never had a hiring hall and therefore has never enjoyed the unilateral control over employment that other construction unions have. Thus, even the possession by black carpenters of a union working card was no guarantee of steady employment. For example, though employed, they might face difficulties gaining overtime work from white contractors or foremen. As a result, only the best black carpenters could withstand the discouragement and maintain their position in the trade.

Meanwhile, racial hostility from white carpenters reinforced the discrimination felt by blacks. It is a common complaint among black carpenters that they are often shunned on the job by their white co-workers and given the most disagreeable work by the foreman. White carpenters were hardly unique among American workingmen in exhibiting racism; it was only in the mid–1960s, however, that something began to be done to address this situation within the union.[22]

The first impetus came from the civil rights movement. In 1965 the United States Department of Labor set new apprenticeship standards to comply with the 1964 Civil Rights Act. There was considerable opposition both locally and nationally to implementing what became known as affirmative action goals. Ultimately, the carpenters apprenticeship program based at Washburne Trade School had to be revamped and expanded. During the Depression, the apprenticeship program had shriveled and decayed. When Adolph "Duffy" Dardar took over the program in 1965 it had only ninety apprentices with three instructors. Under Dardar, whose leadership receives high marks from the Chicago Urban League, the program underwent major changes. Instead of contractors signing up apprentices and funneling them into the program—a decentralized, ad hoc system riddled with discriminatory practices—apprentices were required to sign up with a joint union-contractor apprenticeship committee. Individual contractors were also relieved of the responsibility of funding the system; instead, an apprenticeship fund was set up based on an employers' contribution of $.01 (now $.12) per journeyman carpenter. The new system enabled the trade to meet Department of Labor goals that 23 percent of all apprentices be minorities. The carpenters also moved to a variety of community outreach programs to feed apprentices into the Washburne program.

Four years later, however, minorities were still not entering the trades in significant numbers. Between 1960 and 1970 the number of black carpenters had risen by but little more than four hundred. In 1969, after a series of protest demonstrations called by black community groups shut down many construction sites in the city, building trades unions accepted a voluntary plan to facilitate direct entry into the trades. Even then many minority apprentices were not completing their apprenticeship training. In 1975 at the direction of the Department of Labor the union adopted a variety of affirmative action programs to help minorities upgrade their educational background so that they could compete in the apprenticeship program. Partly as result, the number of black carpenters in the Chicago area rose to 1,705 in 1980, 6.9 percent of employed carpenters. Though these census figures include nonunion as well as union carpenters, the 61 percent increase over 1970 is roughly indicative of a significant though modest improvement in the position of blacks in the trade.[23]

One of the most successful programs contributing to the participation of minorities in carpentry was the 18th Street Development Corporation, funded by federal CETA grants and the Mayor's Office. In this program, which funneled Hispanics and blacks from the Mexican-American community of Pilsen into the apprenticeship program, a group of seventeen to thirty-five teenagers supervised by five skilled journeymen carpenters learned basic skills by rehabilitating abandoned buildings taken over by the city. Once completed, the buildings were given away by lottery. Because of their "hands-on" experience and the pride they acquired in improving their own community, graduates of the program were highly successful in completing the Washburne program and becoming solid union members. Before the program less than 2 percent of the entering class at Washburne consisted of Hispanics. Since then, that share has hovered at 15 percent. One of the journeyman carpenters employed by the program, Richard de Vries, still serves as the major recruiting agent for the carpenters' apprenticeship program in the Hispanic community.

Outside of the apprenticeship program, Mexican-American carpenters have faced special difficulties with the union. The large majority of Mexican-Americans had come into the Chicago area as pieceworkers installing drywall in the freewheeling home-building market. Many of these so-called "rockers" (as in Sheetrock or drywall) were nonunion men; many others joined the union, and received union scale, but were forced to kick back part of their pay to the contractors for the "privilege" of working. Though formal members of the union, the Mexican drywallers lacked the language skills and the self-confidence that comes from being skilled to demand that the union enforce their grievances. In the early 1980s the Mexican Drywallers Association, an ad hoc group of one hundred and fifty to two hundred "rockers" organized by Luis Muñoz, sued the union and individual contractors for nonenforcement of contract provisions. They were particularly concerned about being forced by contractors to buy tools, beyond those required by the contract, such as screwguns, extension cords, ladders, and stilts. What the drywallers really wanted was full integration into the union, including into its steward selection system in which they felt they were underrepresented. The matter of integration is still a festering problem in the union.[24]

The goal of increasing the participation of women in the carpenters' union is relatively new. Though early federal affirmative action goals included women, few applied to the union's apprenticeship program and even fewer completed it. Women's issues were first raised in 1974 by Toni Hayes, a black woman cabinetmaker, who had entered the apprenticeship program through the Urban League's Project Leap. Hayes and fifteen other women, out of an applicant pool of five hundred, felt that to require high school shop courses as a condition of entrance discriminated against female students who had been advised in high school to take home economics courses. Led by Hayes, the women wrote a position paper that served as the basis of a successful class-action suit filed with the Equal Employment Opportunity Commission and that asked that home economics courses be accepted as an entrance criterion. Hayes was admitted to the apprenticeship program and graduated in 1979, finding a job at Woodwork Corporation of America. During the three-month 1985 millworkers' strike she served as union steward and helped organize picketing.

Afterwards, she formed a caucus within the union, called the "Chicago Women Carpenters." Initially a support group for women carpenters to discuss their particular problems on the job, the caucus expanded its activities to include lobbying with the union leadership to have women included in its outreach programs. In the course of that dialogue, the women confronted and argued with the widespread idea that women were not interested in carpentry. Ultimately, with the cooperation of Dardar, Hayes developed a video cassette on women carpenters to encourage women to enter the carpenters' apprenticeship program. Thereafter, the caucus developed into a broader group that covers all construction trades. A strong trade unionist, Hayes is an active member of the Chicago chapter of Coalition of Labor Union Women (CLUW).[25]

Though changes within the union itself have been less remarkable than those in the apprenticeship program, they are also reflective of the growing commitment to racial equality. One local that has partially made this transition is Local 13. Originally an old Knights of Labor local with a plurality of Irish members, it continues to be dominated by its Irish faction led by its president Mike Sexton, Jr., son of the District Council president (1941–51), and its business agent Tom Ryan. To expand its membership and maintain its influence within the District Council, the local has aggressively signed up black, Hispanic, and women members and processed their job grievances. One local official even took college courses in Spanish so that he could better communicate with his Hispanic members. Local 13 was also the first District Council local to have a woman steward. It seems no coincidence that apprenticeship coordinator Duffy Dardar, whose commitment to opening up the union stems in part from his interest in the Catholic Church's social justice movement, also hails from Local 13.[26]

In the 1980s the affirmative action thrust of the union has been blunted. The two presidential terms of Ronald Reagan with their cutbacks of federal funding of social programs such as CETA and his promotion of an antiunion and antiminority public environment have taken their toll. Thus, the 18th Street Development Corporation endured funding cutbacks and the appointment of a new antiunion coordinator who has broken his ties with the carpenters. Meanwhile, the end of the building boom Chicago had enjoyed through most of the postwar period has made it far more difficult for graduate apprentices, many of whom are minorities or women, to find steady work and thereby consolidate their positions within the union. Indeed, the steady rise and persistence of unemployment and underemployment in the local construction industry in the 1980s has been the single greatest factor in the inability of minorities to make greater inroads into the trade.

Finally, the union has been affected by the flaring racial tensions associated with the election of Chicago's first black mayor, Harold Washington. In 1987 the Chicago Board of Education, led by Washington appointees, responded to a suit charging it with discrimination, by demanding that the few remaining unions operating apprenticeship programs at Washburne accept affirmative action goals of 40 percent for blacks, 20 percent for women and 14 percent for Hispanics. The carpenters replied that their program covered a ten-county area, not just Chicago, and that the Department of Labor's 23 percent figure more adequately reflected the demographics of that broader area. The Board also demanded that Board shop teachers be employed in place of teachers approved by the joint apprenticeship committee in order to integrate the program. After months of deadlock the carpenters pulled out of Washburne and in September 1987 moved their trade school to suburban Elk Grove Village. The pullout was a great setback to the goal of forging ties to Chicago's minority communities, and it also raised the prospect that the Board would continue to operate its trade school but under nonunion auspices. Though the union continues to adhere to Department of Labor guidelines, the stance it will take on these issues in the future is in doubt.[27]

The approach of the carpenters' union to the participation of minorities and women will be a critical gauge of the union's future viability. The emerging social and political power of self-conscious disadvantaged groups in Chicago can either be allied with that of the union—and in the course of that alliance transform the union—or be used by antiunion forces to undermine the power of the union, including its past accomplishments. More than most unions, the carpenters have been in the past a microcosm of the city's ethnic working class. This was one key to its success and its leadership of Chicago's labor movement through the early twentieth century. In the preservation and expansion of the union's open door policy lies much of the hope of the union for progressive leadership in the labor movement and in the city.

Conclusion

Over one hundred years after the establishment of the Brotherhood, and one hundred and twenty-four years since the formation of the first carpenters' protective union during the Civil War, the Chicago carpenters' union is in many ways barely recognizable. The early union was a fragile, temporary, makeshift operation that could enroll thousands of members in a few weeks and then lose them all when a strike failed or when work became scarce. Today's carpenters' District Council boasts an extensive, full-time administration and the loyalty of the vast majority of its members. The basic reason for the formation of the early union—the elimination of piecework—has been substantially achieved, though it remains an ever-present threat. The journeyman carpenter is a highly paid, highly respected craftsman and no major contractor in the city or its environs dares to challenge the union's power head-on within the trade.

But to achieve these advances the carpenters have paid substantial costs. While the union continues to uphold as one of its primary goals the integrity of carpenter craftsmanship, throughout this century it has acquiesced in the replacement of its traditional material, wood, and traditional wood craftsmanship, with new materials and skills. In return, it has gained a vast extension of its jurisdiction. Carpentry still requires a considerable degree of intelligence, skill, and experience, but the term has come to encompass areas of work that last century's carpenters would never have dreamed of claiming: the setting of concrete forms and the installation of interior systems, not to mention the union's various specialty skills.

Some changes in the union have mirrored developments in the American labor movement as a whole. In the late nineteenth century, union carpenters believed that they were part of a movement that was destined to remake the world, not merely to fight for better wages, conditions, and defend jurisdiction. Commitment to the union and to the labor "cause" was a deep, lifelong affair for union activists. In those early days carpenters wanted to replace the "middleman" contractor with union-run cooperatives—a goal that imbued unionism with purpose and vision. In the twentieth century this world view has gradually disappeared. Modern unionists have no ambition to rival the private contractor except as individuals. Since the early 1920s the union has also ceased to back independent labor politics and radical challenges to the city's local establishment. Within the Chicago labor movement the carpenters are known today as a conservative union, a far cry from the carpenters of the 1880s, 1890s, and the second decade of the twentieth century.

Yet some things remain the same. Despite all the technological and business-related developments in the trade that have contributed to the decline in skill and the rise of semiskilled specialty areas of work, about a quarter of all union men in the Chicago area remain highly skilled general carpenters—about the same percentage as in the late nineteenth century. These men maintain a high level of craftsmanship within the trade and continue to be the backbone of the union, a persistent hedge against the tendency of carpentry to degenerate into a semiskilled occupation.

Like their brothers of yesteryear, contemporary carpenters must still search the metropolitan area several times a year for work, and they are subject to summary dismissal by their employers if they cannot meet minimum skill requirements or when there is no work. Carpenters still buy their own tools, and they still take pride in their craft and completed product. Among unionists, carpenters still stand out for their qualities of personal independence and stubborn combativeness when pushed on an issue of union principle. As the 1972 strike demonstrated, most rank and file carpenters remain loyal to one another in a pinch and can defeat their adversaries in an extended conflict. As the union enters what seems to be a new period of stagnation in construction activity, antiunion drives, and intensified industrial conflict, members, activists, and leaders alike can take pride and renewed confidence in a history replete with utopian vision, discipline and practical organization, recuperation and triumph following defeat, and most important of all, a legacy of union brotherhood.

Appendixes
Notes
Index

Appendix I

Development of the Chicago District Council of Carpenters, 1863–1888

1863–1870	C & J Protective Union	
1872–1873	C & J Consolidated Union	
1879–1880	C & J Union[1]	
1880–1881[2]	C & J Benevolent Association ("Benevolents")	C & J Protective and Benevolent Association ("Protectives")
1881–1882	Local 3	Local 4—Local 4 (rump union)[3]

1882–1885   Local 21 (twelve ethnic branches)
1, 2, 4, 6, 9, 11 English-speaking; 3, 7, 10, 12 German; 5 Bohemian; 8 Scandinavian

1885–1886   Local 21 (consolidated into three branches)[4]
1 and 2 English-speaking; 3 French-Canadian

1886–1887   Branch system replaced by multiple locals chartered by Brotherhood[5]
Locals 1 (formerly Local 21, Branch 1), 10, 21 (formerly French-Canadian Branch 3), 23, 28 (formerly Local 21, Branch 2), 54 (formerly independent Bohemian Carpenters Union), 71, 88, 162 Hyde Park, 181, 199 South Chicago, 240–44 (formerly five branches of German-speaking International Society of Carpenters), 256 (formerly independent Bohemian Carpenters Union), 284, 291, and 430 (formerly independent Bohemian Carpenters Union)

1888   Chicago District Council of Carpenters organized

1. In 1880, the C & J Union split into two rival organizations—the so-called "Benevolent" Association and the "Protective" Association.

2. The "Benevolent" Association and the "Protective" Association co-hosted the first national convention ofthe United Brotherhood of Carpenters and Joiners in August 1881, receiving UBC Charters 3 and 4, respectively.

3. This rump organization bolted from the main body of Local 4, when it merged with its rival, Local 3, as a result of pressure from the national office. Local 4 was denied a separate charter at the Brotherhood's national convention in 1882. Consequently, it was reported in *The Carpenter* that its members affiliated with the Knights of Labor.

4. Following a disasterous strike in 1884, most of the German and Bohemian carpenters seceded from Local 21 to form the German-speaking International Society of Carpenters and the Bohemian Carpenters Union respectively. In 1887, these German and Bohemian carpenter unions reaffiliated with the UBC, each receiving a separate charter. The remaining branches consolidated into three branches under Local 21's charter.

5. In order to restore unity in Chicago, the UBC abandoned the Branch system in 1886 and encouraged the various ethnic and political factions to join the Brotherhood by issuing separate charters in the city.

Appendix 2

Consolidation of Chicago Carpenters' Unions under the Chicago District Council, 1887–1914

1886	United Carpenters Committee
	   20 United Brotherhood of Carpenters and
	      Joiners locals
	    3 Amalgamated Society of Carpenters branches

1887–1894[1]	United Carpenters' Council Chicago District Council of Carpenters Knights of Labor Amalgamated Society of Carpenters Progressive Carpenters and Joiners Stairbuilders Union Independent Carpenters Union Carpenters and Joiners Progressive Association
July 1894	United Carpenters' Council adjourned *sine die*[2]
1895–1914	Carpenters Executive Council Chicago District Council of Carpenters Knights of Labor[3] Amalgamated Society of Carpenters[4]

1. In order to coordinate their strike for the eight-hour day, a United Carpenters Committee was organized in 1886. This informal committee became a permanent organization as the United Carpenters Council in 1888. Other independent organizations subsequently joined it.

2. By July 1894, only three Knights of Labor assemblies and three branches of the Amalgamated Society remained. All of the other locals affiliated with the Brotherhood.

3. The last remaining Knights of Labor Assembly in Chicago, Local Assembly 6570, joined the UBC in 1896 as Local 13.

4. The Carpenters Executive Council was dissolved in 1914, when the Amalgamated Society of Carpenters merged with the UBC.

Appendix 3

Chicago Carpenter Hourly Wages, 1870–1987

1870	$2.12*	1903	.45
1871	2.6125	1904	.50
1872	2.5825	1905	.50
1873	2.2725	1906	.50
1874	1.9475	1907	.50
1875	1.965	1908	.5625
1876	1.91	1909	.60
1877	2.1075	1910	.60
1878	2.11	1911	.60
1879	2.2325	1912	.65
1880	2.20	1913	.65
1881	2.375	1914	.65
1882	2.315	1915	.70
1883	2.3275	1916	.70
1884	2.3975	1917	.70
1885	2.3575	1918	.80
1886	2.4425	1919	1.00
1887	2.48	1920	1.00
1888	2.475	1921	1.25
1889	2.32	1922	1.00
1890	.35†	1923	1.15
1891	.35	1924	1.25
1892	.35	1925	1.375
1893	.35	1926	1.50
1894	.35	1927	1.50
1895	.35	1928	1.50
1896	.35	1929	1.5625
1897	.35	1930	1.625
1898	.375	1931	1.625
1899	.425	1932	1.3125
1900	.425‡	1933	1.3125
1901	.425	1934	1.3125
1902	.45	1935	1.3125

Appendix 3 (cont.)

1936	1.50	1944	1.70
1937	1.625	1945	1.775
1938	1.625	1946	1.95
1939	1.625	1947	2.15
1940	1.625	1948	2.35
1941	1.625	1949	2.45
1942	1.70	1950	2.55
1943	1.70	1951	2.7011

	Wage[1]	Welfare[2]	Pension[2]	Apprenticeship[2]	MCIA[3]
1952	$2.95§	$.05	$.00	$.00	
1953	3.05	.10	.00	.00	
1954	3.20	.10	.00	.00	
1955	3.275	.10	.00	.00	
1956	3.35	.10	.00	.00	
1957	˙3.45	.10	.10	.00	
1958	3.65	.10	.10	.00	
1959	3.75	.10	.10	.00	
1960	3.91	.10	.10	.00	
1961	4.08	.10	.10	.00	
1962	4.23	.15	.15	.00	
1963	4.43	.15	.15	.00	
1964	4.60	.15	.15	.00	
1965	4.85	.15	.15	.00	
1966	5.20	.15	.15	.01	
1967	5.45	.15	.25	.02	
1968	5.75	.15	.305	.02	
1969	6.05	.19	.335	.03	
1970	6.85	.25	.475	.07	
1971	7.65	.30	.625	.08	
06/72-12/72	8.30	.45	.625	.06	
01/73-05/73	8.65	.45	.625	.06	
06/73-05/74	9.15	.50	.63	.06	
06/74-05/75	9.65	.55	.63	.06	
06/75-11/75	10.15	.55	.73	.06	
12/75-05/76	10.15	.65	.83	.06	
06/76-05/77	10.55	.78	.88	.06	
06/77-05/78	11.00	.88	.98	.07	.01

Appendix 3 *(cont.)*

	Wage[1]	Welfare[2]	Pension[2]	Apprenticeship[2]	MCIA[3]
06/78-05/79	11.50	.98	1.08	.08	.01
06/79-05/80	12.70	1.08	1.08	.08	.01
06/80-05/81	14.00	1.23	1.08	.10	.01
06/81-08/81	15.40	1.38	1.08	.10	.02
09/81-11/81	15.40	1.43	1.08	.10	.02
12/81-03/82	15.50	1.43	1.08	.10	.02
04/82-05/82	15.50	1.43	1.08	.12	.02
06/82-05/83	16.50	2.18	1.08	.12	.02
06/83-12/83	16.50	2.48	1.08	.12	.02
01/84-08/84	16.50	2.58	1.08	.12	.02
09/84-05/85	16.75	2.58	1.08	.12	.02
06/85-08/85	17.00	2.58	1.08	.12	.02
09/85-05/86	17.00	2.43	1.23	.12	.02
06/86-05/87	18.00	1.93	1.23	.12	.02

*Average daily wages at ten hours a day; Source: U.S. Bureau of Labor Statistics, *History of Wages in the United States from Colonial Times to 1928* (Washington D.C.: Government Printing Office, 1928), p. 673.

†Beginning in 1890 the wage rate is the official union hourly rate at eight hours; Source: *History of Wages in the United States*, p. 165.

‡Source: Chicago and Cook County Building and Construction Trades Council.

§Figures as of June 1. Source: Chicago and Northeast Illinois District Council of Carpenters.

[1]Not including benefits.

[2]Contributed by employer.

[3]Midwest Construction Industry Advancement Fund. Contributed by employer.

Appendix 4

Compensation for Millmen, *1973–1987*

Rate	Welfare	Pension	Apprentice	Wage
06/73–05/74	$ .50	$ .00	$.06	$ 6.23
06/74–05/75	.55	.00	.06	6.58
06/75–05/76	.60	.25	.06	6.88
06/76–05/77	.60	.35	.06	7.28
06/77–11/77	.75	.35	.07	7.78
12/77–05/78	.75	.35	.07	7.93
06/78–11/78	.85	.40	.08	8.38
12/78–05/79	.85	.45	.08	8.49
06/79–11/79	.91	.50	.08	9.17
12/79–05/80	.91	.50	.08	9.25
06/80–05/81	1.01	.55	.10	10.43
06/81–05/82	1.20	.60	.10	10.53
06/82–05/83	1.66	.65	.12	11.28
06/83–05/84	1.96	.70	.12	11.73
06/84–11/84	1.96	.70	.12	12.33
12/84–05/85	1.96	.75	.12	12.43
06/85–11/85	1.96	.75	.12	13.08
12/85–05/86	1.96	.85	.12	13.08
06/86–11/86	1.96	.85	.12	13.78
12/86–05/87	1.96	1.00	.12	13.78

Appendix 5

United Carpenters Committee and
United Carpenters Council Presidents

United Carpenters Committee
1886   (April 1886–January, 1887)—J. B. Parks
                (Carpenters and Joiners Progressive Association).

United Carpenters Council
1887   (February–March)—T. Sterling.
1888   (January–June)—R. B. Hall (Local 28);
                (July)—H. F. Hogan (Local 141);
                (August–September)—Thomas Schulkins (KOL
                Assembly 10312);
                (October)—G. W. Blackford (Local 162);
                (November)—Charles Armstrong (Local 162);
                (December)—James Morahan (Local 1).
1889   (January–October)—Joseph Langlois (Local 21);
                (October–December)—Joseph Parks (Carpenters and
                Joiners Progressive Association).
1890   (January–March)—R. B. Hall (Local 28);
                (April–September)—James O'Connell (Local 1).
1890–1891   (October 1890–June 1891)—J. G. Ogden (KOL
                Assembly 9272).
1891–1892   (July 1891–June 1892)—Robert Swallow (Local 28).
1892–1893   (July 1892–July 1893)—J. B. Cogswell (Local 28).
1893–1894   O. E. Woodbury (Local 1).

Appendix 6

Presidents and Secretary-Treasurers of the Chicago and Northeast Illinois District Council of Carpenters

	Presidents		Secretary-Treasurers
1889*	James Brennock (Local 1, formerly KOL 6507); C. J. Johnson (Local 181).	1889	R. B. Hall (Local 28—now 10); W. S. Weeks (Local 28)
1890	John Bumb (Local 73, now 10); R.B. Hall (Local 28).	1890	W. S. Weeks (Local 28).
1891	J. E. Cogswell (Local 28).	1891	R. L. Hassell (Local 1).
1892	J. B. Cogswell (Local 28); R. B. Hall (Local 28).	1892	S. S. Baker (Local 162—now 10).
1893	R. B. Hall (Local 28); Robert McCulloch (Local 269).	1893	Fred Carr (Local 1).
1894	A. C. Cattermull (Local 28).	1894	H. M. McCormick (Local 1).
1895	O. E. Woodbury (Local 23—now 10).	1895	W. R. Bowes (Local 28).
1896	J. B. McKinlay (Local 62).	1896	Asa Hodgman (Local 141).
1897	Timothy Cruise (Local 1).	1897	H. M. McCormick (Local 1).
1898	Timothy Cruise (Local 1).	1898–1902	Thomas Neale (Local 1).
1899	O. E. Woodbury (Local 23).		
1900–1902	Timothy Cruise (Local 1).		
1903	A. W. Simpson (Local 13, formerly KOL 9272).	1903–1907	K. G. Torkelson (Local 181).

Appendix 6 *(cont.)*

Presidents	Secretary-Treasurers
1903–1905 James Kirby (Local 199).[1]	
1905–1917 John Metz (Local 10).	1907–1922 Daniel Galvin (Local 13).
1917–1922 William Brims (Local 80).	
1922–1927 Harry Jensen (Local 181).	1922–1948 Charles H. Sand (Local 58).
1927–1937 Thomas F. Flynn (Local 13).	
1937 Henry J. Mock (Local 242).	
1937–1941 John R. Stevenson (Local 80).[2]	
1941–1951 Michael J. Sexton (Local 13).	1948–1950 Stanley Johnson (Local 141).[3]
	1950–1951 Hjalmar Erickson (Local 62).
1951–1966 Ted Kenny (Local 1922).	1951–1973 Chas. A. Thompson (Local 58).
1966-Pres. George Vest, Jr. (Local 141).	1973–Pres. Wesley Isaacson (Local 58).

*District Council officers were elected to six-month terms from 1889 until 1913 when a one-year term was instituted. A three-year term was inaugurated in 1948; and a four-year term in 1957.

[1]Resigned to become president of the Structural Building Trades Alliance; he was later general president of the Brotherhood, 1912–1915.

[2]Resigned to become second vice president of the Brotherhood.

[3]Resigned to become secretary of the Illinois State Federation of Labor.

Appendix 7

Total Employed Construction Carpenters in Chicago

	Total Carpenters*	Number Unionized	Percentage Unionized
1870	6,210		
1880	6,712	1,000[a]	15
1890	20,082	6,000[b]	30
1900	17,717	5,230[c]	30
1910	24,048	11,000–14,000[d]	46–58
1920	24,404	18,000[e]	77
1930	27,927	26,000[f]	93
1940	10,480 (employed)	14,700[g]	100
1950	22,829		
1960	22,239		
1970	21,594		
1980	24,889		

*Note: Before 1950 the percent of unionized carpenters tends to be slightly overstated because the number of carpenters counted in the United States Census does not include those living in the Chicago suburbs. Since 1950, the United States Census figure counted all of the carpenters in the Chicago Standard Metropolitan Statistical Area (SMSA).

[a]*Chicago Tribune*, January 20, 1881, p. 8.

[b]*U.C.C. Proceedings* and *U.C.C. Roll Book of Delegates*, 1890.

[c]Ernest Bogart, "The Chicago Building Trades Dispute," in J. R. Commons, ed., *Trade Union Problems* (New York: Ginn & Co., 1921), p. 91.

[d]*The Carpenter* reported 11,000 members in May 1906 and the *Chicago Tribune* gave 14,000 on April 1, 1912, p. 3.

[e]Membership fluctuated between 18,000 and 21,000 from 1911-1921; see Royal E. Montgomery, *Industrial Relations in the Chicago Building Trades* (Chicago: University of Chicago Press, 1927), p. 169.

[f]This estimate is based on figures in the *Chicago District Council Proceedings*, December 1929.

[g]Approximate figures based on *Chicago District Council Proceedings* figures for March 1941.

Appendix 8

Locals of the Chicago and Northeast Illinois District Council of Carpenters

Information provided includes: Geographical Area, Ethnicity, Date Established, Membership (1891, 1925, 1981, and 1987), Special Comments (includes information on locals merged Jan. 1, 1984).

Local	Geographical Area (1987)	Ethnicity	Date Established	Membership	Special Comments
1	Loop and Near North Side	Formerly German and Scots	1887	1308(1891) 2114(1925) 1014(1981) 1309(1987)	Leading local in 1890s; prominent leaders: William Schardt, Dick Garnet.
10	Southeast	Formerly Irish; now Black/mixed	1895	1289(1925) 1084(1981) 1234(1987)	Always one of the leading locals.
13	Near North Side West Side	Irish	1896	1521(1987) 1616(1987)	A leading local headed by Tom Flynn; later by the Sexton family; close to Mayor Thompson and then to the Democrats.
21	West Side	French	1882	194(1891) 255(1925) 88(1981)	Formerly a branch of the original Local 21, which included all Chicago; merged into 199 (1984).

Appendix 8 *(cont.)*

Local	Geographical Area (1987)	Ethnicity	Date Established	Membership	Special Comments
54	West Side	Czech	1887	210(1981) 1068(1987)	Formerly anarchist in 1880s, always progressive, now included 419 and 643.
58	Far North Side	Swedish; now mixed	1896	2510(1981) 1306(1987)	One of the leading locals in Council and contributor of council secretaries.
62	South Side	Danish; Norw.; Dutch; now mixed	1889	227(1891) 2086(1925) 1142(1981) 1014(1987)	One of the most progressive and militant locals in early 20th century.
80	West Side West Suburbs	Scots, Irish/ mixed	1889	20(1891) 1724(1925) 1081(1981) 1083(1987)	Dominated by Scotsmen, including John R. Stevenson; one of leading locals.
141	South Side	Swedish; now mixed	1887	94(1891) 1137(1925) 882(1981) 815(1987)	The local of Stanley Johnson and George Vest, Jr.
174	Will County		1897	913(1987)	
181	Northwest Side	Scandinavian (Danish, Norwegian)	1886	280(1891) 2056(1925) 1399(1981) 1301(1987)	The leading left, opposition local throughout much of 20th century.
199	Far Southwest Side	Mixed	1888	116(1891) 701(1925) 445(1981) 647(1987)	Pile drivers; since 1984, includes 21, 70, 578.

Appendix 8 *(cont.)*

Local	Geographical Area (1987)	Ethnicity	Date Established	Membership	Special Comments
242	West Side	Polish/ German	1903	50(1891) 865(1925) 701(1981) 848(1987)	A leading local led by Henry J. Mock for many years; since 1984 includes *416.*
250	Lake County	Mixed	1892	92(1925) 58(1981) 1453(1987)	Since Jan. 1981 includes *448, 461, 1996.*
271	Far South Side (Now unassigned)		1907	140(1925)	Former Amalgamated Woodworkers local; then a millmen's local; merged into *1922* in 1969.
272	South Cook County	Italian; mixed.	1899	470(1925) 831(1981) 808(1987)	
341	Near North Side	Polish	1910	323(1925) 149(1981)	Millmens' local; former AWW; since 1984 merged into *1027.*
416	West Side	German; now mixed	1888	93(1891) 920(1925) 353(1981)	Includes several dozen city workers; since 1984 merged into *242.*
419	North Side	German	1888	474(1891) 313(1925)	Since 1984 merged into *54.*
434	South Cook County	Dutch	1890	67(1891) 1057(1925) 955(1981) 923(1987)	
448	Waukegan	Mixed		550(1925) 556(1981)	Since 1984 merged into *250.*

Appendix 8 *(cont.)*

Local	Geographical Area (1987)	Ethnicity	Date Established	Membership	Special Comments
461	Highland Park	Mixed	1900	266(1925) 343(1981) 215(1987)	Since 1984 merged into *250.*
504	West Side (now unassigned)	Jewish	1900	958(1925) 208(1981)	Led for eighty years by the Holzman family; one of the several leading progressive locals; since 1984 merged into *1539.*
558	North Du Page County	Mixed	1908	523(1981) 1044(1987)	Since 1984 includes *1527* and *2004.*
578	Downtown	Finnish	1917	272(1981)	Pile drivers; since 1984 merged into *199.*
643	Downtown	Mixed	1909	616(1925) 353(1981)	Originally the Ship Carpenters and Caulkers Union founded in 1860; member Knights of Labor; merged into *54* in 1984.
839	Northwest Cook County	Mixed	1924	229(1925) 1233(1981) 1663(1987)	Since 1984 includes *1196* and *2014.*
916	Kendall and Grundy counties		1901	567(1987)	
1027	Millwork		1984	2268(1987)	Includes *341, 1027, 1367, 1784, 1786, 1922.*

Appendix 8 *(cont.)*

Local	Geographical Area (1987)	Ethnicity	Date Established	Membership	Special Comments
1045			1967	228(1981)	Merged into 1539 in 1984.
1128	La Grange	Mixed	1910	409(1925) 394(1981)	
1196	Arlington Heights		1925	43(1925) 218(1982)	Merged into 839 since 1984.
1185	Metro Area	Mixed	1942	988(1981) 1015(1987)	Carpet and linoleum workers.
1307	North Cook County	Mixed	1906	687(1925) 543(1981) 1154(1987)	Shinglers, insulators, and siders.
1367	North Side	Swedish	1904	1291(1925) 392(1981)	Millmen; first president: Anton Johannsen; merged into 1027 since 1984.
1527	Du Page		1903	323(1981)	Merged into 558 since 1984.
1539	North Shore	Czech/Jewish	1935	426(1981) 865(1987)	Floor resurfacers, now includes 2094.
1693	Downtown	Mixed	1910	389(1985) 836(1981) 784(1987)	Millwrights
1784	North Side	German	1906	759(1925) 617(1981)	Millmen; formerly the International Furniture Workers Union (1872); then the AWW (1895); leading progressive millmen's local; merged into 1027 in 1984.

Appendix 8 *(cont.)*

Local	Geographical Area (1987)	Ethnicity	Date Established	Membership	Special Comments
1889	South Du Page County	Mixed	1912	877(1981)	Now includes 1128.
1922	South Side	Mixed	1907	855(1925) 713(1981)	Millmen; the local of Ted Kenny and Charles Svec; merged into 1027 in 1984.
1954	Brookfield		1943	288(1981) 202(1987)	Plant Maintenance Workers.
1996	Libertyville		1928	425(1981)	Merged into 250.
2004	Itasca		1927	115(1981)	
2014	Barrington		1937	320(1981)	
2087			1937	346(1987)	
2094	Metro Area		1937	320(1981)	Merged into 1307.
3025			1954	29(1981)	
74L			1901	361(1981) 357(1987)	Lathers, joined United Brotherhood of Carpenters in 1979.

Notes

Chapter 1
The Beginnings of Carpenters' Unionism, 1863–1877

1. Taken from testimony before the United States Industrial Commission. See *Report of the United States Industrial Commission*, 19 Vols. (Washington D.C.: Government Printing Office, 1901), 8:465.

2. Ibid.

3. *The Carpenter*, Sept. 19░░, p. 10; James Brennock, "History of the Chicago District Council of Carpe░░░░ (1902 manuscript in possession of the Chicago and Northeast Illinoi░ ░░t Council of the United Brotherhood of Carpenters and Joiners of Ame░░░░seph Buchanan, *The Story of a Labor Agitator* (New York: Outlook C░░░░), p. 351.

4. Robert Christie, *Em░░░░ Wood: A History of the Carpenters Union* (Ithaca, N.Y.: Cornell ░░░░ess, 1956), pp. 19–20; Bob Reckman, "Carpentry: The Craft and Tra░░░░Case Studies on the Labor Process*, ed. Andrew Zimbalist (New Yor░░░░ly Review Press, 1979), pp. 78–80.

5. Christie, *Empire i░░░░1, pp. 20–21; Reckman, "Carpentry," pp. 82–85.

6. *Industrial Chicago*, 6 Vols. (Chicago: Goodspeed Publishing Co., 1891–96), *The Building Interest*, 1:327–31, 702.

7. Harold Mayer and Richard C. Wade, *Chicago: Growth of a Metropolis* (Chicago: Lakeside Publishing Co., 1973), pp. 20, 22, 256; Reckman, "Carpentry," pp. 80–82.

8. James Brennock, "Twenty Years Ago and Now in the Carpenter Trade," *Worker's Magazine* in *Chicago Tribune*, Jan. 7, 1906, sec. 6.

9. *Industrial Chicago*, 2:357–65, 382, 383; United States Department of the Interior, Census Office, *Eighth United States Census, 1860, Manufactures of the United States* (Washington D.C.: Government Printing Office, 1865), pp. 86–87; *Ninth United States Census* vol. 8: *Wealth and Industries of the United States* (Washington D.C.: Government Printing Office, 1872), p. 649; *Tenth Census of the United States*, vol. 2, *Manufactures of the United States* (Washington, D.C.: Government Printing Office, 1883), pp. 392–93. The 1860 and 1870 figures are for Cook County. However, almost all of these factories were located in Chicago. In 1880 there were only three factories of this kind outside of Chicago.

10. For a general discussion of piecework, see Christie, *Empire in Wood*, pp. 25–29; for reports on piecework and subcontracting in this period, see United States Department of the Interior, United States Census Office, *Eighth*

United States Census, 1860, Manufactures   Jnited States, pp. 86–87;
The Carpenter, Jan. 1882, p. 4; Apr. 1883   ιy 1884, p. 3; Mar. 1886, p.
4; Fourth Biennial Report of the Illinois P   Labor Statistics (Springfield,
Ill.: H. W. Rokker Co., 1886), p. 157. (revalance of piecework in the
industrialization process in mid-nin   century America, see Sean Wilentz, Chants Democratic: New York (the Rise of the American Working
Class, 1788–1850 (New York: Macı   Co., 1984), pp. 108–44.

11. The Carpenter, June 188 , p. 3.

12. Ibid., July 1884, p. 3.

13. Second Biennial Report of the Illinois Bureau of Labor Statistics (Springfield, Ill.: H. W. Rokker Co., 1882), p. 2.

14. McGuire is quoted in the Chicago Daily Inter-Ocean, May 22, 1884, p. 6; Doran is quoted in the Progressive Age, Mar. 28, 1881, p. 4; for typical references to itinerant carpenters, see Chicago Tribune, May 9, 1872, p. 6; May 14, 1872, p. 7.

15. Third Biennial Report of the Illinois Bureau of Labor Statistics, (Springfield, Ill.: H. W. Rokker Co., 1884), p. 352; Fourth Biennial Report, pp. 244, 248, 336, 341.

16. United States Department of the Interior, Census Office, Tenth Census of the United States: 1880 vol. 1, Statistics of the Population (Washington D.C.: Government Printing Office, 1883), p. 870.

17. Bessie Louise Pierce, A History of Chicago, vol. 3, The Rise of the Modern City, 1871–1893 (Chicago: Univ. of Chicago Press, 1957), pp. 20–23.

18. P. H. McCarthy quoted in L. A. O'Donnell, "From Limerick to the Golden Gate: Odyssey of an Irish Carpenter," Studies (Ireland) (Spring-Summer 1979), pp. 76–91.

19. Progressive Age, Feb. 25, 1882, p. 5.

20. The Carpenter, June 1882; for other carpenter references to the ethic of solidarity, see Aug. 1882, p. 4; and Progressive Age, Feb. 11, 1882, p. 3.

21. The following model of the "simple protective union" is based on a study of the behavior of carpenter unions between 1872 and 1886. See especially Workingman's Advocate, Sept. 28, 1872, p. 3. This model also benefited from David Montgomery's discussion of trade unonism in this period in Beyond Equality: Labor and the Radical Republicans, 1862–1872 (New York: Alfred A. Knopf, Vintage Books, 1967), pp. 139–60.

22. The Carpenter, June 1882, p. 3.

23. Workingman's Advocate, Jan. 30, 1875, p. 2; on the producers' ethic, see Leon Fink, Workingmen's Democracy: The Knights of Labor and American Politics (Urbana: Univ. of Illinois Press, 1983), pp. 3–37; Wilentz, Chants Democratic, pp. 153–68.

24. Chicago Tribune, Jan. 25, 1875, p. 2.

25. The Carpenter, Mar. 1885, p. 3; Perry R. Duis and Glen E. Holt, "Little Boxes, Big Fortune," Chicago Magazine (Nov. 1977):114–18; Workingman's Advocate, Sept. 21, 1872, p. 3; Sept. 28, 1872, p. 3; The Carpenter, Oct. 1887, p. 4.

26. Bessie Louise Pierce, A History of Chicago, vol. 2, From Town to City, 1848–1871 (New York: Alfred A. Knopf, 1940), pp. 160, 166n71, 445;

Frank Duffy, *History of the United Brotherhood of Carpenters and Joiners of America* (Indianapolis: Union Printers, 1941), pt. 2, p. 87; *Illinois Staats Zeitung*, Jan. 28, 1861, p. 3; Feb. 10, 1862, p. 4.

27. *Illinois Staats Zeitung*, Mar. 7, 1863, p. 4 (translation by John B. Jentz); *Chicago Tribune*, Mar. 17, 1863, p. 4; *Illinois Staats Zeitung*, Mar. 15, 1864, p. 1; Mar. 22, 1864, p. 1; Mar. 31, 1864, p. 1.

28. *Chicago Tribune*, Mar. 7, 1863, p. 4.

29. Ibid., May 3, 1867, pp. 3, 4; May 4, 1867, pp. 3, 4.

30. Ibid., Jan. 9, 1867, p. 3; May 18, 1867, p. 4; Oct. 12, 1867, p. 2; Nov. 9, 1867, p. 3; Nov. 16, 1867, p. 2; Nov. 23, 1867, p. 2; Apr. 18, 1868, p. 4.

31. *Workingman's Advocate*, Apr. 17, 1869, p. 3.

32. Pierce, *History of Chicago*, 3:3-6; *Workingman's Advocate*, Apr. 11, 1871, p. 3; *Chicago Tribune*, May 8, 1872, p. 2.

33. *Chicago Tribune*, Jan. 16, 1872, p. 2; Jan. 17, 1872, p. 2; Jan. 18, 1872, p. 2; Feb. 11, 1872, p. 4; Feb. 13, 1872, p. 2.

34. *Workingman's Advocate*, Jan. 27, 1872, pp. 2, 3; Feb. 17, 1872, p. 3; Mar. 9, 1872, p. 3; *Chicago Tribune*, May 7, 1872, p. 2; May 8, 1872, p. 5; May 9, 1872, p. 6; May 14, 1872, p. 6.

35. *Chicago Tribune*, May 8, 1872, p. 2.

36. Ibid., May 4, 1872, p. 5.

37. *Workingman's Advocate*, Feb. 17, 1872, p. 6; Mar.13, 1872, p. 3; July 13, 1872, p. 3; Sept. 21, 1872, p. 2; Sept. 28, 1872, p. 2.

38. *Chicago Tribune*, Sept. 17, 1872, p. 6; Sept. 23, 1872, p. 6; Sept. 24, 1872, p. 6; Sept. 25, 1872, p. 6; Sept. 28, 1872, p. 6; *Workingman's Advocate*, Sept. 21, 1872, p. 3; Oct. 5, 1872, p. 3; July 5, 1873, p. 5.

39. *Workingman's Advocate*, July 4, 1868, p. 2; Sept. 28, 1872, p. 3; July 13, 1875, p. 7.

40. *Workingman's Advocate*, Sept. 28, 1872, p. 2; see also Mar. 30, 1872, p. 3; June 28, 1873, p. 3.

41. Alfred T. Andreas, *History of Chicago from the Earliest Period to the Present Time*, 3 vols. (Chicago: A. T. Andreas Co., 1886), 3:606-8; *Investigation by a Select Committee of the House of Representatives Relative to the Causes of the General Depression in Labor and Business; and as to Chinese Immigration* (Washington D.C.: Government Printing Office, 1879), 46th Cong., 2nd Sess., p. 104; *Chicago Tribune*, Sept. 5, 1876, p. 6.

42. *Workingman's Advocate*, Feb. 14, 1873, p. 3; Aug. 22 & 29, 1874, p. 3; July 17, 1875, p. 3; Jan. 8, 1876, p. 3.

43. On the Knights nationwide, see Norman J. Ware, *The Labor Movement in the United States, 1860-1895: A Study in Democracy* (New York: Random House, 1929), and Leon Fink, *Workingman's Democracy*; on Chicago Knights and their relation to the socialists, see Richard Schneirov, "The Knights of Labor in the Chicago Labor Movement and in Municipal Politics, 1877-1887" (Ph.d. diss., Northern Ill. Univ., 1984).

44. Richard Schneirov, "Chicago's Great Upheaval of 1877," *Chicago History* 9 (Winter 1980):3-17.

45. John P. Altgeld, *The Chicago Martyrs* (San Francisco: Free Press Society, 1899), pp. 147-48.

Chapter 2
Forging of the Modern Union,
1878–1891

1. The Carpenter, Mar. 1885, p. 5.

2. Chicago Tribune, July 13, 1878, p. 8; Nov. 17, 1879, p. 8; Frank Duffy, History of the United Brotherhood of Carpenters (Indianapolis: Union Printers, 1941), pp. 97, 98.

3. Chicago Tribune, Sept. 12, 1879, p. 8; Sept. 13, 1879, p. 8; Progressive Age, July 9, 1881, p. 4; The Carpenter, June 1883, p. 6; Duffy, History of the United Brotherhood, p. 98.

4. Progressive Age, July 9, 1881, p. 4; Proceedings of the First Annual Convention of the Brotherhood of Carpenters and Joiners of America, Chicago, Ill., Aug. 8–12, 1881, pp. 8, 9; The Carpenter, June 1882, p. 3; Chicago Tribune, Apr. 17, 1882, p. 8.

5. Robert Christie, Empire in Wood: A History of the Carpenters' Union (Ithaca, N.Y.: Cornell Univ. Press, 1956), pp. 23–25; 38–43; Duffy, History of the United Brotherhood, pp. 113–16.

6. Chicago Tribune, Sept. 11, 1882, p. 8; The Carpenter, May 1882, p. 5; June 1882, pp. 1, 13.

7. Progressive Age, Oct. 23, 1881, p. 4.

8. Chicago Tribune, Sept. 11, 1882, p. 8; Progressive Age, Feb. 25, 1882, p. 4.

9. The Carpenter, June 1883, p. 4; May 1884, p. 4.

10. Chicago Tribune, May 5, 1884, p. 5; May 10, 1884, p. 6; The Carpenter, June 1884, p. 1; Sept. 1884, p. 5; Oct. 1884, p. 5; Feb. 1885, p. 8.

11. Proceedings of the Fourth Annual Convention of the Brotherhood of Carpenters and Joiners of America, Cincinnati, Ohio, Aug. 5–9, 1884 (Cincinnati: Unionist Printing, 1884), p. 11; "History of Local 54," translated from the minutes by H. Hydra (manuscript in the possession of Local 54), pp. 7–10; The Carpenter, Feb. 1885, p. 8; July 1885, p. 1.

12. For a social history of the anarchists, see Bruce Nelson, "Culture and Conspiracy: A Social History of Chicago Anarchism, 1870–1900" (Ph.D. diss., Northern Ill. Univ., 1985). For general histories of the Chicago anarchists, see also Henry David, The History of the Haymarket Affair, 3rd rev. ed. (New York: Crowell-Collier Books, 1963); Paul Avrich, The Haymarket Tragedy (Princeton: Princeton Univ. Press, 1984); Haymarket Scrapbook, ed. Dave Roediger & Franklin Rosemont (Chicago: Charles H. Kerr Publishing Co., 1986).

13. The Carpenter, Mar. 1885, p. 3; Dec. 1885, p. 5; Chicago Tribune, Nov. 16, 1885, p. 8; Nov. 18, 1885, p. 8; Nov. 23, 1885, p. 8.

14. The Carpenter, June 1882, p. 3; Sept. 1882, p. 8; for testimony of James Brennock, see United States Industrial Commission, Report of the United States Industrial Commission (Washington D.C.: Government Printing Office, 1901) 19 vols., 8:469; James Brennock, "History of the Chicago District Council of Carpenters," (1902 manuscript in the possession of the Chicago District Council of Carpenters), p. 2.

15. Based on our reading of The Carpenter from 1881 through 1890,

there is a decline in complaints about piecework after 1886; see also Christie, *Empire in Wood*, p. 65.

16. On the use of scabs and boycotts in this period in Chicago, see Richard Schneirov, "The Knights of Labor in the Chicago Labor Movement and in Municipal Politics, 1877–1887" (Ph.D. diss., Northern Ill. Univ., 1984), pp. 146–269; for New York, see David M. Gordon, "The Labor Boycott in New York City, 1880–1886," *Labor History* 16 (Spring 1975):185–229; on the street-car strike, see *Chicago Tribune*, July 4, 1885, pp. 1, 2.

17. *Chicago Tribune*, Apr. 7, 1881, p. 6.

18. Ibid., July 7, 1879, p. 8.

19. On the role of the Knights in the eight-hour strikes, see Richard Schneirov, "The Knights of Labor in Chicago," pp. 404–82; *Report of the United States Industrial Commission*, 8:465, 469; Brennock, "History of the Chicago Carpenters," p. 2.

20. *The Knights of Labor*, Mar. 1886, p. 2.

21. *Report of the United States Industrial Commission*, 8:465.

22. Sample was taken from the *Progressive Age*, 1881–82, and checked against the United Carpenters Council, *Roll Book of Delegates, 1888–1892*.

23. United Labor Party, "Executive Committee Minutes, September 25, 1886," Reel 7, T. J. Morgan Papers, Illinois Historical Survey, Univ. of Illinois, Urbana.

24. For important references to the triumvirate see *The Knights of Labor*, Feb. 12, 1887, p. 3; *Chicago Tribune*, Apr. 4, 1887, p. 5; May 1, 1887, p. 3; Apr. 11, 1891, p. 4; *Labor Enquirer*, Oct. 22, 1887, p. 1; Joseph R. Buchanan, *Story of a Labor Agitator* (New York: Outlook Co., 1903), p. 351; *Report of the United States Industrial Commission*, 8:467.

25. *Chicago Daily Inter-Ocean*, Apr. 15, 1886; *Chicago Tribune*, Apr. 24, 1886, p. 10.

26. For accounts of the Haymarket events, see note 12 above.

27. Abraham Bisno, *Abraham Bisno, Union Pioneer* (Madison: Univ. of Wisconsin Press, 1967), pp. 80, 81.

28. *The Knights of Labor*, June 19, 1886, p. 4; *Chicago Tribune*, July 16, 1884, p. 6; Apr. 30, 1886, p. 2; "History of Local 1784," (manuscript in possession of Local 1784).

29. On Jackson, see *Chicago Tribune*, Oct. 1, 1886, p. 3; Dec. 22, 1886, p. 3; Sept. 18, 1915; *Saturday Evening Post*, June 1, 1907; articles on Jackson for the last two dates courtesy of Donald Smith, Univ. of Calgary, Alberta, Canada; see also his article "William Henry Jackson: Riel's Disciple," in *Pelletier-Lathlin Memorial Lecture Series. Brandon University, 1979–1980*, ed. A. S. Lussier (Brandon, Manitoba: Department of Native Studies, 1980).

30. The quote is from an unidentified carpenter cited in Luke Grant, *The National Erectors' Association and the International Assosociation of Bridge and Structural Ironworkers* (Washington D.C.: Government Printing Office, 1915), p. 118; based on the similarity of the descriptions in this quote and the accounts cited in note 29 above, we have concluded that Grant was quoting Jackson.

31. Though the various carpenters' unions never acknowledged defeat

in 1886, the carpenters' 1887 demands indicate that eight hours was at best partially established.

32. *The Carpenter*, Mar. 1887, p. 7; "History of Local 54," pp. 16–18; on the relation between the free thought community, the labor movement, and socialism, see Richard Schneirov, "Free Thought and Socialism in the Czech Community in Chicago, 1875–1887," in Dirk Hoerder, ed., *Struggle a Hard Battle: Essays on Working-Class Immigrants* (De Kalb: Northern Ill. Univ. Press, 1986).

33. *The Knights of Labor*, Dec. 30, 1886, p. 6; *Chicago Daily Inter-Ocean*, Dec. 5, 1886, p. 5; *Chicago Tribune*, Oct. 26, 1886, p. 8; untitled newspaper article Dec. 2, 1886, Reel 6, T. J. Morgan Papers, Illinois Historical Survey.

34. United Carpenters Council, *Minute Book*, Jan. 28, 1887; May 6, 1887; June 3, 1887; Buchanan, *Labor Agitator*, p. 351.

35. *Chicago Tribune*, Apr. 2, 1887, p. 1; Apr. 4, 1887, p. 1; Apr. 12, 1887, p. 3; Buchanan, *Labor Agitator*, pp. 352–54.

36. *Chicago Tribune*, Apr. 13, 1887, p. 3; Apr. 14, 1887, p. 3; Apr. 20, 1887, p. 3; *The Knights of Labor*, Apr. 16, 1887, p. 9.

37. *Chicago Tribune*, May 13, 1887, p. 1; May 16, 1887, p. 1; May 17, 1887, p. 1; May 27, 1887, p. 9; *The Knights of Labor*, May 14, 1887, pp. 1, 8; for quote, see May 16, 1887, p. 1; for a general account, see James Beeks, *30,000 Locked Out: The Great Strike of the Building Trades in Chicago* (Chicago: F. Gindele Publishing Co., 1887).

38. *Chicago Tribune*, May 13, 1887, p. 1; May 27, 1887, p. 9; June 14, 1887, p. 6; June 22, 1887, p. 8; June 23, 1887, p. 3.

39. For quotes, see *Chicago Tribune*, July 9, 1887, p. 1, and Aug. 3, 1887, p. 2; see also July 23, 1887, p. 3; Aug. 3, 1887, p. 8; Aug. 7, 1887, p. 13; Sept. 29, 1887, p. 1.

40. Ibid., Sept. 7, 1887, p. 1; Sept. 8, 1887, p. 3; in 1886, 800 carpenters marched in the Labor Day parade, see Sept. 6, 1887, p. 2.

41. *Report of the United States Industrial Commission*, 8:469; for McGuire's statements on the Knights, see *The Carpenter*, Mar. 1886, p. 4; Nov. 1887, p. 4; *Chicago Tribune*, Nov. 21, 1886, p. 6.

42. *Report of the United States Industrial Commission*, 8:469; *Proceedings of the General Assembly of the Knights of Labor of America Eleventh Regular Session held at Minneapolis, Minnesota, October 4 to 9, 1887*, p. 1423, Reel 67, Terence V. Powderly–John W. Hayes Papers, Catholic University, Washington D.C. (microfilm, Northern Illinois Univ. Library).

43. *Proceedings of the Minneapolis General Assembly of the Knights of Labor, 1887*, p. 1423; Chicago Trade and Labor Assembly, *Ledger Book, 1887*, Chicago Historical Society, Chicago, Ill.; *The Carpenter*, June 1887, p. 4; *Chicago Tribune*, Dec. 14, 1887, p. 7.

44. United Carpenters Council, *Minute Book*, Feb. 14, 24, 1887; June 1, 15, 1887; *The Carpenter*, Mar. 1888, p. 4; *Chicago Tribune*, Apr. 15, 1889; Brennock, "History of the Carpenters," p. 4.

45. United Labor Party, *Delegate List Book*, p. 4, Reel 7, T. J. Morgan Papers, Illinois Historical Survey; Chicago Trade and Labor Assembly, *Ledger Book, Delegates, 1887–1889*, Chicago Historical Society; United Carpenters

Council, *Minute Book, 1887–1889*, passim; *The Carpenter*, Feb. 1887, p. 4; Apr. 1887, p. 4. With the major exception of July–December 1890, the delegates from Locals 1 and 28 comprised between 50 percent and 80 percent of the UCC's Executive Council between March 1888 and March 1891.

46. *Chicago Tribune*, Apr. 9, 1890, p. 3; on hourly payments, see Feb. 28, 1890, p. 3.

47. Ibid., Mar. 21, 1890, p. 3; Apr. 7, 1890, p. 1; for quote, see Apr. 8, 1890, p. 1.

48. Ibid., Apr. 15, 1890, p. 5.

49. Ibid., Aug. 23, 1890, p. 5.

50. Ibid., June 1, 1890, p. 6; June 7, 1890, p. 3; June 8, 1890, p. 9.

51. Ibid., Apr. 15, 1890, p. 5; Apr. 17, 1890, p. 1; Apr. 19, 1890, p. 2; Apr. 23, 1890, p. 3; Apr. 27, 1890, p. 2; May 8, 1890, p. 7; *The Carpenter*, July 1890, p. 4.

52. *Chicago Tribune*, May 4, 1890, p. 1; July 31, 1890, p. 3; see especially Aug. 17, 1890, p. 3.

53. Ibid., Aug. 3, 1890, 1890, p. 4; Aug. 10, 1890, p. 6; Aug. 17, 1890, p. 3; Sept. 4, 1890, p. 1; Sept. 10, 1890, p. 3; *The Carpenter*, Sept. 1890, p. 4.

54. Figures derived from *Third Annual Report of the United States Commissioner of Labor, 1887. Strikes and Lockouts* (Washington, D.C.: Government Printing Office, 1888), pp. 112–70, and *Tenth Annual Report of the United States Commissioner of Labor, 1894. Strikes and Lockouts* (Washington: Government Printing Office, 1896), pp. 163–250. We would like to thank Steven Sapolsky for pointing out the relevance of this source to us.

55. *Chicago Tribune*, Mar. 6, 1891, p. 2; Mar. 7, 1891, p. 2; Mar. 9, 1891, p. 2; Mar. 22, 1891, p. 4; Brennock, "History of the Chicago Carpenters," pp. 5–13.

56. McGuire quoted in Walter Galenson, *The United Brotherhood of Carpenters: The First Hundred Years* (Cambridge: Harvard Univ. Press, 1983), p. 387.

57. Residences and occupations checked in *Lakeside Annual Directory of the City of Chicago* (various Chicago publishers), 1881–94.

58. On the role of the Knights in popularizing sympathy strikes, see Fred Hall, *Sympathetic Strikes and Sympathetic Lockouts* (New York: Columbia Univ. Press, 1898), pp. 19, 33, 87; *Knights of Labor*, Apr. 16, 1887, p. 13. It should be noted that the Knights attempted to form the first unified council of building trades run by walking delegates, *Chicago Tribune*, Jan. 5, 1887, p. 6.

59. *Daily Labor Bulletin*, May 26, 1905, p. 3, John Fitzpatrick Papers, Chicago Historical Society. We would like to thank Steven Sapolsky for bringing this quote to our attention.

Chapter 3
Moderates and Radicals: The Struggle for Control, 1891–1901

1. Testimony published in United States Industrial Commission, *Report of the United States Industrial Commission* (Washington D.C.: Government Printing Office, 1901) 19 vols., 8:467.

2. Charles B. Spahr, *America's Working People* (New York: Longmans, Green and Co., 1900), p. 190.

3. *The Carpenter*, Oct. 1893, p. 8.

4. On Brennock see *Report of the United States Industrial Commission*, 8:469; on Woodbury, see The Sunset Club, *Yearbook, 1899–1901* (Chicago: Sunset Club, 1901), p. 58.

5. Gompers quoted in Alan Trachtenberg, *The Incorporation of America: Culture and Society in the Gilded Age* (New York: Hill and Wang, 1982), p. 95. Support for the interpretation that the pure and simple unionism of Gompers and other labor leaders was compatible with the goal of cooperative commonwealth is found in Stuart Bruce Kaufman, *Samuel Gompers and the Origins of the A.F. of L., 1848–1896* (Westport, Conn.: Greenwood Press, 1973), esp. ch. 6; William M. Dick, *Labor and Socialism in America: The Gompers Era* (Port Washington, N.Y.: Kennikat Press, 1972), esp. chs. 2 and 5; H. M. Gittleman, "Adolph Strasser and the Origin of Pure and Smple Unionism," *Labor History* 6 (Winter 1965):71–83.

6. United Carpenters Council, *Rollbook of Delegates*, Apr. 25, 1891; May 1, 2, 20, 1891; July 6, 11, 13, 1891; United Carpenters Council (hereafter UCC), *Proceedings*, May 18, 1893.

7. *Chicago Tribune*, Aug. 17, 1890, p. 3; Apr. 24, 1893, p. 2; *The Carpenter*, Jan. 1891, p. 5.

8. *Chicago Tribune*, Mar. 19, 1891, p. 1.

9. James Brennock, "History of the Chicago District Council of Carpenters," (1902 manuscript in possession of the Chicago District Council of Carpenters), p. 9; on the contractors' attitude toward the union, see *Chicago Tribune*, Mar. 11, 1891, p. 3; Mar. 13, 1891, p. 5; July 4, 1891, p. 4.

10. Brennock, "History of the District Council," pp. 5, 11; Royal E. Montgomery, *Industrial Relations in the Chicago Building Trades* (Chicago: Univ. of Chicago Press, 1927), p. 17; *The Carpenter*, Mar. 1896, p. 1; May 1897, p. 2; *Chicago Tribune*, Apr. 4, 1890, p. 3.

11. H. H. Bancroft, *Book of the Fair* (New York: Bounty Books, 1894), p. 332; beside Lyman Gage, the fair's Board of Directors included H. N. Higgenbotham, Thomas Palmer, Charles Yerkes, Thomas Bryan, and C. K. G. Billings, see *Chicago Tribune*, Apr. 9, 1891, p. 1.

12. *Chicago Tribune*, Mar. 9, 1891, p. 2; Apr. 9, 1891, p. 1.

13. Ibid., May 9, 1891, p. 1; July 4, 1891, p. 7.

14. Rossiter Johnson, ed., *A History of the World's Columbian Exposition* (New York: D. Appleton and Co., 1897), p. 153; *The Carpenter*, Feb. 1892, p. 1; *Chicago Tribune*, Apr. 20, 1891, p. 1; Apr. 22, 1891, p. 3; Apr. 24, 1891, p. 2; for an account of what it was like to work at the fair as a laborer, see Walter Wyckoff, *The Workers: An Experiment in Reality, The West* (New York: Charles Scribners & Sons, 1898), pp. 247–87.

15. UCC, *Proceedings*, June 4, 1891, July 9, 1891; *Chicago Tribune*, May 9, 1891, p. 1; May 14, 1891, p. 2; June 18, 1891, p. 1.

16. Quote is from UCC, *Proceedings*, June 30, 1892; see also Jan. 11, 1892, Jan. 28, 1892; Aug. 25, 1892; Nov. 17, 1892; Dec. 8, 1892; see also *The Carpenter*, Jan. 1892, p. 2.

17. For the text of Gompers' report on his visit to the fair, see *The*

Carpenter, Mar. 1892, p. 2; complaints directed at Gompers are to be found in the UCC, *Proceedings*, July 4, 1892, and *The Carpenter*, Feb. 1893, p. 2.

18. *Chicago Tribune*, Apr. 10, 1893, pp. 1, 2; H. N. Higgenbotham, *Report of the President to the Board of Directors of the World's Columbian Exposition* (Chicago: Rand McNally and Co., 1898), p. 36; Brennock, "History of the District Council," p. 11.

19. UCC, *Proceedings*, Feb. 23, 1893; Mar. 23, 1893.

20. *Chicago Tribune*, Apr. 4, 1893, p. 2; Apr. 5, 1893, p. 2; Apr. 10, 1893, pp. 1, 2; Apr. 11 1893, pp. 1, 2; Apr. 24, 1893, p. 2; UCC *Proceedings*, Apr. 13, 1893.

21. UCC, *Proceedings*, Apr. 13, 1893; *Chicago Tribune*, Apr. 14, 1893, p. 1; quote is from Apr. 24, 1893, p. 2; see also Apr. 25, 1893, p. 6.

22. For an insightful discussion of the White City on which we rely, see Trachtenberg, *The Incorporation of America*, pp. 208–34; quote is from Chester McArthur Destler, *American Radicalism, 1865–1901: Essays and Documents* (New London, Conn.: Conn. College, 1946), p. 177.

23. UCC, *Proceedings*, May 18, 25, 1893; June 22, 1893; *Chicago Tribune*, June 19, 1893, p. 2; Brennock, "History of the District Council," p. 11.

24. UCC, *Proceedings*, June 13, 15, 22, 1893; *Chicago Tribune*, June 19, 1893, p. 2; Brennock, "History of the District Council," pp. 11, 12; disenchantment with arbitration is expressed in *The Carpenter*, Dec. 1899, p. 3.

25. UCC, *Proceedings*, Aug. 31, 1893; Dec. 21, 28, 1893; the 6,000 membership figure is an estimate based on the following sources: Chicago District Council of Carpenters, *Proceedings*, Dec. 23, 1893; Mar. 23, 1894; UCC, *Proceedings*, Mar. 1, 1894; *The Carpenter*, July 1894, p. 8; for 1898 membership, see District Council, *Proceedings*, Mar. 29, 1898.

26. *Chicago Tribune*, Aug. 18, 1893, p. 1; Aug. 19, 1893, p. 1; Aug. 22, 1893, p. 1; Aug. 24, 1893, p. 1; Aug. 29, 1893, p. 5; Aug. 30, 1893, p. 2.

27. Ibid., Aug. 16, 1893, p. 3; Aug. 19, 1893, p. 1; Aug. 25, 1893, p. 1; Aug. 26, 1893, p. 1; Aug. 27, 1893, p. 1; Aug. 28, 1893, p. 1.

28. Ibid., Aug. 26, 1893, p. 1; Aug. 27, 1893, p. 1; Aug. 28, 1893, p. 1; Aug. 29, 1893, p. 1; Aug. 30, 1893, p. 1; Aug. 31, 1893, p. 1.

29. Ibid., Sept. 2, 1893, p. 2.

30. Ibid., Apr. 27, 1891, p. 9.

31. The quote and the comparison between the White City and Pullman is made in Trachtenberg, *The Incorporation of America*, p. 224.

32. A daily account of the Pullman strike is to be found in the *Chicago Tribune*, July 1–14, 1894. See also Altmont Lindsey, *The Pullman Strike* (Chicago: Univ. of Chicago Press, 1942); on the actions of McGuire and Gompers, see District Council, *Proceedings*, July 11, 1894, and *Chicago Tribune*, July 14, 1894, p. 1.

33. *Chicago Tribune*, July 5, 1894, pp. 5, 9; July 6, 1894, p. 12; Sept. 17, 1894, p. 7; UCC, *Proceedings*, July 27, 1893.

34. *Chicago Tribune*, Aug. 1, 1894, p. 3; Aug. 17, 1894, p. 1; Aug. 22, 1894, p. 1.

35. The best account of the rise and fall of the Cook County Peoples' party is in Destler, *American Radicalism*, pp. 162–211; quote is from *Chicago Tribune*, Aug. 18, 1894, p. 1.

36. *Chicago Tribune*, Aug. 19, 1894, p. 1; Aug. 22, 1894, p. 1; Aug. 25, 1894, p. 1; Sept. 17, 1894, p. 7.

37. Lloyd's speech is published in Destler, *American Radicalism*, pp. 212–21.

38. The political conflict between "free silver and collectivism" is discussed in Destler, *American Radicalism*, pp. 222–54.

39. UCC, *Proceedings*, Mar. 1, 1894; *The Carpenter*, July 1894, p. 8.

40. Quote is from *The Carpenter*, Feb. 1895, p. 9. See also District Council, *Proceedings*, Mar. 5, 1891; July 16, 1892; Oct. 1, 1892; Nov. 19, 1892; Dec. 3, 1892; United Brotherhood of Carpenters and Joiners of America, *Proceedings of the Seventh Biennial Convention held at St. Louis, August 1–8, 1892*, p. 52; UCC, *Proceedings*, Nov. 17, 1893.

41. Brennock, "History of the District Council," pp. 12–15; UCC, *Proceedings*, Dec. 1, 21, 1893; July 5, 1894; *The Carpenter*, July 1894, pp. 8, 9; Nov. 1894, p. 1; Feb. 1895, p. 1; Aug. 1895, p. 2; District Council, *Proceedings*, July 28, 1894; Nov. 10, 17, 1894; *Chicago Tribune*, Nov. 11, 1894, p. 1; Dec. 4, 1894, p. 6; Jan. 3, 1895, p. 8.

42. Ernest Bogart, "The Chicago Building Trades Dispute," in *Trade Unionism and Labor Problems*, ed. John R. Commons (New York: Ginn and Co., 1921), pp. 94, 95; District Council, *Proceedings*, Jan. 1896; Oct. 30, 1897; Mar. 1898; *The Carpenter*, Oct. 1897, p. 10; May 1897, p. 13; *Report of the United States Industrial Commission*, 8:457; *Chicago Tribune*, Jan. 7, 1900, p. 7.

43. On the limiting of production by union-contractor agreement, see Montgomery, *Industrial Relations in the Chicago Building Trades*, passim.; limitations of production are explored more generally in the *Report of the United States Industrial Commission*.

44. *Report of the United States Industrial Commission*, 8:458–59; Bogart, "The Chicago Building Trades Dispute," p. 97.

45. Architect quote is from *The Carpenter*, Dec. 1899, p. 3; Craig's statement is from "Memoirs," (typescript in possession of the Chicago Historical Society, n.d.).

46. First quote from Spahr, *America's Working People*, p. 178; Woodbury statement from Sunset Club, *Yearbook, 1899–1901*, p. 59.

47. *Report of the United States Industrial Commission*, 8:466; Sunset Club, *Yearbook, 1899–1901*, p. 60.

48. Quoted in Spahr, *America's Working People*, p. 177.

49. Woodbury quote from *Chicago Tribune*, Nov. 13, 1899, p. 1; Brennock, "History of the District Council," p. 18; District Council, *Proceedings*, July 17, 1897; *Report of the United States Industrial Commission*, 8:457.

50. *Chicago Tribune*, Nov. 11, 1899, pp. 1, 2.

51. Brennock, "History of the District Council," p. 18; *Chicago Tribune*, Apr. 7, 1898, p. 7; District Council, *Proceedings*, Mar. 29, 1898.

52. Craig, "Memoirs," pp. 3, 4; Spahr, *America's Working People*, p. 176.

53. Craig, "Memoirs," pp. 3, 4; Bogart, "The Chicago Building Trades Dispute," pp. 88–92.

54. *Report of the United States Industrial Commission*, 8:446.

55. *Chicago Tribune*, Nov. 7, 1899, p. 31; see also Nov. 10, 1899, pp. 1, 2; Craig, "Memoirs," pp. 4–8; Bogart, "The Chicago Building Trades Dispute," pp. 92–94.

56. *The Carpenter*, Dec. 1899, p. 13; see also S. V. Lindblom, "Analysis of the Building Trades Conflict in Chicago From the Trades-Union Standpoint," *Journal of Political Economy* 28 (June 1900):342.

57. Bogart, "The Chicago Building Trades Dispute," pp. 112, 113.

58. Montgomery, *Industrial Relations in the Building Trades*, pp. 80–84, 169, 170; Craig, "Memoirs," p. 50; interview of the authors with Stanley Johnson, carpenter leader.

59. Craig, "Memoirs," pp. 15, 16.

60. Ibid., pp. 21–25; *Chicago Tribune*, Dec. 2, 1899, p. 5; Dec. 3, 1899, p. 7; Dec. 7, 1899, p. 6; Dec. 11, 1899, p. 2; Bogart, "The Chicago Building Trades Dispute," pp. 99–101.

61. *Chicago Tribune*, Jan. 7, 1900, p. 7; Craig, "Memoirs," pp. 25, 26; Bogart, "The Chicago Building Trades Dispute," p. 101.

62. *The Carpenter*, Feb. 1900, p. 1; see also *Chicago Tribune*, Feb. 17, 1900, p. 4.

63. *Report of the United States Industrial Commission*, 8:CI–CVIII, 469, 534–39; *Chicago Tribune*, Feb. 24, 1900, p. 7; Mar. 1, 1900, p. 12; Mar. 17, 1900, p. 3; May 14, 1900, p. 2; May 18, 1900, p. 1; May. 21, 1900, p. 3; Bogart, "The Building Trades Dispute," pp. 117–19.

64. *Chicago Tribune*, Apr. 13, 1900, p. 1; Apr. 27, 1900, p. 1; Spahr, *America's Working People*, pp. 172, 173, 175.

65. *Chicago Tribune*, Mar. 10, 1900, p. 9; Apr. 20, 1900, p. 1; Apr. 27, 1900, p. 1; Apr. 29, 1900, p. 9; May 13, 1900, p. 6; May 15, 1900, p. 2; June 16, 1900, p. 1; Aug. 4, 1900, p. 3; Bogart, "The Chicago Building Trades Dispute," pp. 118–20.

66. *Chicago Tribune*, Aug. 10, 1900, p. 2; Aug. 12, 1900, p. 1; Aug. 22, 1900, p. 1; Aug. 24, 1900, p. 1; Jan. 9, 1901, p. 4; Feb. 6, 1901, p. 7; Feb. 10, 1901, p. 1; District Council, *Proceedings*, Sept. 1, 1900.

67. *Chicago Tribune*, Feb. 8, 1901, p. 1. The text of the agreement is published in the *Report of the United States Industrial Commission*, 8:528–30.

Chapter 4
The New Unionism and the Uniform Agreement, 1901–1929

1. Edward Craig, "Memoirs," (typescript in possession of the Chicago Historical Society, n.d.), p. 79.

2. *Chicago Tribune*, Apr. 19, 1915, pp. 1, 8.

3. Chad Wallin, *The Builders' Story: An Interpretive Record of the Builders' Association of Chicago* (Chicago: Chicago Builders' Association, 1960), pp. 5, 10, 11.

4. Figures derived from Homer Hoyt, *One Hundred Years of Land*

Values in Chicago: The Relationship of the Growth of Chicago to the Rise in its Land Value, 1830-1933 (New York: privately published, 1933).

5. *The Carpenter*, May 1910, pp. 9-11; Dec. 1913, pp. 2-5; Craig, "Memoirs," pp. 82, 101; on the "Chicago system," see Walter Galenson, *The United Brotherhood of Carpenters: The First Hundred Years* (Cambridge: Harvard Univ. Press, 1983), pp. 157, 158

6. *Chicago Tribune*, Apr. 18, 1915, p. 6; on the general policy of the carpenters during this period, see Royal E. Montgomery, *Industrial Relations in the Chicago Building Trades*, (Chicago: Univ. of Chicago Press, 1927), pp. 33-45.

7. *The Carpenter*, June 1908, pp. 15-18; Robert Christie, *Empire in Wood: A History of the Carpenters Union*, (Ithaca, N.Y.: Cornell Univ. Press, 1956), pp. 79-83; Wallin, *The Builders Story*, pp. 5-9.

8. Christie, *Empire in Wood*, pp. 108-10; the latest discussion of the carpenters' jurisdictional history can be found in Galenson, *The United Brotherhood of Carpenters*, pp. 96-122.

9. Chistie, *Empire in Wood*, pp. 120-36.

10. *The Carpenter*, Mar. 1898, p. 4; May 1898, p. 9.

11. Christie, *Empire in Wood*, pp. 86, 87, 116-19; Galenson, *The United Brotherhood of Carpenters*, pp. 76-78, 105; *Chicago Tribune*, Apr. 15, 1915, p. 1. For examples of carpenters protesting millworkers doing outside work, see Chicago District Council of Carpenters, *Proceedings*, Feb. 17, 1912; Oct. 5, 1912; Aug. 19, 1916.

12. District Council, *Proceedings*, Aug. 5, 1911; Jan. 27, 1912; Mar. 9, 1912; *Chicago Record Herald*, Oct. 23, 1906, p. 6; Frederick Deibler, *The Amalgamated Woodworkers International Union of America: A Historical Study of Trades Unionism in its Relationship to the Development of an Industry*, (Madison: Univ. of Wisconsin Press, 1912), pp. 161-93; *The Carpenter*, Dec. 1906, p. 33, 34; *Chicago Daily Socialist*, Mar. 19, 1909, p. 2; Apr. 5, 1909, p. 2; *Souvenir of Dedication of Carpenters Council Building*, (Chicago: District Council of Carpenters, 1925).

13. For criticisms of the stance of the Brotherhood, see Deibler, *Amalgamated Woodworkers*, pp. 191-93; Christie, *Empire in Wood*, pp. 118-19; Galenson defends the Brotherhood against this criticism, see *The United Brotherhood of Carpenters*, pp. 99-107.

14. District Council, *Proceedings*, Sept. 4, 1912, Oct. 12, 1913; May 15, 1920; Apr. 14, 1938; *The Carpenter*, Dec. 1906, pp. 33, 34; Mar. 1911, pp. 49, 50; interview with Charles Svec, millmen's business agent.

15. Montgomery, *Industrial Relations in the Building Trades*, pp. 12-26.

16. Ibid., pp. 34-45; 53-57.

17. *Chicago Tribune*, June 26, 1915, p. 3; June 27, 1915, p. 11; Craig, "Memoirs," pp. 142, 158.

18. Craig, "Memoirs," pp. 90-93; Montgomery, *Industrial Relations in the Building Trades*, pp. 46-48.

19. Craig, "Memoirs," pp. 16-18, 128; Montgomery, *Industrial Relations in the Building Trades*, pp. 74-76.

20. Hoyt, *One Hundred Years of Land Values*, p. 337. On the growth

of the new locals, see District Council, *Proceedings*, Aug. 12, 1911; Sept. 13, 1911; Feb. 10, 1912; we wish to thank Steven Sapolsky for sharing with us his insights about the impact of building decentralization on unionism during this period.

21. David Montgomery, "The New Unionism and the Transformation of Workers' Consciousness, 1909–1922," *Journal of Social History* 7 (Summer 1974):509–29; James R. Green, *The World of the Worker: Labor in Twentieth-Century America* (New York: Hill and Wang, 1980), pp. 67–99.

22. *Chicago Tribune*, Apr. 18, 1915, p. 6; Apr. 19, 1915, p. 8.

23. District Council, *Proceedings*, Sept. 23, 1911. Quote is from *Chicago Daily Inter-Ocean*, Mar. 31, 1912, p. 2.

24. *Chicago Daily Socialist*, Apr. 9, 1912, p. 3; Apr. 13, 1912, p. 2; Apr. 14, 1912, p. 2; District Council, *Proceedings*, Apr. 21, 1912.

25. Montgomery, *Industrial Relations in the Building Trades*, pp. 72–74.

26. Ibid., pp. 74–76; Craig, "Memoirs," pp. 140–143.

27. Montgomery, *Industrial Relations in the Building Trades*, p. 75; Craig, "Memoirs," pp. 145–48.

28. *Chicago Tribune*, Apr. 17, 1915, p. 4; Apr. 18, 1915, pp. 1, 8.

29. Ibid., Apr. 18, 1915, p. 1; Apr. 21, 1915, p. 15; *The Carpenter*, Sept. 1915, pp. 8–10; Craig, "Memoirs," p. 153.

30. Quote is from *The Carpenter*, Sept. 1915, pp. 8–10; see also *Chicago Tribune*, Apr. 18, 1915, p. 1; Apr. 21, 1915, p. 15; Craig, "Memoirs," p. 153.

31. *Chicago Tribune*, July 1, 1915, pp. 1, 4; July 3, 1915, p. 1; July 8, 1915, p. 1; July 11, 1915, p. 1; *The Carpenter*, Sept. 1915, pp. 8–10; Craig, "Memoirs," pp. 154–55.

32. District Council, *Proceedings*, Apr. 13, 1919; Apr. 27, 1919; *Chicago Tribune*, Jan. 20, 1921, p. 5; Jan. 22, 1921, p. 1; Montgomery, *Industrial Relations in the Building Trades*, pp. 199–201.

33. *The Carpenter*, Nov. 1919, pp. 22, 23; on the radicalism of 1919, see Savel Zimand, *Modern Social Movements: Descriptive Summaries and Bibliographies* (New York: H. W. Wilson and Co., 1921). For a summary of work on this period, see Melvin Dubofsky, *Industrialism and the American Worker, 1865–1920* (Arlington Heights, Ill.: AHM Publishing Co., 1975), pp. 128–33.

34. *Chicago Tribune*, Sept. 1, 1919, p. 1; Sept. 2, 1919, p. 1; Graham Taylor, "An Epidemic of Strikes," *The Survey*, Aug. 2, 1919. The national strike wave of 1919 is summarized and discussed in Jeremy Brecher, *Strike!* (San Francisco: Straight Arrow Books, 1972), pp. 101–43.

35. District Council, *Proceedings*, Feb. 8, 1919; see also Mar. 8, 1919; Apr. 26, 1919; Feb. 14, 1920; Mar. 13, 1920; *New Majority*, Apr. 5, 1919, p. 15.

36. District Council, *Proceedings*, Sept. 6, 1919; Mar. 20, 1920; Mar. 26, 1920.

37. Ibid., Aug. 23, 1913; Feb. 7, 14, 1920; Mar. 27, 1920; Mar. 12, 1921. One labor paper at this time was reported as saying that the carpenters were

"hopelessly split" between conservatives and a large group of "English-speaking socialists." See *Chicago Tribune*, July 19, 1919, p. 2.

38. On Sand, see *Chicago Daily Socialist*, Aug. 13, 1909, p. 2; Aug. 14, 1909, p. 1; Aug. 17, 1909, p. 2; July 6, 1910, p. 3; August 11, 1911, p. 3; on Galvin, see *Chicago Tribune*, Apr. 18, 1915, p. 6; on Johanssen, see Hutchins Hapgood, *The Spirit of Labor* (New York: Duffield & Co., 1907); on DeGroot and Kjar, see District Council, *Proceedings*, Sept. 18, 1930; *The Carpenter*, Mar. 1929; and Steve Nelson, James R. Barrett, and Rob Ruck, *Steve Nelson, American Radical* (Pittsburgh: Univ. of Pittsburgh Press, 1981); see also The Progressive Building Trades Worker, *What's Wrong in the Carpenters' Union* (Chicago: The Progressive Building Trades Worker, 1925).

39. District Council, *Proceedings*, Dec. 13, 1919; Feb. 14, 1920; Mar. 13, 1920; Nov. 20, 1920; Dec. 11, 1920; *Chicago Herald Examiner*, July 13, 1913, pt. 2, p. 4.

40. District Council, *Proceedings*, June 28, 1919; July 5, 12, 1919; Aug. 2, 1919; *Chicago Tribune*, July 20, 1919, p. 2.

41. *Chicago Tribune*, Sept. 6, 1919, p. 10; Sept. 7, 1919, p. 18; Sept. 16, 1919, p. 19; District Council, *Proceedings*, Aug. 16, 1919; Sept. 11, 20, 1919; Feb. 7, 1920; Mar. 27, 1920; May 15, 1920.

42. *American Contractor*, July 17, 1920; Nov. 13, 1920; *New Majority*, Sept. 24, 1921, pp. 1, 2; Oct. 8, 1921, p. 1; Nov. 12, 1921, p. 4; Montgomery, *Industrial Relations in the Building Trades*, pp. 234–35.

43. *American Contractor*, Apr. 30, 1921; Chicago Association of Commerce, *Executive Committee Minutes*, Aug. 13, 1920; Oct. 10, 1920; Employers Association of Chicago, *Executive Committee Minutes*, Sept. 3, 1920; Dec. 8, 1920; District Council, *Proceedings*, Aug. 28, 1920; Montgomery, *Industrial Relations in the Building Trades*, pp. 103–7; Savel Zimand, *The Open Shop Drive: Who Is Behind It and Where Is It Going* (New York: Bureau of Industrial Research, 1921).

44. The Dunne column is reprinted from *The Carpenter*, Jan.-Feb. 1920.

45. *Building Construction Employers Association Bulletin*, Feb. 1921; *The Carpenter*, Jan. 1921; District Council, *Proceedings*, June 12, 19, 26, 1920; Aug. 14, 1920; Sept. 11, 18, 1920; Jan. 29, 1921; Feb. 20, 1921; Mar. 5, 1921; Apr. 23, 1921; June 16, 1921; *Chicago Tribune*, June 16, 1921, p. 7; quote is from Mar. 26, 1921.

46. District Council, *Proceedings*, Mar. 12, 1921; Apr. 2, 30, 1921; May 2, 14, 1921; June 18, 1921.

47. Ibid., June 25, 1920; Mar. 23, 1921; *Chicago Tribune*, June 24, 1921, p. 7; June 26, 1921, p. 5; July 1, 1921, p. 11; "Draft Agreement Between the Building Trades Council and the Building Construction Employers Association," June 10, 1921 (typescript in the files of the Chicago and Cook County Building And Construction Trades Council).

48. Montgomery, *Industrial Relations in the Building Trades*, pp. 239–55.

49. Ibid., pp. 256–69.

50. *Chicago Tribune*, Sept. 9, 1921, p. 1; Sept. 10, 1921, p. 1; October

1, 1921, p. 1; Montgomery, *Industrial Relations in the Building Trades*, pp. 271–75.

51. *Chicago Tribune*, Nov. 6, 1921, p. 18; Employers Association, *Minutes*, Oct. 12, 1921; BCEA, *Bulletin*, Nov. 1921; *New Majority*, Dec. 31, 1921, p. 1.

52. "Address of T. E. Donnelley Before the Millwork Cost Bureau, Eighth Annual Convention, Apr. 19, 1922," T. E. Donnelley Papers. R. R. Donnelley & Sons Co., Chicago.

53. Employers Association, *Minutes*, Sept. 14, 1921; District Council, *Proceedings*, Oct. 13, 22, 1921; Nov. 19, 1921; *Chicago Tribune*, Nov. 17, 1921, p. 17.

54. *New Majority*, Sept. 23, 1923; *Chicago Commerce*, Oct. 20, 1923; Nov. 13, 1924; T. E. Donnelley, "The Fight for Fairplay in Chicago," Spring 1923, Landis Award Collection, Chicago Historical Society.

55. District Council, *Proceedings*, Dec. 3, 31, 1921; *Chicago Tribune*, Nov. 17, 1921, p. 17; Nov. 21, 1921, p. 12.

56. District Council, *Proceedings*, Oct. 15, 1921; Jan. 7, 28, 1922; *Chicago Daily News*, Oct. 16, 1921.

57. Luke Grant, *The National Erectors Association and the International Association of Bridge and Structural Iron Workers* (Washington D.C.: United States Commission on Industrial Relations, 1915), pp. 115, 116, 119; *Chicago Commerce*, May 13, 1922; *Chicago Tribune*, Apr. 10, 1922, p. 1; Apr. 11, 1922, p. 1; Apr. 12, 1922, p. 1; Apr. 16, 1922, p. 1. On labor racketeering in Chicago, see Louis Adamic, *Dynamite: The Story of Class Violence in America* (New York: Viking Press, 1931), pp. 325–49, esp. 341–43.

58. District Council, *Proceedings*, Jan. 28, 1922; Feb. 4, 18, 1922; *Chicago Tribune*, Nov. 21, 1921, p. 21.

59. District Council, *Proceedings*, Feb. 11, 1922.

60. Ibid., June 30, 1922; July 14, 1922.

61. Ibid., Apr. 4, 1922; *New Majority*, Dec. 17, 1921; Jan. 14, 21, 1922; May 6, 1922.

62. Montgomery, *Industrial Relations in the Building Trades*, pp. 287–92; District Council, *Proceedings*, May 5, 1922; Feb. 16, 1923.

63. *Dedication of the Carpenters Building, 1925*; District Council, *Proceedings*, Feb. 25, 1922; Sept. 25, 1927.

64. Quote is from Wallin, *Builders' Story*, p. 60; BCEA, *Bulletin*, Aug. 1922; Associated Builders, *Bulletin*, Feb. 1923.

65. District Council, *Proceedings*, Mar. 23, 1923; Apr. 27, 1923; May 25, 1923; June 15, 1923; Aug. 17, 1923; Nov. 9, 1923; Dec. 7, 1923; Jan. 18, 1924; Jan. 16, 1925; *The Carpenter*, July 1923, p. 24; BCEA, *Bulletin*, July 1924; *Chicago Commerce*, May 24, 1924; Dec. 13, 1924.

66. District Council, *Proceedings*, June 6, 13, 20, 1924; Sept. 19, 1924; Oct. 17, 1924; Feb. 20, 1925.

67. *Dedication of Carpenters Building, 1925*; District Council, *Proceedings*, July 14, 1922; Sept. 19, 1924; Frederick L. Ryan, *Industrial Relations in the San Francisco Building Trades* (Norman, Okla.: Univ. of Okla. Press, 1936).

68. "Address of T. E. Donnelley Before the Fifth Annual Meeting of

the General Contractors of America, January 21, 1924," T. E. Donnelley Papers, R. R. Donnelley & Sons Co., Chicago.

69. District Council, *Proceedings*, June 20, 1924; Sept. 19, 1924; Oct. 17, 1924; Feb. 20, 1925; May 29, 1925.

70. Ibid., Mar. 5, 1926; see also June 4, 11, 1926; Oct. 22, 1926; Nov. 19, 1926; Dec. 3, 1926; May 19, 1928; Galenson, *The United Brotherhood of Carpenters*, pp. 206–15.

71. District Council, *Proceedings*, June 25, 1926; July 2, 9, 23, 1926; June 24, 1927; July 1, 1927; Oct. 14, 1927; Nov. 4, 1927; Apr. 6, 1928; June 29, 1928; July 27, 1928; Dec. 14, 21, 1928; Feb. 8, 1929; for a short biographical sketch of Flynn, see *Federation News*, May 27, 1933.

72. District Council, *Proceedings*, Mar. 2, 1928.

73. District Council, *Proceedings*, Nov. 30, 1928; Dec. 1, 1928.

74. Ibid., Feb. 8, 28, 1929; Mar. 1, 1929.

75. Ibid., Mar. 7, 14, 21, 1929; quote from leaflet entitled "Carpenters' Attention," filed at Chicago District Council of Carpenters Headquarters.

76. District Council, *Proceedings*, Apr. 18, 1929; May 9, 1929; June 13, 1929; *Federation News*, May 18, 1929; June 15, 1929.

77. District Council, *Proceedings*, Apr. 18, 1929.

78. Ibid., Sept. 30, 1930; leaflet entitled "A Personal Appeal from Nels Kjar," n.d., filed at District Council headquarters; Galensen, *The United Brotherhood of Carpenters*, pp. 215–22; for an account of the anti-Communist movement within the carpenters nationally, see Christie, *Empire in Wood*, pp. 253–68.

Chapter 5
The Carpenters and the Federal Government:
From the New Deal to Taft-Hartley,
1929–1947

1. Quoted in Walter Galenson, *The United Brotherhood of Carpenters: The First Hundred Years* (Cambridge: Harvard Univ. Press, 1983), p. 266.

2. Ibid.

3. On the relationship of A.F. of L. unions to the state before the New Deal, see Christopher L. Tomlins, *The State and the Unions: Labor Relations, Law, and the Organized Labor Movement in America, 1880–1960* (Cambridge: Cambridge Univ. Press, 1985), pp. 3–95.

4. Figures from Chicago District Council of Carpenters, *Proceedings*, Feb. 26, 1931; Homer Hoyt, *One Hundred Years of Land Values in Chicago: The Relationship of the Growth of Chicago to the Rise in its Land Values, 1830–1933* (New York: Privately published, 1933).

5. District Council, *Proceedings*, Sept.4, 1930; Oct. 2, 1930; *Federation News*, Feb. 20, 1932; interview with Stanley Johnson, veteran unionist Local 141.

6. Membership reports by Secretary Charles Sand scattered in District Council, *Proceedings*.

7. District Council, *Proceedings*, Apr. 21, 1932; Dec. 22, 1932; on the numbers of carpenters in Chicago, see United States Department of the Interior, Census Office, *Fifteenth U.S. Census*, 1930, vol. 4: *Census of Population* (Washington D.C.: Government Printing Office, 1933), p. 447; *Sixteenth United States Census*, vol 3: *Census of Population* (Washington D.C.: Government Printing Office, 1943), p. 874.

8. District Council, *Proceedings*, Apr. 30, 1931; Oct. 22, 1931; Dec. 17, 1931; Feb. 4, 21, 1932; Oct. 2, 30, 1932; Mar. 30, 1933; Apr. 6, 13, 20, 1933; July 13, 1933.

9. Ibid., Mar. 12, 1931; July 15, 1937.

10. Ibid., Mar. 16, 1931; "Sand To Affiliated Locals," District Council, *Proceedings*, Mar. 16, 1931; see also the statement of the First General Vice President George Talry in District Council, *Proceedings*, Jan. 28, 1932.

11. See "Notes for a Special Meeting Called for Discussing Labor Day Policy," in John Fitzpatrick Papers, Box 17, Folder 23, Chicago Historical Society; interview with Michael J. Connolly.

12. District Council, *Proceedings*, Apr. 15, 1927; Apr. 2, 1931.

13. Interview with Stanley Johnson; District Council, *Proceedings*, June 30, 1938; Mar. 2, 30, 1939; Nov. 30, 1939.

14. District Council, *Proceedings*, Nov. 6, 1930; May 21, 1931.

15. Ibid., July 17, 1930; Dec. 4, 1930; Sept. 10, 1931; Sept. 1, 1932; Oct. 27, 1932.

16. Ibid., Jan. 12, 1932; interview with Stanley Johnson.

17. Cathy Cahan and Richard Cahan, "The Lost City of the Depression," *Chicago History* 5 (Winter 1976–77):233–42.

18. District Council, *Proceedings*, Dec. 1, 29, 1932.

19. Ibid., Dec. 8, 1932; Jan. 12, 19, 1933.

20. Ibid., Feb. 2, 1933; on the Imperial Hall meeting, see Dec. 3, 1931; interview with Michael J. Connolly and Joseph McAlinden.

21. District Council, *Proceedings*, Feb. 2, 9, 1933; Mar. 30, 1933; Mar. 1, 15, 1934.

22. Ibid., May 25, 1933; July 2, 1931; interview with Michael J. Connolly and Joseph McAlinden.

23. "Sand to Illinois State Senators, June 22, 1939," in District Council, *Proceedings*; see also Jan. 28, 1932; Dec. 8, 1932; Apr. 13, 1933; May 17, 1934; interview with Stanley Johnson.

24. Lawrence C. Christenson, *Collective Bargaining in Chicago, 1929–30* (Chicago: Privately published, 1933), pp. 22–25; *The Economist*, June 30, 1933.

25. District Council, *Proceedings*, Apr. 29,, 1927; May 6, 20, 1927; June 17, 1927; Aug. 29, 1929; Aug. 7, 1930; Sept. 4, 25, 1930; Apr. 2, 1931; May 14, 1931; June 4, 1931; July 30, 1931.

26. Ibid., May 5, 1932; June 2, 30, 1932; Sept. 15, 1932.

27. Ibid., Aug. 11, 25, 1932; Sept. 8, 1932.

28. Ibid., Oct. 13, 1932; Nov. 3, 17, 1932; Mar. 23, 1933.

29. See the speech of President Flynn in District Council, *Proceedings*, July 6, 1933.

30. Tomlins, *The State and the Unions*, 99–147.

31. William E. Leuchtenburg, *Franklin D. Roosevelt and the New Deal* (New York: Harper & Row, 1963), pp. 57, 58, 70; District Council, *Proceedings*, Feb. 26, 1931; July 28, 1932.

32. *Federation News*, May 5, 1934; District Council, *Proceedings*, Aug. 17, 1933; Nov. 13, 1933; Galenson, *The United Brotherhood of Carpenters*, pp. 239, 240.

33. District Council, *Proceedings*, Sept. 7, 1933; Oct. 5, 19, 28, 1933; "Mill Conference Proceedings" (in District Council, *Proceedings*), Feb. 24, 1934; May 3, 1934; Nov. 15, 1934; May 7, 1936.

34. District Council, *Proceedings*, Feb. 23, 1933; July 27, 1933.

35. Ibid., Jan. 18, 25, 1934; Aug. 10, 17, 1933; Feb. 15, 1934; Tomlins, *The State and the Unions*, p. 105.

36. District Council, *Proceedings*, May 10, 17, 31, 1934.

37. Ibid., June 14, 28, 1934; July 12, 19, 24, 1934; Aug. 31, 1934.

38. Ibid., July 5, 1934; Sept. 1934; Oct. 11, 1934.

39. Hyman Meites, *History of the Jews of Chicago* (Chicago: Jewish Historical Society of Illinois, 1924), pp. 468, 469; interview with Art Holzman, president of Local 504; "Report of the Organization Committee recommending that Union 504 be Revoked," District Council, *Proceedings*, June 17, 1911.

40. Interviews with Stanley Johnson and Joseph McAlinden; District Council, *Proceedings*, Oct. 18, 1934; Nov. 2, 1934; Dec. 13, 1934; Feb. 28, 1935; Mar. 14, 1935; Apr. 4, 11, 1935.

41. Leuchtenberg, *F.D.R. and the New Deal*, pp. 70, 121–24.

42. District Council, *Proceedings*, Jan. 4, 1933; Nov. 23, 1933; Dec. 14, 28, 1933; Mar. 14, 1935.

43. Ibid., Oct. 5, 1933; Nov. 9, 16, 1933; Mar. 29, 1934; Apr. 12, 1934; Apr. 19, 1934; Oct. 18, 1934; Feb. 14, 1935; Apr. 11, 1935.

44. Ibid., May 2, 1935.

45. "Secretary Sand to Affiliated Locals, September 7, 1934," in District Council, *Proceedings*; see also June 18, 1936.

46. Interview with Stanley Johnson.

47. District Council, *Proceedings*, June 21, 1934; Aug. 16, 1934; Apr. 8, 1937; Robert Christie, *Empire in Wood: A History of the Carpenters Union* (Ithaca, N.Y.: Cornell Univ. Press, 1956), pp. 269–84.

48. District Council, *Proceedings*, Jan. 17, 24, 1935.

49. Tomlins, *The State and the Unions*, pp. 99–147.

50. James R. Green, *The World of the Worker: Labor in Twentieth Century America* (New York: Hill and Wang, 1980), p. 139; Leuchtenburg, *F.D.R. and the New Deal*, p. 124–30; "Report on the Proceedings of the the the 53rd Illinois State Federation of Labor Convention, September 9–14, 1935," in District Council, *Proceedings*.

51. Donald S. Howard, *The W.P.A. and Federal Relief Policy* (New York: Russell Sage Foundation, 1943), p. 215; District Council: *Proceedings*, Sept. 26, 1935; *Chicago Tribune*, July 2, 1939, p. 3.

52. District Council, *Proceedings*, Nov. 14, 21, 28, 1935; Dec. 5, 12, 1935.

53. Ibid., Oct. 3, 1935; Frank A. Randell, *History of the Development of Building Construction of Chicago* (Urbana: Univ. of Illinois Press, 1949), p. 298.

54. District Council, *Proceedings*, May 28, 1936; July 23, 30, 1936; Apr. 8, 1937; Dec. 16, 1937; June 30, 1938; Jan. 4, 1940; interview with Stanley Johnson.

55. District Council, *Proceedings*, Jan. 3, 28, 1935; Mar. 21, 1935; Jan. 30, 1936; Nov. 12, 1936; Feb. 18, 24, 1937; July 29, 1937; Oct. 7, 1937; for membership figures from 1938 through 1940, see Mar. 3, 1941.

56. Associated Builders of Chicago, *Bulletin*, Aug. 1935; District Council, *Proceedings*, Aug. 13, 1936; Gordon Hotstetter to T. E. Donnelley, Apr. 14, 1944, T. E. Donnelley Papers, R. R. Donnelley & Sons Co., Chicago.

57. District Council, *Proceedings*, Jan. 4, 1937; Mar. 11, 1937; Apr. 29, 1937; May 6, 20, 1937; "Report of Arbitration Board on Proposed New Agreement," in District Council *Proceedings*, Apr. 29, 1937.

58. Galenson, *The United Brotherhood of Carpenters*, pp. 252–54; Tomlins, *The State and the Unions*, p. 142.

59. Christie, *Empire in Wood*, pp. 285–300, 324, 325; District Council, *Proceedings*, Aug. 19, 1937; "Sand to Contractors et al., May 10, 1938," and "Sand to Affiliated Locals, Oct. 19, 1938" in District Council *Proceedings*.

60. District Council, *Proceedings*, Dec. 2, 1937; Jan. 20, 1938; Apr. 7, 14, 1938.

61. Ibid., Jan. 5, 1939; Feb. 1, 1940; for a biography of Flynn, see *Federation News*, Apr. 17, 1937; Christie, *Empire in Wood*, pp. 307–16.

62. Leuchtenburg, *F.D.R. and the New Deal*, pp. 244–49.

63. District Council, *Proceedings*, Mar. 24, 1938; Apr. 14, 1938; May 5, 19, 26, 1938; June 2, 9, 1938; July 28, 1938; May 11, 1939; *Federation News*, May 14, 1938; Howard, *The W.P.A.*, pp. 222–24.

64. District Council, *Proceedings*, July 6, 20, 1939; Aug. 3, 1939; Nov. 16, 1939; *Chicago Tribune*, July 2, 1939, p. 3; July 13, 1939, p. 3; July 14, 1939, p. 5, 6; July 15, 1939, p. 3; July 21, 1939, p. 3; Howard, *The W.P.A.*, pp. 148, 214–16, 519–22.

65. District Council, *Proceedings*, Oct. 3, 1940; see "Report on the Proceedings of the 58th General Illinois State Federation of Labor Convention, September 16–21, 1940," in ibid.; interview with Stanley Johnson.

66. Leuchtenburg, *F.D.R. and the New Deal*, pp. 299, 300.

67. District Council, *Proceedings*, Dec. 12, 1940; Apr. 3, 1941; Oct. 30, 1941; Feb. 12, 1942; Jan. 27, 1944.

68. "Report on Proceedings of the 60th Annual A.F. of L. Convention, November 1940" in District Council, *Proceedings*; see also Oct. 24, 1940; Dec. 5, 1940; Jan. 9, 1941; Feb. 13, 20, 1941.

69. District Council, *Proceedings*, Aug. 7, 1941; Joel Seidman, *American Labor from Defense to Reconversion* (Chicago: Univ. of Chicago Press, 1953), pp. 29, 30; on C.I.O. organizing in the building trades see District Council, *Proceedings*, June 17, 1937; August 17, 1939; May 16, 1940; Sept. 4, 1941; Oct. 16, 1941.

70. District Council, *Proceedings*, Dec. 26, 1941; Jan. 8, 22, 1942; Sept. 30, 1943.

71. Ibid., Dec. 11, 1941; Jan. 8, 1942; June 4, 1942; July 2, 1942.

72. Ibid., July 23, 30, 1942; Aug. 13, 27, 1942; standard agreement reprinted Nov. 12, 1942.

73. Ibid., Mar. 11, 25, 1943; May 6, 1943; Feb. 17, 1944; *Chicago Tribune*, Mar. 24, 1943, p. 15.

74. Sullivan quoted in District Council, *Proceedings*, July 1, 1943; see also Apr. 24, 1941; May 22, 1941; July 29, 1943; Aug. 5, 1943; Sept. 9, 1943; Feb. 24, 1944; Mar. 2, 16, 1944; Apr. 20, 1944; Sept. 21, 1944; Mar. 8, 1945.

75. "Report on 60th Illinois State Federation of Labor Convention, Sept. 21–26, 1942," in District Council, *Proceedings*; see also Apr. 27, 1944; May 25, 1944; June 8, 1944, Aug. 16, 17, 1944; Sept. 7, 14, 1944; Nov. 30, 1944; Feb. 22, 1945; on relations with the Department of Labor, see Sand to Secretary Perkins, Aug. 28, 1944, and Perkins to Secretary-Treasurer Herbert Rivers of the Building Trades Department, Jan. 15, 1944, in District Council, *Proceedings*; Seidman, *From Defense to Reconversion*, pp. 158–61.

76. District Council, *Proceedings*, June 22, 1944; July 13, 27, 1944; Oct. 12, 1944; July 5, 1945; Aug. 2, 1945; Aug. 30, 1945; Sept. 6, 13, 27, 1945.

77. On the outside men, see District Council, *Proceedings*, Feb. 6, 1947; on the climate of this period, see Seidman, *From Defense to Reconversion*, pp. 239–41; on Taft-Hartley, see Harry Millis and Emily Clark Brown, *From the Wagner Act to Taft-Hartley: A Study of National Labor Policy and Labor Relations* (Chicago: Univ. of Chicago Press, 1950), pp. 420–81.

78. Galenson, *The United Brotherhood of Carpenters*, pp. 296–98.

79. District Council, *Proceedings*, Feb. 19, 1948; interview with Stanley Johnson; for a reconsideration of the effect of Taft-Hartley on the labor movement, see Tomlins, *The State and the Unions*, pp. 282–316, esp. 284–300.

Chapter 6
The Era of Union-Contractor Cooperation,
1948–1987

1. Quote from an interview with George Vest, Jr.

2. Housing figures from *Bell Federal Savings Annual Survey of New Building* (Chicago: Bell Federal Savings and Loan Association, 1948–81).

3. This discussion on the importance of jurisdiction is based on the interview with George Vest, Jr.

4. Based on interviews with George Vest, Jr., and Irwin Klass.

5. Based on interviews with Irwin Klass and Joseph L. Donahue.

6. Interview with George Vest, Jr.

7. Interview with Adolph Dardar.

8. Based on interview with Irwin Klass.

9. For evidence that the tendencies of bureaucratization, centralization, and the decline in rank and file participation were consolidated before 1920 in most American unions, see Warren Van Tine, *The Making of a Labor Bureaucrat: Union Leadership in the United States, 1870–1920* (Amherst:

Univ. of Massachusetts Press, 1973); for the carpenters, Robert Christie and Walter Galenson both concur on this point.

10. Quote from interview with George Vest, Jr.

11. Chicago District Council, *Proceedings*, Jan. 25, 1929; Feb. 8, 1929; Jan. 9, 1947; July 1, 1948.

12. *Chicago Tribune*, Sept. 4, 1887, p. 8; Robert Christie, *Empire in Wood: A History of the Carpenters' Union* (Ithaca N.Y.: Cornell Univ. Press, 1956), pp. 62-67.

13. Christie, *Empire in Wood*, pp. 61-78.

14. This section based on interviews with Stanley Johnson (former BA, Local 141) and Stanley Macenas (BA, Local 558).

15. This discussion of the home-building industry based on interviews with George Vest, Jr., and Stanley Macenas.

16. Interview with George Vest, Jr.

17. On open shop construction and the dual wage rate nationally, see Clinton C. Burdon and Raymond E. Leavitt, *Union and Open Shop Construction* (Lexington, Mass: D. C. Heath, Lexington Books, 1980), pp. 12, 13.

18. *Chicago Tribune* Apr. 17, 1972; May 29, 1972; interview with George Vest, Jr..

19. Chicago District Council of Carpenters, *News Release*, July 1, 1972.

20. Interview with Charles Svec.

21. On the equalitarian approach of the national union to blacks, see *The Carpenter* Mar. 1882, p. 4; Oct. 1882, p. 4; Oct. 1883, p. 4; Nov. 1885, p. 5; Oct. 1886, p. 2; see also Walter Galenson, *The United Brotherhood of Carpenters, The First Hundred Years* (Cambridge, Mass.: Harvard Univ. Press, 1983), pp. 38, 39, 127, 128, 199, 228, 180, 181.

22. This discussion of racism is based on interviews with Richard de Vries and Toni Hayes of the Carpenters and Taylor Cotton of the Chicago Urban League.

23. Interview with Adolph Dardar.

24. Interview with Richard de Vries.

25. Interview with Toni Hayes.

26. Interview with Richard de Vries.

27. Interviews with Adolph Dardar, Toni Hayes, and Richard de Vries; see also *Chicago Tribune*, Nov. 14, 1986, p. 39; Dec. 4, 1986, p. 8.

Index

Richard Schneirov is presently teaching in the Department of History at The Ohio State University and has previously lectured under a Fulbright grant at the University of Frankfurt, West Germany. He has also co-directed a study of the formation of Chicago's industrial working class, 1848–77, funded by the National Endowment for the Humanities and based at the Newberry Library in Chicago.

Thomas J. Suhrbur is currently a union organizer for the Illinois Education Association-National Education Association. He also serves on the Executive Board of the Illinois Labor History Society. He previously worked as a carpenter in Local 558 and taught social studies at Geneva (Illinois) High School.